Harvey "Smokey" **Daniels**

Nancy **Steineke**

Texts AND Lessons

for TEACHING LITERATURE

with

65 *Fresh Mentor Texts* from

Dave Eggers • Nikki Giovanni

Tim O'Brien • Jesus Colon

Pat Conroy • Judith Ortiz Cofer

and many more

HEINEMANN
Portsmouth, NH

Literature Selection:
Each lesson is accompanied by a short piece of fiction or poetry, a historic image, or an excerpt from a longer work. For most lessons, you may copy and distribute the pieces to students. (For four selections, the authors were unable to grant classroom copying rights, and we indicate this on the footers for those texts.) Kids must be able to write and mark directly on the page, so *make copies for everyone*—not just one set that gets passed from class to class. Also keep in mind that you can substitute your own selection and adapt our language to teach—or revisit—these skills.

Title: Names the teaching strategy.

Introduction: This brief introductory note gives background on the strategy, structure, or text being used, and explains its value for students.

Time: Tells the expected length of the lesson. Most strategy lessons range from 10 to 50 minutes, averaging 30. Each text set lesson fills at least one 50-minute class period—and we give you steps and language to dig deeper over several additional periods.

Grouping Sequence: Tells how lesson shifts among pairs, small-group, and whole-class configurations.

Used in Text Sets: Lists the text sets in Chapter 10 that use the lessons.

Steps & Teaching Language: This is the core of the lesson, where all the activities and teacher instructions are spelled out in sequence and in detail. Text that appears in regular typeface indicates our suggestions for the teacher. Text in *italic* is suggested teaching language that you can try on and use. If you substitute your own selection, check to see where the language might need to be adapted.

Choices Made

Jim O'Loughlin

Part 1

Later, he would be able to consider all that he had left behind and never saw again: the wedding album, the birth certificates, the kids' favorite toys, even the laptop. In the moment though, with the storm surging and blow back peeling off the roof like masking tape, he only had time to grab what he could on the way out.

Part 2

Still, even as he ran to the car, dripping sweat and bleeding from the gash in his forehead, with the river already up to the wheel wells, he realized that the choices he had just made said something about who he was. In his arms, he held a phone book, the cantaloupe that had just turned ripe, and a gallon of milk. And he had made sure to lock the front door.

CHAPTER 3

SHARING LITERATURE ALOUD

Wise classroom practices—and the Common Core Standards—recognize the importance of both teachers and students reading short literature selections aloud, and paying close attention to the language, the ideas, and their own thinking as they do so.

LESSON 3.1

TEXT ▶ "Choices Made," by Jim O'Loughlin

TIME ▶ 10 Minutes

GROUPING SEQUENCE ▶ Pairs, whole class

USED IN TEXT SETS ▶ 3, 8

Steps & Teaching Language ▶

Pair Share

This fifty-five-word story embodies a classic conversation starter: if you had to suddenly flee your home, what three things would you take?

Well, it does happen. Every August, hurricane season begins in earnest. People who live near the Atlantic coast must face the weather predictions with a combination of dread, fear, and distrust. As we all know, for every prediction that is dead-on, it seems like the previous ninety-nine—or more—have fizzled. In the Midwest, we don't have hurricanes; we have tornadoes, mostly tornado watches and warnings that seldom become tornadoes. But when those storms do make a direct hit, it's often with little or no advance notice—especially if it's the middle of the night and people are sleeping. In the rest of the country, depending on where you live and the season, you might be worrying about floods, mudslides, brush/forest fires, or earthquakes. So, unlike the unwary character in this story, be prepared!

PREPARATION

Copy the two-paragraph story and cut it in half. Good news: if you have a class of thirty, you'll only need to make fifteen copies! Be sure to put all the beginnings in one pile and the endings in another.

STEP 1 **Organize pairs.** Whenever kids will be working in pairs, they need to know who their partner is *beforehand*, and they need to move into a good conversation position—face to face, eye to eye, knee to knee (probably not cheek to cheek). This setup encourages the use of "indoor voices" and prevents noisy, time-wasting shuffling around midlesson. For pairs, we like to have the kids simply push their desks together or sit directly across a table from each other. In this lesson, sitting side by side works best because both students will be reading from the same page.

Chapter 4 offers seven lessons, each dedicated to one of these cognitive strategies, in the above order. But these seven core reading strategies are fully incorporated throughout the book; kids will practice each one repeatedly as you lead them through the readings, activities, and conversations.

Assessment

If you are going to devote ten minutes or twenty-five minutes or a whole class period to one of these lessons, the question naturally arises: How do I grade this? After all, in today's schools, it seems like we have to assess, or at least assign a grade to, almost any activity kids spend time on.

It is important to recognize that these lessons, by themselves, do not lead to final public outcomes, such as polished essays or crafted speeches. They can and often do serve as *starting points* for just such projects, which require extra time and support for their completion. But as they stand, our lessons are more like guided practice, opportunities for kids to read and write and talk *to learn*. That requires an appropriate approach to assessment.

Participation Points

You can certainly give kids points or grades for effective participation in these lessons. But if you start *qualitatively* grading every piece of kids' work on activities like these, trying to defend the difference between a 78 and a 23, you're going to give up huge chunks of your own time marking, scoring, and justifying. Maybe this is some of our old Chicago "tough love" creeping in, but for smaller everyday assignments, we use binary grading: yes/no, on/off, all/nothing. We give 10 points for full participation and 0 points for non-full participation. No 3s, no 7.5s. Ten or zero, that's it.

Our colleague Jim Vopat has brought some poetry to this kind of grading in his book *Writing Circles* (2009). Jim calls this "good faith effort." If a student shows up prepared to work, having all the necessary materials (reading done, notes ready), joins in the work with energy, and carries a fair share of the work—that's a "good faith effort" and earns full points. From a practical point of view, this means we only need to keep track of the few kids who *don't* put forth that GFE, and remember to enter that zero in our gradebook later on.

Still, let's be honest. Giving points is not assessment, it's just grading. When we want to get serious and really scrutinize kids' thinking in these activities, we have to take further steps.

Collect and Save Student Work

As kids do the activities in these forty-five lessons, they naturally create and leave behind writings, lists, drawings, notes, and other tracks of their thinking. So why pop a quiz? Instead, collect, study, and save the naturally occurring by-products of kids' learning. These authentic artifacts, this residue of thinking, are far more meaningful than a disembodied "72" in your gradebook. The kids' own creations are also far more relevant in a parent conference or a principal evaluation than a string of point totals in a gradebook.

OBSERVATION CHART

STUDENT NAME	"GOOD FAITH"	QUOTE	THINKING	SOCIAL SKILLS
1.				
2.				
3.				
4.				
5.				

Observe Kids at Work

The form on page 16 is a tool we use when sitting with a group of kids, watching them work on a lesson together. As you can see, this form incorporates Vopat's good faith idea and then goes much further. As we listen in on kids, we jot down one memorable quote from each student and reflect on what kind of thinking this comment or question represents; we also take notes on any conspicuous use (or neglect) of the collaboration skills called for in the lesson.

Offer Meaningful Performance Opportunities

When the time comes to assign grades for kids' work over long stretches of time and big chunks of content, we traditionally make up a big test and add that score to the points kids have earned along the way. Even as we do this, we quietly recognize that this assessment system invites cramming, superficiality, and the wholesale forgetting of content.

Instead, we like to devise authentic events at which kids share or perform their learning for an engaged audience—and then we use a rubric that carefully defines a successful performance to derive each kid's grade. This might mean a polished essay published on the web, a series of tableaux performed with a group, or a full-scale public debate or talk show enactment. Nancy has written a whole book with ideas on this kind of performance process called *Assessment Live: 10 Real-Time Ways for Kids to Show What They Know—and Meet the Standards* (Heinemann 2009).

Have Fun

We're serious about putting this "F-word" back into school. The two of us had a blast searching out these amazing short texts and using them with kids around the country. In those classrooms, everyone seemed to have a good time reading, savoring, analyzing, debating, and even rereading these little literary gemstones. Field-testing these lessons with kids has reminded us that "all adolescents want to work hard and do well," as the brilliant British educator Charity James once wrote in her book *Young Lives at Stake: The Education of Adolescents*.

Or you can just call it "*rigor* without the *mortis*."

Enjoy!

Smokey and Nancy

The Limited

Sherman Alexie

I saw a man swerve his car
And try to hit a stray dog,
But the quick mutt dodged
Between two parked cars

And made his escape.
God, I thought, did I just see
What I think I saw?
At the next red light,

I pulled up beside the man
And stared hard at him.
He knew that I'd seen
His murder attempt,

But he didn't care.
He smiled and yelled loud
Enough for me to hear him
Through our closed windows:

"Don't give me that face
Unless you're going to do
Something about it.
Come on, tough guy,

What are you going to do?"
I didn't do anything.
I turned right on the green.
He turned left against traffic.

I don't know what happened
To that man or the dog,
But I drove home
And wrote this poem.

Why do poets think
They can change the world?
The only life I can save
Is my own.

WELCOME

GREETINGS, COLLEAGUES. We are Smokey Daniels and Nancy Steineke, joining you again with a new resource that we hope you'll find useful.

Over the past several years, we have worked with students and teachers in twenty-two states, conducting reading workshops and giving demonstration lessons in middle and high school classrooms. Nancy's day job is at Victor J. Andrew High School in suburban Chicago, where she has taught language arts (and once upon a time, home economics, but that's another story) for thirty-five years. Since Smokey no longer has a classroom of his own, he now logs frequent-flier miles as a cross-country guest teacher, including stints at schools in Chicago, Appalachia, Arkansas, New York, Texas, New Mexico, Wisconsin, and Hawaii (someone has to do it), along with writing books and leading workshops.

In 2011 we published *Texts and Lessons for Content-Area Reading*, which included collaborative comprehension lessons and kid-friendly nonfiction articles from a crazy array of sources (*Rolling Stone*, the Discovery Channel, the *New York Times*, etc). Since that book came out, English language arts teachers have been requesting a companion volume that uses *literature* instead of informational text to teach deep comprehension and collaborative discussion. They wanted a book that's just for us ELA folks, not those greedy history and science teachers served by the previous book. Our first love is literature, too. Who are we to refuse?

So here's the product of our two-year search for the best, freshest, and most engaging short literature for young people—and a collection of new, step-by-step lessons that guide kids into, through, and beyond these texts. As with the nonfiction edition, these lessons use engaging short selections to teach close reading and deep comprehension through collaborative conversation and lively debate. And every lesson in the book is correlated with the Common Core Anchor Standards for Reading—as well as many standards for Speaking and Listening, Language, and Writing.

Meeting and Exceeding the Common Core State Standards

The experiences provided by our upcoming thirty-seven lessons closely parallel the readings and tasks recommended by the Common Core State Standards (CCSS) as well as the performances required in tests from the Partnership for Assessment of Readiness for College and Careers (PARCC) and Smarter Balanced Assessment Consortium (SBAC). The main difference is that our lessons put student curiosity and engagement first. The experiences are highly active and student centered, unlike so many of the CCSS prep materials being developed around the country.

In recent years, the Common Core Standards have had a dramatic and sometimes unsettling impact on schools and teachers. We have plenty to say about the challenges of the Core, but luckily for you, we are not going to do it here. This book is about addressing the standards, not critiquing them. Smokey and our colleagues Steve Zemelman and Arthur Hyde recently released the fourth edition of *Best Practice: Bringing Standards to Life in America's Classrooms* (Heinemann 2012). That book offers an extended and balanced treatment of the CCSS—and the many other standards documents and research studies that, together, provide a full vision of what excellent teaching and learning look like today.

For now, we'll just show how this resource can help you engage your kids and meet the CCSS for the English Language Arts, and in particular the Reading Standards for Literature 6–12. To begin with, here are the anchors:

College and Career Readiness Anchor Standards for Reading

KEY IDEAS AND DETAILS

1. Read closely to determine what the text says explicitly and to make logical inferences from it; cite specific textual evidence when writing or speaking to support conclusions drawn from the text.

2. Determine central ideas or themes of a text and analyze their development; summarize the key supporting details and ideas.

3. Analyze how and why individuals, events, and ideas develop and interact over the course of a text.

CRAFT AND STRUCTURE

4. Interpret words and phrases as they are used in a text, including determining technical, connotative, and figurative meanings, and analyze how specific word choices shape meaning or tone.

5. Analyze the structure of texts, including how specific sentences, paragraphs, and larger portions of the text (e.g., a section, chapter, scene, or stanza) relate to each other and the whole.

6. Assess how point of view or purpose shapes the content and style of a text.

INTEGRATION OF KNOWLEDGE AND IDEAS

7. Integrate and evaluate content presented in diverse formats and media, including visually and quantitatively as well as in words.

8. Delineate and evaluate the argument and specific claims in a text, including the validity of the reasoning as well as the relevance and sufficiency of the evidence.

9. Analyze how two or more texts address similar themes or topics in order to build knowledge or to compare the approaches the authors take.

RANGE OF READING AND LEVEL OF TEXT COMPLEXITY

10. Read and comprehend complex literary and informational texts independently and proficiently.
   (www.corestandards.org/assets/CCSSI_ELA%20Standards.pdf)

When you think about this list, you realize that any good reading lesson should incorporate *all* of these goals. Why would we ever design a lesson in which kids *didn't* take all text details into account, pay attention to the author's craft, build knowledge, and gain proficiency with challenging materials? Students deserve it all. So every lesson in this book helps students gain practice with most or all of the reading anchor standards.

While our main aim in this book is to enhance the reading of literature, we also address other Common Core Standards in Speaking and Listening, Language, and Writing, and these correlations are prominently noted. For example, every lesson includes both small-group and whole-class discussion, as explicitly called for in the Speaking and Listening Standards. And, since all sixty-five of the reading selections reproduced here model excellence in language use, the lessons also help students meet key Language Standards. And finally, most lessons require some kind of student writing or note taking. While the written assignments are mostly brief and informal, each one helps to build the fluency, skills, and process knowledge students need to meet the Writing Standards.

Prominent sidebars will help you see which Common Core Standards and skills are receiving special focus and attention all the way through the book. Then, in the appendix, we offer a chart that helps you correlate the lessons with all relevant standards.

About the Readings: What's Fresh in the Market?

Sometimes it seems as though the same fifty short stories and the same fifteen poems are anthologized over and over. Partly, that's because the major textbook companies want to offer students time-tested readings from celebrated authors. But there are plenty of other works of great literature out there, if you know where to look for something fresh.

So where do *we* look? Both of us are inveterate and passionate collectors of short-short fiction and short poems, in both their tree-based and digital forms. If you looked at our voluminous email correspondence, or eavesdropped on our weekly Saturday morning phone calls, you'd mainly hear us trading and reading aloud great short pieces.

We are also inveterate and passionate teachers of reading comprehension, thinking, and discussion strategies. That means we need a constant supply of short texts to use in quick, lively, in-class lessons. When we introduce our students to almost any literary idea or device, it's only natural to pull out a short literature piece from our collections. We came to call these texts "one-page wonders" (OPW in shorthand) because we shopped for kid-friendly reading selections that could be photocopied on one or two pages.

The reading selections we've collected here cover the genres of short stories, poems, drama, and novels, with some essays and accompanying nonfiction pieces appearing in the text sets (see Chapter 10). When choosing OPWs, we favor selections that:

- are engaging, complex, and mostly contemporary
- feature newer, up-and-coming writers (or, if written by famous authors, are not widely anthologized)
- are fresh to us teachers, too, so we can have the joy of discovery right along with our kids
- have sufficient sensory detail and rich language to conjure up vivid images of places and characters
- have enough depth and craft to reward second, closer readings
- address themes that can stimulate lively discussion and debate among students
- are short enough to be read during class, so that a whole lesson can be completed in one period or less
- allow photocopying, so kids can annotate their own copies
- help students practice key comprehension and thinking strategies
- can be extended into more days, or tied into broader literature units

We want to be especially clear about *text complexity,* a key focus of the Common Core Standards. A few of our chosen readings are intentionally easy to enter, enjoy, and talk about. And why not? As the standards say, "Students need opportunities to stretch their reading abilities but also to experience the satisfaction and pleasure of easy, fluent reading, both of which the Standards allow for" (2010, p. 39).

But our main job, year in and year out, is to lead our students up a ladder of challenge, building their stamina and pushing them along to literature that requires more intentional thinking. But along that ladder, it's also our duty to provide just the right amount and type of support to keep kids progressing.

Every class period is not a high-stakes test; it is one more step upward toward college and career readiness. So, even as we respect the CCSS focus on complex text, we also think carefully about what makes that text accessible to young readers along that upward path of their growth. Here are the considerations we keep in mind:

FACTORS THAT MAKE COMPLEX TEXT MORE ACCESSIBLE

- The text is shorter rather than longer.
- The reader has chosen the text, versus it being assigned.
- The reader has relevant background knowledge.
- The topic has personal interest or importance.
- The text evokes curiosity, surprise, or puzzlement.
- The text has high coherence, meaning that it explains itself (e.g., "John Langdon, a farmer and signer of the Constitution . . .").

- The teacher evokes and builds the reader's background knowledge.
- The teacher teaches specific strategies for monitoring comprehension, visualizing, inferring, connecting to background knowledge, questioning, determining importance, and synthesizing.
- Readers can mark, write, or draw on text as they read.
- Readers are encouraged to talk about the text during and after reading.
- Readers can hear text read aloud by the teacher, by a classmate, or in a small group.
- Readers have experience writing in the same genre.

Still, make no mistake about it: 90 percent of the pieces in this collection are plenty complex. That's because they are *full-strength adult literature*, which we think middle and high school students should be engaging with regularly. So we didn't worry so much about Lexiles; instead, we picked selections that grown-up, lifelong readers have paid to read. Trust us, there are plenty of pieces here that give us English majors a run for our interpretive money, but are still intriguing enough to keep teen readers digging and thinking.

Which brings us back to the question in our subhead, What's fresh in the market? You hear that expression a lot on those TV cooking shows when the cameras follow a Famous Chef through the farmer's market, right? She is looking for the dewiest veggies, the most exotic meats, the strangest grains (*freekeh*, seriously? *kamut berries*, really?), the revelatory ethnic treats. Great cooks seek the latest, the newest, the weirdest. They want challenge. They want to create a dish they've never cooked before. They want to work on the edge, take some risks, and dazzle their diners.

If we literature teachers are chefs too, then we really need some fresh produce. To begin with, you just get tired of teaching *To Kill a Mockingbird* for the twenty-third time (unless you're Nancy). More importantly, when we teach a novel or story to our students, they too often see us "read" texts we have read many times before, thought about, talked about, maybe even written about. We know it cold from all our previous encounters.

But this is not the same job we ask kids to do when they come in the classroom each day. We place unfamiliar text in front of them and ask them to read it "cold." They almost never see *us* encountering unknown text, working to build meaning the first time through. Well, if reading unfamiliar text is the students' actual task, then we teachers better be demonstrating that job, early and often. That means we need new texts to refresh and challenge *ourselves*.

Now, these sixty-five little jewels won't be our favorite literary clips forever; we're always finding and adding new ones to the repertoire—and you should, too. As you work with these pieces, you'll start to internalize what makes a one-page wonder, and start collecting your own. Hope you get as geeky about finding them as we are.

So, shall we move on to the nuts and bolts of the lessons?

HOW TO USE THIS BOOK

Coming right up, Chapters 3 through 9 present thirty-seven strategy lessons for improving students' literary comprehension and discussion, using very short texts. In Chapter 10, we offer eight text set lessons, thematically connected assortments of pieces designed to be studied, compared, and debated together. Then, in Chapter 11, we bring forward three commonly taught whole-class novels and show how you can use selected lessons from this book to teach those works—and countless others—in a highly interactive, engaging way. And finally, in Chapter 12, we explain how to grow your own inventory of special texts for teaching literary thinking. Here's the rundown.

Chapters 3–9: Strategy Lessons

Yes! It's OK to photocopy! We secured permission from the publisher for each piece that we've asked you to photocopy, so it's perfectly OK to slap those on the photocopier and run them off for your kids. In fact that's the whole idea.

The strategy lessons are each accompanied by at least one "one-page wonder"— an enticing poem, short-short story, essay, or image that engages students in close reading, thinking, and discussion. We selected these pieces with literary quality and student engagement foremost in our minds. They cover a wide range of genres and themes; only a few are abridged. The lessons accompanying these readings offer specific suggestions and language you can use to teach them. They are written as generally as possible, so you can use (and reuse) the steps and language with any compatible text you choose. And the strategy lessons are quick: they are designed to be completed within ten to fifty minutes.

We have grouped the lessons into seven families based on their thinking focus as well as their standards connections.

Sharing Literature Aloud

Smart-Reader Strategies

Lively Discussions

Closer Readings

Up and Thinking

Literary Arguments

Coping with Complex and Classic Texts

The strategy lessons appear in what we'd call a "mild sequential order." For example, kids can't do arguing both sides unless they first know how to pair share with a classmate. Very generally, the lessons become more complex and socially demanding as they unfold. But, that being said, use them in whatever order you like; so far, no fatalities have been reported due to reordering. You can also mix and match—any lesson with any reading selection, ours or yours. If a piece looks too easy or hard for your kids, don't give up on the lesson—find an alternative text elsewhere in the book or in your own collection, and carry on. And remember, always study any potential lesson text carefully to be sure it is appropriate for your students and the community where you would like to continue teaching.

Chapter 10: Text Set Lessons

The text sets follow a similar lesson format, but each one offers multiple coordinated reading selections. Now students can range though two to five texts representing different genres and authors, each of them taking a different angle on a common topic or literary theme. This formula includes nonfiction selections and various media in the mix, much as PARCC and Smarter Balanced assessments do. Among our themes:

Memory

Citizenship

Life Stories

Mothers and Daughters

Narcissism

Labels

Abuse

Soldiers and Heroes

Text set lessons about these rich topics offer multiple points of entry for different students, and provide for a deep and sustained engagement in reading and thinking. They can easily lead to multiday units in which students do their own research to shed further light on the theme.

The suggested sequence of activities for a text set is built from strategy lessons in the first part of the book. Therefore, the instructions for text sets are more compact, since the necessary lesson steps are given in earlier chapters. Don't worry, we'll clearly signal where you should look for each lesson step.

Chapter 11: Keeping Kids at the Center of Whole-Class Novels

Whole-class novels are still a big part of the English language arts curriculum in most middle and high schools (thank goodness). But now teachers are wondering: How can I teach these great books in a way that's harmonious with the Common Core Standards? How do I ensure my students are grasping all important details, noticing the author's craft and structure, improving their academic vocabularies, and always stepping up their thinking skills? All while still being deeply engaged with the story and with each other?

We looked up the most commonly taught novels in middle and high school, and three of the top titles were:

The Giver, by Lois Lowry

To Kill a Mockingbird, by Harper Lee

The Great Gatsby, by F. Scott Fitzgerald

Literature Selection:
Each lesson is accompanied by a short piece of fiction or poetry, a historic image, or an excerpt from a longer work. For most lessons, you may copy and distribute the pieces to students. (For four selections, the authors were unable to grant classroom copying rights, and we indicate this on the footers for those texts.) Kids must be able to write and mark directly on the page, so *make copies for everyone*—not just one set that gets passed from class to class. Also keep in mind that you can substitute your own selection and adapt our language to teach—or revisit— these skills.

Title: Names the teaching strategy.

Introduction: This brief introductory note gives background on the strategy, structure, or text being used, and explains its value for students.

Time: Tells the expected length of the lesson. Most strategy lessons range from 10 to 50 minutes, averaging 30. Each text set lesson fills at least one 50-minute class period—and we give you steps and language to dig deeper over several additional periods.

Grouping Sequence: Tells how lesson shifts among pairs, small-group, and whole-class configurations.

Used in Text Sets: Lists the text sets in Chapter 10 that use the lessons.

Steps & Teaching Language: This is the core of the lesson, where all the activities and teacher instructions are spelled out in sequence and in detail. Text that appears in regular typeface indicates our suggestions for the teacher. Text in *italic* is suggested teaching language that you can try on and use. If you substitute your own selection, check to see where the language might need to be adapted.

Choices Made
Jim O'Loughlin

Part 1

Later, he would be able to consider all that he had left behind and never saw again: the wedding album, the birth certificates, the kids' favorite toys, even the laptop. In the moment though, with the storm surging and blow back peeling off the roof like masking tape, he only had time to grab what he could on the way out.

Part 2

Still, even as he ran to the car, dripping sweat and bleeding from the gash in his forehead, with the river already up to the wheel wells, he realized that the choices he had just made said something about who he was. In his arms, he held a phone book, the cantaloupe that had just turned ripe, and a gallon of milk. And he had made sure to lock the front door.

CHAPTER 3
SHARING LITERATURE ALOUD

Wise classroom practices—and the Common Core Standards—recognize the importance of both teachers and students reading short literature selections aloud, and paying close attention to the language, the ideas, and their own thinking as they do so.

LESSON 3.1

TEXT ▸ "Choices Made," by Jim O'Loughlin

TIME ▸ 10 Minutes

GROUPING SEQUENCE ▸ Pairs, whole class

USED IN TEXT SETS ▸ 3, 8

Pair Share

This fifty-five-word story embodies a classic conversation starter: if you had to suddenly flee your home, what three things would you take?

Well, it does happen. Every August, hurricane season begins in earnest. People who live near the Atlantic coast must face the weather predictions with a combination of dread, fear, and distrust. As we all know, for every prediction that is dead-on, it seems like the previous ninety-nine—or more—have fizzled. In the Midwest, we don't have hurricanes; we have tornadoes, mostly tornado watches and warnings that seldom become tornadoes. But when those storms do make a direct hit, it's often with little or no advance notice—especially if it's the middle of the night and people are sleeping. In the rest of the country, depending on where you live and the season, you might be worrying about floods, mudslides, brush/forest fires, or earthquakes. So, unlike the unwary character in this story, be prepared!

PREPARATION

Copy the two-paragraph story and cut it in half. Good news: if you have a class of thirty, you'll only need to make fifteen copies! Be sure to put all the beginnings in one pile and the endings in another.

Steps & Teaching Language ▸

STEP 1 **Organize pairs.** Whenever kids will be working in pairs, they need to know who their partner is *beforehand*, and they need to move into a good conversation position—face to face, eye to eye, knee to knee (probably not cheek to cheek). This setup encourages the use of "indoor voices" and prevents noisy, time-wasting shuffling around mid-lesson. For pairs, we like to have the kids simply push their desks together or sit directly across a table from each other. In this lesson, sitting side by side works best because both students will be reading from the same page.

Shoptalk: Here we offer comments about when to use the lesson, how to coordinate it with your textbook (if you have one), and other teaching topics we'd like to share.

Common Core Standards Supported: Lists CCSS skills and principles addressed in the lesson.

Shoptalk ▶

If you are using a basal or anthology, it probably tells you little or nothing about how to set up successful partner or small-group work in your class. (You may find some notes about social skills in the teacher's edition). If you skipped our Chapter 2, check it out: there's some helpful information about training kids for small-group work back on pages 10–13. Making these crucial advance moves, such as setting up partners first and making sure they are positioned to communicate, makes a huge difference with our lessons—or the ones in your textbook.

Still have kids who don't want to work with each other? Tell them that *your* standard is that "everybody works with everybody in here." Then form partners daily, by random drawing, so the pairing is not about you—and so that everyone eventually does work with everyone else. Acquaintance builds friendliness.

STEP 2   **Turn and talk.**   Pose the question that we previewed earlier: *If you had to escape from your house with only three things (assuming your family and pets are OK), what would you take? Turn to your partner and share your answers. Don't forget to explain why these items are important to you. What do they symbolize or represent?*

STEP 3   **Introduce and pass out the story.**   Each pair receives two handouts, the beginning and the end of the story, face down. *OK, first figure out which of you two has the earliest birthday in the year. Got it? OK, the person with the earliest birthday gets the first half of the story, and the other gets the ending. As I pass this story out to you, I want you to keep them* face down *for the time being. No peeking!*

STEP 4   **Give instructions.**   *Early birthdays, ready? When I say go, turn your paper over and begin reading aloud. Make sure you put the story in the middle so that your partner can follow along. Once you finish reading, stop and talk. Share your reactions, talk about what's going on and why the character chose not to take those items. Be sure that both you and your partner contribute and that you actively challenge each other to go into detail and really explain your thoughts.*

When you are finished discussing the first half, the late birthdays should turn their sheet over, put it between you, and then read aloud as your partner follows along. After reading, have another discussion following the same guidelines. Except this time, you need to talk about what the character did take with him.

STEP 5   **Concluding pairs discussion.**   *I see that most of you have finished. Before we share in a large group, I want you to recall the items you would have taken in an emergency and compare yourselves to the story character. What did you have in common? What things were different?*

STEP 6   **Share with the whole class.**   *How did you explain what this character actually took versus what he might have taken when he thought about it later? What might these items symbolize? How did your "emergency items" compare with the character's choices?*

Don't prolong the sharing. Just get a few quick responses to each of the questions. The important conversational work took place as the pairs discussed together.

Even simpler: While we usually complicate things in these variations, this lesson actually has some fun wrinkles already. So we'll just mention a *simpler* version for this one. Eliminate the cutting in half and just let partners gobble the story in one gulp (thirty seconds?), then get into that turn-and-talk.

COMMON CORE STANDARDS SUPPORTED

- Read closely to determine what the text says explicitly and to make logical inferences from it; cite specific textual evidence when writing or speaking to support conclusions drawn from the text. *(CCRA.R.1)*

- Interpret words and phrases as they are used in a text, including figurative meanings. *(CCRA.R.4)*

- Assess how point of view shapes the content and style of a text. *(CCRA.R.6)*

- Participate effectively in a range of conversations and collaborations. *(CCRA.SL.1)*

◀ *Variation*

Variations: In this section you'll find specific ways you can vary, modify, or extend the lesson. Some of these variations can extend the lesson into the following class period.

Web Support: All the charts, lists, or forms that need to be projected for any lesson are on our website, www.heinemann.com /textsandlessonsliterature.

Lesson 3.1 / Pair Share   **19**

So we chose these three books as "exemplar texts" in showing how you can use our lessons to teach a novel. Basically, you'll see us stringing together a logical sequence of strategy lessons from Chapters 3 through 9, with bits of connective tissue added where needed. Of course, the point of this chapter is not these three specific books, but the process by which you can build an engaged, interactive, and standards-friendly approach to *any* novel.

Chapter 12: Extending the Texts and Lessons

While this book provides sixty-five great reading selections, there are about 180 days in most of our school years! Hmm, doing the arithmetic, you could run out of text around New Year's and be hungry for more. In this short chapter, we give away all of our secrets for finding more short, kid-friendly literature selections. We offer bibliographies for the short-short story genre, for poetry, and for images and artworks. We also explain how you can write your own one-page wonders for kids. Really, you can.

Working in Groups

These lessons are all highly interactive and collaborative, because that's what part of what engages kids and gets them thinking. The Common Core Standards also push pretty hard for us to get students working with each other. The Speaking and Listening anchor standards are quite general, and most of our lessons address many or all anchors.

But just for fun, let's drill down into the more specific Speaking and Listening Standards for grades 9–10 as an example. Students should:

1. *Initiate and participate effectively in a range of collaborative discussions (one-on-one, in groups, and teacher-led) with diverse partners on* grades 9–10 *topics, texts, and issues, building on others' ideas and expressing their own clearly and persuasively.*

   a. *Come to discussions prepared, having read and researched material under study; explicitly draw on that preparation by referring to evidence from texts and other research on the topic or issue to stimulate a thoughtful, well-reasoned exchange of ideas.*

   b. *Work with peers to set rules for collegial discussions and decision-making (e.g., informal consensus, taking votes on key issues, presentation of alternate views), clear goals and deadlines, and individual roles as needed.*

   c. *Propel conversations by posing and responding to questions that relate the current discussion to broader themes or larger ideas; actively incorporate others into the discussion; and clarify, verify, or challenge ideas and conclusions.*

   d. *Respond thoughtfully to diverse perspectives, summarize points of agreement and disagreement, and, when warranted, qualify or justify their own views and understanding and make new connections in light of the evidence and reasoning presented.*

In every one of our lessons, students are interacting in just these ways.

If you worry that your students might not be ready to collaborate as the CCSS requires, you are not alone. For a variety of reasons, teenage students may find it hard to manifest the focus, friendliness, and support that these face-to-face meetings require. So we have designed our lessons to enhance on-task conversations.

- The readings are interesting.
- The instructions are explicit.
- Every kid-kid meeting is highly structured.
- Every lesson follows a "socially incremental" design. Kids typically begin working with just one other person (more controlled than starting in groups of four or five).
- Once collaboration is established, kids can move from pairs to small groups.
- Finally (and always) lessons finish in a whole-class discussion, orchestrated by the teacher.

As you can already see, we rely extensively on *pairs* or *partners* in these lessons—and in all our work with young people. When students are meeting with just one other learner, they experience maximum "positive social pressure." That means both persons totally need each other to complete the task. There's no chance to slough off and hope other group members will pick up the slack. There are no other members—you two are it! So you have to pay attention, listen carefully, speak up, and take on your share of the work. With pairs, there tend to be fewer distractions, sidetracks, and disputes of the kind we sometimes have to manage in larger groups.

MATERIALS AND EQUIPMENT

These lessons are generally pretty low-tech. Mostly, you just photocopy the articles and prepare kids to have meaningful conversations. But there are a few supplies we like to have around:

- Post-it notes of various sizes
- Index cards, 3x5-inch and 4x6-inch varieties
- Large chart paper or newsprint and tape
- Fat and skinny markers in assorted colors
- Clipboards: When kids are working with short selections, they may be moving around the room, sitting on the floor, meeting in various groups. They'll need to bring a hard writing surface. A weighty textbook works, but feather-light clipboards were made to be portable desks.
- A projector that allows you to show the lesson instructions we've parked for you on our website, as well as images, work samples, and web pages related to the lessons.
- In our ideal classroom, kids would also have individual tablet computers, on which we can preload great text and images, and then kids can annotate and write about them, joining in digital conversations in live or online settings. However, every student must have the exact same device and be able to use it as fluently as paper and pencil, or the technology can actually distract from the brisk pace of these lessons.

In almost every lesson, you'll have to decide how to form pairs (or groups of three or four), and there is a lot to think about. You already know what happens when you let friends work with each other; lots of kids get left out, while the friend partners have plenty to talk about, other than your lesson. Instead, keep mixing kids up, arranging different partners for every activity, every day. This is part of your community building. Everyone gets to know everyone. No one gets to say, "I won't work with him." Let's learn from kindergarten: write each kid's name on a popsicle stick and keep them in a coffee mug. When it's time to pick partners, students draw from the mug. This way, pairings are random; it's never about you personally forcing certain kids to work together. No arguments and no groaning allowed. As the weeks unfold and kids' collaboration skills are honed in pair work, we feel more comfortable putting them in small groups during our lessons. And later in the year, kids will have partners or groups that stay together over many days, as in book clubs, writing circles, and inquiry circles.

Maybe you have a class that needs even more support to succeed at student-led discussion. In such situations, the key is to explicitly teach the social skills kids need, *before* they head off into small groups. This is a topic we have treated extensively in other books, and won't re-spout our wisdom here. But for those who want more information on explicit social skill lessons, we have posted some links on the book's website.

Below is a chart showing seven key collaboration strategies kids need to develop, adapted from Smokey and Stephanie Harvey's *Comprehension and Collaboration* (2009). As you can see, the chart gives both positive and negative examples of each skill. Maybe you will recognize some of your own students there, hopefully not in the right-hand column.

STRATEGY	EXAMPLES/ACTIONS	SOUNDS LIKE	DOESN'T SOUND LIKE
1. **Be responsible to the group**	• Be prepared: work completed, materials and notes in hand • Bring interesting questions/ideas to the discussion • Fess up if unprepared • Focus on the work and members • Establish and live by your group's ground rules • Settle issues within the group	"Does everyone have their reading? Good, let's get going." "I'm sorry, guys, I didn't get the reading done." "OK, then today you'll take notes on our conversation."	"What? There's a meeting?" "I left my stuff in my locker." "Teacher, Bobby keeps distracting our group."
2. **Listen actively**	• Use names • Make eye contact • Nod, confirm, look interested • Lean in, sit close together • Summarize or paraphrase	"Joe, pull your chair up closer." "Fran, I think I heard you say . . ." "So you think . . ."	"I'm not sitting by you." Huh?"

STRATEGY	EXAMPLES/ACTIONS	SOUNDS LIKE	DOESN'T SOUND LIKE
3. Speak up	• Join in, speak often, be active • Use a moderate voice level • Connect your ideas with what others just said • Overcome your shyness • Ask lead and follow-up questions • Use your notes or annotations, or drawings	"What you said just reminded me of . . . " "What made you feel that way?"	(silence) Not using/looking at notes when conversation lulls
4. Share the air and encourage others	• Take turns • Be aware of who's contributing, and work to even out the airtime • Monitor yourself for dominating or shirking the conversation • Invite others in • Receive others' ideas respectfully • Use talking stick or poker chips if needed	"What do you think, Wendy?" "I better finish my point and let someone else talk." "That's a cool idea, Tom." "Can you say more about that, Chris?"	"Blah blah blah blah blah blah blah blah . . . " "I pass."
5. Prove your point/support your view	• Explain, give examples • Refer to specific passages • Read aloud important sections • Dig deeper into the text, reread important parts	"I think Jim treats Huck as a son because . . . " "Right here on page 15 it says that . . ."	"This book is dumb." "Why open the book?" "Well, that's my opinion anyway."
6. Disagree agreeably	• Be tolerant of other's ideas • Speak up—offer a different viewpoint and don't be steamrolled • Use neutral language: "I was thinking of it this way" • Celebrate and enjoy divergent viewpoints	"Wow, I thought of something totally different." "I can see your point, but what about . . . " "I'm glad you brought that up; I never would have seen it that way."	"You are so wrong!" "What book are *you* reading?" "No way!"
7. Reflect and correct	• Identify specific behaviors that helped or hurt the discussion • Talk openly about problems • Make plans to try out new strategies at the next meeting and then review their effectiveness	"What went well today and where did we run into problems?" "OK, so what will we do differently during our next meeting?" "Let's write down our plan."	"We rocked." "We sucked." "It was OK."

These seven strategies are embedded over and over again in this book's lessons. As you teach them, your kids will be getting plenty of practice and becoming better partners and group members—and meeting the Speaking and Listening Standards for the Common Core or your state.

How Proficient Readers Think

Here's a question: How do effective, veteran readers *think* when they are reading stories, poems, literary essays, or plays? What goes on in their minds? Exactly how do they turn those little marks on the page into understanding and knowledge in their brains—especially when the text is hard or old or boring? If there are some effective patterns and strategies, we need to know what they are, so we can teach them to the kids. Like ASAP.

Happily for us, some reliable and well-replicated research (Pearson and Gallagher 1983; Pearson, Roehler, Dole, and Duffy 1992; Daniels 2011) give us a very pretty clear picture of the key cognitive strategies in play. Powerful readers:

Monitor their comprehension

Connect to background knowledge

Visualize and make sensory images

Ask questions of the text

Draw inferences

Determine what's important

Synthesize and summarize meaning

ALL IN THE FAMILY

This resource stands on its own, offering immediately usable readings and language for collaborative lessons in thinking about literature. But it was also created to be used with several recent books by our "family" of coauthors. Over the past ten years, our own collaborative group has created a library of books focused on building students' knowledge and skill through the direct teaching of learning strategies in the context of challenging inquiry units, extensive peer collaboration, and practical, formative assessments.

Among these books are:

- *Best Practice: Bringing Standards to Life in America's Classrooms*, 4th edition (Zemelman, Daniels, and Hyde 2012)

- *Best Practice Video Companion* (Zemelman and Daniels 2012)

- *Comprehension Going Forward* (Daniels 2011)

- *Texts and Lessons for Content-Area Reading* (Daniels and Steineke 2011)

- *Assessment Live: 10 Real-Time Ways for Kids to Show What They Know—and Meet the Standards* (Steineke 2009)

- *Comprehension and Collaboration: Inquiry Circles in Action* (Harvey and Daniels 2009)

- *Mini-lessons for Literature Circles* (Daniels and Steineke 2006)

- *Content-Area Writing: Every Teacher's Guide* (Daniels, Zemelman, and Steineke 2005)

- *Subjects Matter: Every Teacher's Guide to Content-Area Reading* (Daniels and Zemelman 2004)

- *Reading and Writing Together* (Steineke 2003)

Chapter 4 offers seven lessons, each dedicated to one of these cognitive strategies, in the above order. But these seven core reading strategies are fully incorporated throughout the book; kids will practice each one repeatedly as you lead them through the readings, activities, and conversations.

Assessment

If you are going to devote ten minutes or twenty-five minutes or a whole class period to one of these lessons, the question naturally arises: How do I grade this? After all, in today's schools, it seems like we have to assess, or at least assign a grade to, almost any activity kids spend time on.

It is important to recognize that these lessons, by themselves, do not lead to final public outcomes, such as polished essays or crafted speeches. They can and often do serve as *starting points* for just such projects, which require extra time and support for their completion. But as they stand, our lessons are more like guided practice, opportunities for kids to read and write and talk *to learn.* That requires an appropriate approach to assessment.

Participation Points

You can certainly give kids points or grades for effective participation in these lessons. But if you start *qualitatively* grading every piece of kids' work on activities like these, trying to defend the difference between a 78 and a 23, you're going to give up huge chunks of your own time marking, scoring, and justifying. Maybe this is some of our old Chicago "tough love" creeping in, but for smaller everyday assignments, we use binary grading: yes/no, on/off, all/nothing. We give 10 points for full participation and 0 points for non-full participation. No 3s, no 7.5s. Ten or zero, that's it.

Our colleague Jim Vopat has brought some poetry to this kind of grading in his book *Writing Circles* (2009). Jim calls this "good faith effort." If a student shows up prepared to work, having all the necessary materials (reading done, notes ready), joins in the work with energy, and carries a fair share of the work— that's a "good faith effort" and earns full points. From a practical point of view, this means we only need to keep track of the few kids who *don't* put forth that GFE, and remember to enter that zero in our gradebook later on.

Still, let's be honest. Giving points is not assessment, it's just grading. When we want to get serious and really scrutinize kids' thinking in these activities, we have to take further steps.

Collect and Save Student Work

As kids do the activities in these forty-five lessons, they naturally create and leave behind writings, lists, drawings, notes, and other tracks of their thinking. So why pop a quiz? Instead, collect, study, and save the naturally occurring by-products of kids' learning. These authentic artifacts, this residue of thinking, are far more meaningful than a disembodied "72" in your gradebook. The kids' own creations are also far more relevant in a parent conference or a principal evaluation than a string of point totals in a gradebook.

OBSERVATION CHART

STUDENT NAME	"GOOD FAITH"	QUOTE	THINKING	SOCIAL SKILLS
1.				
2.				
3.				
4.				
5.				

Observe Kids at Work

The form on page 16 is a tool we use when sitting with a group of kids, watching them work on a lesson together. As you can see, this form incorporates Vopat's good faith idea and then goes much further. As we listen in on kids, we jot down one memorable quote from each student and reflect on what kind of thinking this comment or question represents; we also take notes on any conspicuous use (or neglect) of the collaboration skills called for in the lesson.

Offer Meaningful Performance Opportunities

When the time comes to assign grades for kids' work over long stretches of time and big chunks of content, we traditionally make up a big test and add that score to the points kids have earned along the way. Even as we do this, we quietly recognize that this assessment system invites cramming, superficiality, and the wholesale forgetting of content.

Instead, we like to devise authentic events at which kids share or perform their learning for an engaged audience—and then we use a rubric that carefully defines a successful performance to derive each kid's grade. This might mean a polished essay published on the web, a series of tableaux performed with a group, or a full-scale public debate or talk show enactment. Nancy has written a whole book with ideas on this kind of performance process called *Assessment Live: 10 Real-Time Ways for Kids to Show What They Know—and Meet the Standards* (Heinemann 2009).

Have Fun

We're serious about putting this "F-word" back into school. The two of us had a blast searching out these amazing short texts and using them with kids around the country. In those classrooms, everyone seemed to have a good time reading, savoring, analyzing, debating, and even rereading these little literary gemstones. Field-testing these lessons with kids has reminded us that "all adolescents want to work hard and do well," as the brilliant British educator Charity James once wrote in her book *Young Lives at Stake: The Education of Adolescents*.

Or you can just call it "*rigor* without the *mortis*."

Enjoy!

Smokey and Nancy

SHARING LITERATURE ALOUD

Wise classroom practices—and the Common Core Standards—recognize the importance of both teachers and students reading short literature selections aloud, and paying close attention to the language, the ideas, and their own thinking as they do so.

LESSON 3.1

Pair Share

TEXT ▶ "Choices Made," by Jim O'Loughlin

TIME ▶ 10 Minutes

GROUPING SEQUENCE ▶ Pairs, whole class

USED IN TEXT SETS ▶ 3, 8

This fifty-five-word story embodies a classic conversation starter: if you had to suddenly flee your home, what three things would you take?

Well, it does happen. Every August, hurricane season begins in earnest. People who live near the Atlantic coast must face the weather predictions with a combination of dread, fear, and distrust. As we all know, for every prediction that is dead-on, it seems like the previous ninety-nine—or more—have fizzled. In the Midwest, we don't have hurricanes; we have tornadoes, mostly tornado watches and warnings that seldom become tornadoes. But when those storms do make a direct hit, it's often with little or no advance notice—especially if it's the middle of the night and people are sleeping. In the rest of the country, depending on where you live and the season, you might be worrying about floods, mudslides, brush/forest fires, or earthquakes. So, unlike the unwary character in this story, be prepared!

> **PREPARATION**
>
> Copy the two-paragraph story and cut it in half. Good news: if you have a class of thirty, you'll only need to make fifteen copies! Be sure to put all the beginnings in one pile and the endings in another.

Steps & Teaching Language ▶

STEP 1 **Organize pairs.** Whenever kids will be working in pairs, they need to know who their partner is *beforehand*, and they need to move into a good conversation position—face to face, eye to eye, knee to knee (probably not cheek to cheek). This setup encourages the use of "indoor voices" and prevents noisy, time-wasting shuffling around mid-lesson. For pairs, we like to have the kids simply push their desks together or sit directly across a table from each other. In this lesson, sitting side by side works best because both students will be reading from the same page.

STEP 2 **Turn and talk.** Pose the question that we previewed earlier: *If you had to escape from your house with only three things (assuming your family and pets are OK), what would you take? Turn to your partner and share your answers. Don't forget to explain why these items are important to you. What do they symbolize or represent?*

STEP 3 **Introduce and pass out the story.** Each pair receives two handouts, the beginning and the end of the story, face down. *OK, first figure out which of you two has the earliest birthday in the year. Got it? OK, the person with the earliest birthday gets the first half of the story, and the other gets the ending. As I pass this story out to you, I want you to keep* them face down *for the time being. No peeking!*

STEP 4 **Give instructions.** *Early birthdays, ready? When I say go, turn your paper over and begin reading aloud. Make sure you put the story in the middle so that your partner can follow along. Once you finish reading, stop and talk. Share your reactions, talk about what's going on and why the character chose not to take those items. Be sure that both you and your partner contribute and that you actively challenge each other to go into detail and really explain your thoughts.*

When you are finished discussing the first half, the late birthdays should turn their sheet over, put it between you, and then read aloud as your partner follows along. After reading, have another discussion following the same guidelines. Except this time, you need to talk about what the character did take with him.

STEP 5 **Concluding pairs discussion.** *I see that most of you have finished. Before we share in a large group, I want you to recall the items you would have taken in an emergency and compare yourselves to the story character. What did you have in common? What things were different?*

STEP 6 **Share with the whole class.** *How did you explain what this character actually took versus what he might have taken when he thought about it later? What might these items symbolize? How did your "emergency items" compare with the character's choices?*

Don't prolong the sharing. Just get a few quick responses to each of the questions. The important conversational work took place as the pairs discussed together.

Even simpler: While we usually complicate things in these variations, this lesson actually has some fun wrinkles already. So we'll just mention a *simpler* version for this one. Eliminate the cutting in half and just let partners gobble the story in one gulp (thirty seconds?), then get into that turn-and-talk.

◀ *Variation*

COMMON CORE STANDARDS SUPPORTED

- Read closely to determine what the text says explicitly and to make logical inferences from it; cite specific textual evidence when writing or speaking to support conclusions drawn from the text. *(CCRA.R.1)*

- Interpret words and phrases as they are used in a text, including figurative meanings. *(CCRA.R.4)*

- Assess how point of view shapes the content and style of a text. *(CCRA.R.6)*

- Participate effectively in a range of conversations and collaborations. *(CCRA.SL.1)*

If you are using a basal or anthology, it probably tells you little or nothing about how to set up successful partner or small-group work in your class. (You may find some notes about social skills in the teacher's edition). If you skipped our Chapter 2, check it out: there's some helpful information about training kids for small-group work back on pages 10–13. Making these crucial advance moves, such as setting up partners first and making sure they are positioned to communicate, makes a huge difference with our lessons—or the ones in your textbook.

Still have kids who don't want to work with each other? Tell them that *your* standard is that "everybody works with everybody in here." Then form partners daily, by random drawing, so the pairing is not about you—and so that everyone eventually does work with everyone else. Acquaintance builds friendliness.

Choices Made

Jim O'Loughlin

Part 1

Later, he would be able to consider all that he had left behind and never saw again: the wedding album, the birth certificates, the kids' favorite toys, even the laptop. In the moment though, with the storm surging and blow back peeling off the roof like masking tape, he only had time to grab what he could on the way out.

Choices Made

Jim O'Loughlin

Part 2

Still, even as he ran to the car, dripping sweat and bleeding from the gash in his forehead, with the river already up to the wheel wells, he realized that the choices he had just made said something about who he was. In his arms, he held a phone book, the cantaloupe that had just turned ripe, and a gallon of milk. And he had made sure to lock the front door.

Teacher Read-Aloud

TEXT ▶ Preface from *The Winter Room,* by Gary Paulsen

TIME ▶ 20 minutes

GROUPING SEQUENCE ▶ Whole class, pairs, whole class

USED IN TEXT SETS ▶ 2, 3, 8

For many of us who are lifelong readers today, our fascination with books and literature often began with someone in our childhood who read to us out loud. For Nancy, it was her father.

> *I think he read to me just about every night before I went to bed until I was in seventh grade and decided I was "just too old for that." Over fifty years later, I still remember those books:* The City Under the Back Steps *(bitten by the ant queen, children shrink and are taken captive by the colony!). And then there was the book about bees whose title I cannot recall. I liked that one so much my father read it to me twice, but on the second reading I requested he skip the part where most of the bees died in late fall; it was just too sad. By sixth grade, I took an interest in ghost stories, so the author du jour was Edgar Allan Poe. Poe's story about premature burial really creeped me out! The last book my father read to me was* Dracula *by Bram Stoker.*

Whoever our read-aloud partners were, they gave us a huge leg up to literacy—and they helped us fall in love with reading. For those of us lucky enough to have had such transformative experiences, we can remember being delightedly catapulted into unknown times and worlds, materializing amid the lives and adventures of amazing characters, delivered there on the wings of language used well.

The Common Core Standards and many sample units being developed around the country rely very heavily on teachers reading texts aloud to their students at all grade levels. And if oral reading is going to be central to our work with kids, we'd better do it well. Many elementary teachers actually get instruction and practice in oral interpretation as part of their formal teacher training. But middle and high school teachers, unless we also teach speech and drama, may not feel so confident and eager to start doing more reading aloud. So what do we do? Plan ahead, rehearse literature you love, keep it simple, and practice, practice, practice. Here's a simple lesson to start.

PREPARATION

Carefully rehearse this wonderful text, the preface to Gary Paulsen's *The Winter Room* (or another evocative short text that you love). Before you "go live" in class, read it aloud to yourself five times, and develop an interpretation that both highlights the author's words as you understand them, and also brings your own distinctive thinking, feeling, and voice to the text. If you like, mark the text for pauses, volume changes, dramatic effects, and so on. You are ready when you can read the piece aloud while looking mostly at your students, with just a few glances at the page. Doing your final practices in front of a mirror is a way to polish your performance.

In addition to rehearsing the oral interpretation, don't forget to plan your introduction. We've given you the intro this time, but since this is such a versatile reading strategy, we know you'll be using it time and again. Besides mentioning title and author, you might need to give students some story setup about plot in characters, particularly if you have chosen a scene from within a novel. Finally, decide what you want your listeners to do. Are they going to listen for the use of a specific craft technique (which we'll be discussing later), or do you want them to just sit back and enjoy the story, letting them respond afterwards to what stirred them?

We have chosen this text especially for its power to evoke strong feelings and stir vivid visual images. Here we have the power of literature in its most concentrated form. This is the kind of text that kids can fall in love with—and that can help inspire them to be writers themselves, knocking people's socks off with words just like Gary Paulsen's.

COMMON CORE STANDARDS SUPPORTED

- Interpret words and phrases as they are used in a text, including determining connotative and figurative meanings. *(CCRA.R.4)*

- Assess how point of view or purpose shapes the content and style of a text. *(CCRA.R.6)*

- Participate effectively in a range of conversations and collaborations. *(CCRA.SL.1)*

◀ **Steps & Teaching Language**

STEP 1 **Get kids set.** Have kids clear their desktops and determine who will be their pair-share partner after the read-aloud.

In a minute I am going to read you a short excerpt from a book you may know, The Winter Room *by Gary Paulsen. Everyone be sure you know who your partner is so you two can talk afterwards. Ready? Now, just settle back, feel quiet, let these words wash over you, and try to go wherever the author takes you. OK?*

STEP 2 **Read aloud.** Read the selection, using your well-rehearsed dramatic interpretation.

STEP 3 **Pair share.** *OK, turn and talk with your partner. What did you notice? How did you feel? What do you wonder? Where did the author take you? Go ahead . . .*

STEP 4 **Open discussion. Invite a few pairs to share their reactions.** The immediate goal is simply for kids to notice how well-crafted words on a page can reach right into our heads and generate strong sensory images and emotional responses. We are focusing first on response, not analysis.

STEP 5 **Deeper discussion.** Now invite kids to dig deeper into their response to talk about which specific images, what chunks of language, worked to create a visceral response.

Who can point out a specific word or line that created a strong impression? Another? What is it about Paulsen's language that makes it so powerful? This piece is a preface to Paulsen's book The Winter Room. *What do you think the author's purpose was in placing this particular piece right at the front of a novel? And why the title, "Tuning"?"*

Variations ▶

- **Frequency:** Reading aloud is not something we do just once. Many of this book's upcoming lessons will incorporate read-alouds as part of the experience. But just doing this simple, quick version frequently is well worth the time. Some great teachers we know do a literature read-aloud *every day*, just to attune kids' ears to great writing and language. Wow, think of that—180 great passages in a school year!

- **Kid read-alouds:** Have individual kids select, rehearse, and perform brief read-alouds—no more than one per day. Before the first volunteer presents, offer a whole-class lesson on how to be an attentive and supportive audience. Co-create a list of what positive audience members do and say, and keep it posted during the reading. Always have a specific prompt for listeners to report on afterwards (the most powerful word; something I visualized, etc.), so they feel accountable and stay focused.

Shoptalk ▶

- Want to become an even better read-alouder? Check the classic *Read Aloud Handbook* by Jim Trelease. Or listen to some of the many of the adult and YA audiobooks now available on CD or through websites like www.techsupportalert.com/free-books-audio.

- Reading aloud is a great way to introduce difficult text to students when they will need to finish the reading on their own. In the dramatic way we've outlined, read the beginning of the story, essay, or novel aloud. Ahead of time, determine where you will stop and have students turn and talk. What are they going to talk about? What characters have been introduced? What is the attitude of the author toward the topic under discussion? You name it. The point is to get kids talking about and clarifying the issues that are initially confusing. Typically, after a couple of pages of read-aloud, students have the foundation necessary to dive into and finish the text on their own.

Tuning
Preface from *The Winter Room*

Gary Paulsen

If books could be more, could show more, could own more, this book would have smells . . .

It would have the smells of old farms; the sweet smell of new-mown hay as it falls off the oiled sickle blade when the horses pull the mower through the field, and the sour smell of manure steaming in a winter barn. It would have the sticky-slick smell of birth when the calves come and they suck for the first time on the rich, new milk; the dusty smell of winter hay dried and stored in the loft waiting to be dropped down to the cattle; the pungent fermented smell of the chopped corn silage when it is brought into the manger on the silage fork. This book would have the smell of new potatoes sliced and frying in light pepper on a woodstove burning dry pine, the damp smell of leather mittens steaming on the back of the stovetop, and the acrid smell of the slop bucket by the door when the lid is lifted and the potato peelings are dumped in—but it can't.

Books can't have smells.

If books could be more and own more and give more, this book would have sound . . .

It would have the high, keening sound of the six-foot bucksaws as the men pull them back and forth through the trees to cut pine for paper pulp; the grunting-gassy sounds of the work teams snorting and slapping as they hit the harness to jerk the stumps out of the ground. It would have the chewing sounds of cows in the barn working at their cuds on a long winter's night; the solid thunking sound of the ax coming down to split stovewood, and the piercing scream of the pigs when the knife cuts their throats and they know death is at hand—but it can't.

Books can't have sound.

And finally if books could be more, give more, show more, this book would have light . . .

Oh, it would have the soft gold light—gold with bits of hay dust floating in it—that slips through the crack in the barn wall; the light of the Coleman lantern hissing flat-white in the kitchen; the silver-gray light of a middle winter day, the splattered, white-night light of a full moon on snow, the new light of dawn at the eastern edge of the pasture behind the cows coming in to be milked on a summer morning—but it can't.

Books can't have light.

If books could have more, give more, be more, show more, they would still need readers, who bring to them sound and smell and light and all the rest that can't be in books.

The book needs you.

One-Minute Write

TEXT ▶ "The Limited,"
by Sherman Alexie

TIME ▶ 20 Minutes

GROUPING SEQUENCE ▶ Whole
class, pairs, whole class

USED IN TEXT SET ▶ 3

You know how inexplicable anger can suddenly flash between two drivers on the road? Here's a Sherman Alexie poem about that disturbing phenomenon.

But there is more happening in these lines, too, about *machismo* and being a poet and existential despair. So "The Limited" is a made-to-order poem that lets kids respond to its surface events, but also rewards further scrutiny. As we often say, the road to analysis leads through response. If we expect kids to dig into texts, we have to show them how and why—and make it fun.

> ### PREPARATION
>
> Be prepared to read the poem to the class. Make sure kids have blank paper or journals ready for a quick written response. Prearrange partner matchups.

Steps & Teaching Language ▶

STEP 1 **Explain the lesson.** *I'm going to read you a short poem by Sherman Alexie. After I'm done, we are all going to take one minute and jot down our responses and reactions to the poem. OK, ready?*

STEP 2 **Read the poem aloud.** Now, using the expressive skills you brought to the prior lesson, read "The Limited" with drama and energy.

STEP 3 **One-minute write.** *OK, let's write. Wherever the poem takes you, whatever it makes you see or think or wonder, what it reminds you of, why you think Alexie wrote this poem, just jot it down. Use all the time I'm giving you—keep that pen moving for the whole sixty seconds. I'll tell you when time is up. Go.*

As a good model, you should write about the poem also, unless you have kids who cannot function without your help. In that case, prepare your one-minute write beforehand.

STEP 4 **Share with partners.** Have kids meet in pairs and take turns reading aloud their responses to the poem. Circulate and support them as needed. As students share, project the poem and encourage them to reread it and see what else they notice.

STEP 5 **Class discussion.** Allow the projection to remain as you wrap up discussion. *Now let's get a sense of all the different responses that this poem inspired. Who had a partner who had an interesting idea about the poem? Can you summarize their idea for us?* Notice that this is a very precise prompt; you are asking kids to summarize what their partner wrote, not their own response. Get a good sampling around the room, and dig for the whole range of responses. *Who had a partner who had a* *different take on this poem?* At an appropriate moment, chip in your own one-minute write. In this step, you are not seeking to get "correct" interpretations of the poem, but to evoke kids' curiosity and conversation about it.

STEP 6   **Moving toward analysis.** Get ready to read "The Limited" aloud a second time. Tell kids that this time they should be asking themselves: Why did Alexie write this poem? What is his message or theme? What word choices make this poem powerful? What about the poem's structure makes it work? Then, another one-minute write can focus on the author's craft and purpose, with a second whole-class discussion to share and connect.

COMMON CORE STANDARDS SUPPORTED

- Determine central ideas or themes of a text. *(CCRA.R.2)*
- Analyze how specific word choices shape meaning or tone. *(CCRA.R.4)*
- Analyze the structure of texts. *(CCRA.R.5)*
- Participate effectively in a range of conversations and collaborations. *(CCRA.SL.1)*

What makes a poem a poem? "The Limited" supports plenty of attention to its craft, structure, and very sparing use of poetic elements. Here's one engaging follow-up. If these lines were typed in prose form on a page, would they still make a poem? If so, which ingredients cause that?

◀ *Variation*

One-minute writes are especially helpful when you want kids to form an opinion of a character or narrator in the first few paragraphs of a longer work. This can be a helpful predicting/inferring challenge, requiring that kids use text details to project future developments in the work. We also frequently rely on one-minute writes to make sure students develop their own thinking before beginning a discussion with a partner or small group. That way there's less likelihood of students "bandwagoning" on what others say.

◀ *Shoptalk*

"The Limited" makes you wonder: Am I an upstander or a bystander? Though we don't necessarily see someone purposely attempt to kill a dog, we all witness incidents of bullying, discrimination, intimidation. And we all grapple with this moral dilemma: Do I stand by and do nothing, or risk my own safety in order to take a stand? Take a look at the selections in your textbook. Which ones carry this theme? Alexie's poem would make an excellent introduction to these longer works.

The Limited

Sherman Alexie

I saw a man swerve his car
And try to hit a stray dog,
But the quick mutt dodged
Between two parked cars

And made his escape.
God, I thought, did I just see
What I think I saw?
At the next red light,

I pulled up beside the man
And stared hard at him.
He knew that I'd seen
His murder attempt,

But he didn't care.
He smiled and yelled loud
Enough for me to hear him
Through our closed windows:

"Don't give me that face
Unless you're going to do
Something about it.
Come on, tough guy,

What are you going to do?"
I didn't do anything.
I turned right on the green.
He turned left against traffic.

I don't know what happened
To that man or the dog,
But I drove home
And wrote this poem.

Why do poets think
They can change the world?
The only life I can save
Is my own.

Teacher Think-Aloud

Face it, none of us would have gone into English language arts if we hadn't loved to read. We were the kids whose third-grade "bookworms" had more segments than anyone else's. We were the kids who made weekly—maybe daily—trips to the library. When we read, we just cruise. Yeah, sometimes we run into some difficult text, but it doesn't shake us. If we have to read it, we just buckle down and use the strategies we've unconsciously developed over the years. We recognize the text for what it is (perhaps one that is not particularly considerate of its readers) and we deal with it. When it comes down to it, even when we try to empathize with our students' text struggles, it's sometimes difficult because we just haven't felt their struggles in a long, long time—if ever.

Nancy: *If you want to really put yourself in your students' shoes, try learning to do something for which you have little aptitude or background knowledge. A few years ago, I unwittingly put myself in that position when I decided to take guitar lessons. Yes, I had played piano and flute in my teens, so I had a leg up on reading music. But here's the news: eking some real music out of a guitar has nothing in common with the flute or the piano. Besides the fact that the strings literally cut into your fingers until your tips develop calluses, and your useless hand (in my case my left) has to learn how to move its fingers precisely and independently of one another as they stretch and contort to simultaneously hit the strings in three or four different frets.*

Five years later I'm still taking lessons and my left-hand fingers are slowly adapting. Along the way, my guitar teacher regularly says things like "Watch me" or "Try this" or "Do it again this way." What is he doing? He's modeling, guiding, and teaching me strategies, strategies that I am grateful for as a struggling guitarist.

That frustrating, uncomfortable, incompetent feeling I get while learning guitar is exactly the same feeling the kids have when they pick up a challenging text. If my guitar teacher just handed me some music and said, "Play," I'd probably just give up. Though our kids can't officially quit, they do unofficially when they refuse to read or put their heads down. As teachers, we need to check our assumptions at the door and greet the kids as readers ready to progress with our guidance. And the best way to begin the process is to show the kids how we think when we read.

TEXT ▶ "Untitled," by Dan Argent

TIME ▶ 15 Minutes

GROUPING SEQUENCE ▶ Recurrent whole class, pairs, whole class

USED IN TEXT SET ▶ 3

PREPARATION

Make a copy of the story "Untitled" for each student. Cut the copies in two, so students cannot read ahead. This lesson will work best if you can project the text and our ongoing annotation as you read. Determine how pairs will form for quick sharing.

Steps & ▶ Teaching Language

STEP 1 **Pass out the first half of the story.** *Today I'm going to give you a chance to peek inside my brain and see what I'm thinking as I read. Being conscious of your thoughts as you read is probably one of the most important things you can do to understand a text. As I read, I'm also going to mark down some things that stand out to me and seem important, details that give me clues.*

STEP 2 **Read the first paragraph.** As you read, project the text and mark the words and phrases you talk about. Your comments might go something like this.

- *The title of this story is "Untitled." That isn't very helpful in predicting what this story is about. That means I'm going to have to pay close attention to the first clues.*

- *Marlowe-8210-K. That sounds like a robot's name. Is Karl a robot? Maybe this story is taking place in the future.*

- *Seems like the brothers are struggling: shabbier part of city, small apartment.*

- *Societal utility score? That definitely sounds like the future.*

- *The last of our clone line—so Karl isn't a robot, but there are a lot of copies of him. Does that mean he is identical to his brother?*

- *The machines designed . . . Wow, now this future is starting to sound like that film* The Terminator *where the machines took over mankind.*

- *What happens to a clone line that doesn't live up to expectations? If I were Karl, I'd be worried.*

STEP 3 **Invite students to describe your thinking.** *What did you notice about my comments? What was I thinking about? What details in the story did I skip over? Which ones did I home in on? Why? Turn to your partner and talk for a moment.* Give pairs a minute and then share out.

STEP 4 **Invite students to share their thinking.** *Take a moment to reread this first paragraph. Your responses were probably different from many of mine. What details stand out to you that I didn't connect with? What are you thinking?* Give students a minute or two to reread and think.

Turn to your partner and explain your thoughts. Quick share out.

STEP 5 **Pass out the second half of the story.** At this point you need to decide how to continue. You have several options.

- Continue modeling your thinking just as you did with the first half.

- Continue reading aloud but let kids join in and help you (a shared reading). Read a couple of sentences aloud at a time and then stop for students to do a quick pair share to describe their own thinking.

COMMON CORE STANDARDS SUPPORTED

- Read closely to determine what the text says explicitly and to make logical inferences from it; cite specific textual evidence when writing or speaking to support conclusions drawn from the text. *(CCRA.R.1)*

- Summarize the key supporting details and ideas. *(CCRA.R.2)*

- Assess how point of view or purpose shapes the content and style of a text. *(CCRA.R.6)*

- Participate effectively in a range of conversations and collaborations. *(CCRA.SL.1)*

- Have students read the second paragraph silently, marking the places where they stopped to think. Then have pairs share their thoughts and end with pairs sharing in the large group.

STEP 6 **Discuss the story's conclusion.** *How does Karl's description of his life's events build to the ending? What's going to happen to Karl and his brother Jay? What kind of emotional feeling do you get from the end of the story?* Partners trade thoughts and then share with the whole class.

Any piece of text—from your anthology, from this week's *New Yorker,* or from a novel—can be used for a think-aloud. And it's vital for students to regularly listen to a proficient reader's internal running conversation. Too often, kids will push their eyes across a text without demanding that it make sense along the way. Making think-alouds a predictable part of classroom practice helps emphasize this key to mastering more difficult texts.

Also, consider modeling craft think-alouds. Let students first read a piece silently as they monitor their own thinking. Then read the piece aloud the second time, stopping to highlight your thinking when you notice the similes, interesting word play, and so on. But here's the catch. Just briefly *model your thinking*. If you're not careful, your read-aloud can morph into read-aloud-plus-lecture! And of course, after you've read aloud a couple of paragraphs, turn the think-aloud back over to the kids to practice with their partners as you monitor and coach. Think-alouds are totally essential to growing better readers, but a little of this modeling goes a long way; three or four minutes is the longest think-aloud we would ever offer.

◀ *Shoptalk*

Untitled

Dan Argent

My full name is Marlowe-8210-K, but everyone calls me Karl. I live in an apartment with my brother Jay in one of the shabbier parts of the city. Our apartment is pretty small, just the two rooms and a shower cubby, but that's all we can afford these days. Our societal utility score is low, almost zero, and if things don't take a turn for the better soon, I'll be the last of our clone-line born into this world. Sure, the Machines designed our genotype to produce a long line of great artists, but after eleven generations all that the Marlowe-8210 line had to show for itself was a mildly fashionable decade back around brother Frank's day. It's almost funny sometimes—the Machines can calculate the folding of a protein to the nth degree of accuracy, but human biology is still stubbornly imperfect and messy. Most of the time they get what they want, but some clone-lines just don't live up to expectations.

I can hear Jay cursing in the next room. He's a lot older than me, at least three decades, and I think it depresses him living with a younger copy. Right now he's working on something, some kind of mood sculpture, but he finds it hard to concentrate. I suppose he feels responsible for it all, being the older sibling. I tell him not to worry, that when I've finished school I'll create something stupendous, some work of art that will go down in history. Most of the time that cheers him up, but sometimes he gets angry and can't bear to be around me. I don't dare tell him that according to my teacher I'm even worse an artist than he is. Anyway, I'm hiding this recording under the apartment floor with a photo of me and Jay plus a few micro-lithographs that we made together. I know it's stupid, but I just want to leave something, some small indication that once our family existed. Things don't seem so bad when I think that perhaps someday someone will view this.

Remember us,
Karl

Partner Think-Aloud

Have you ever seen a movie that doesn't spell things out? Two that come to mind for us are *The Sixth Sense* and *No Country for Old Men.* After seeing those movies, we just *had* to talk to others who saw them. *What do you think happened when . . . At what point did you realize . . . ? Really? Are you sure that's what happened? What made you think that?*

Those scripts were written to puzzle and keep viewers engaged long after they left the theater. The same is true with literature. We've got to get students to welcome pieces that are challenging and puzzling rather than dreading them because the plot lines and details are not neatly spelled out. Experimenting with some really short stories provides this fun kind of practice.

TEXT ▸ "There's No Place Like It," by Dean Christianson "Death in the Afternoon," by Priscilla Mintling

TIME ▸ 20 minutes (can be split into two lessons over two days)

GROUPING SEQUENCE ▸ Recurrent pairs, whole class

USED IN TEXT SET ▸ 7

PREPARATION

These two stories are designed to be *projected* for your class to read, not copied. Have loose-leaf paper or journals ready for students to jot notes. Determine how students will form partners for sharing.

STEP 1 **Project "There's No Place Like It" and explain reading aloud.** *Take a look at the story on the screen. It's pretty short and written with a combination of narration and dialogue. With your partner, I want one of you to read the narration and the other to read what's in the quotes. After you finish the story, switch parts and read it a second time. Got it? Go.*

As students read, monitor the room so that you can move on to the next step as soon as they are finished.

STEP 2 **What do you notice/think?** *Now that you've read the story twice, look back at it. With your partner, take turns picking out a line and describe what it makes you think about or imagine. Are there any lines that remind you of another story you've read or a movie/television program you've seen? As you talk, jot down a few quick notes so that you'll remember what you talked about when we share in a few minutes.*

STEP 3 **Sharing.** *What did you notice or think when you talked about this story with your partner?* Call on or ask for volunteers. Be sure to elicit some conversation about the irony of the ending if students don't bring it up on their own.

STEP 4 **Project "Death in the Afternoon" and explain reading aloud.** *This story is written in the same style as the previous one: super short and written with a combination of narration and dialogue. Once again, with your partner, I want one of you to read the narration and the other to read*

◀ **Steps** & **Teaching Language**

what's in the quotes. After you finish the story, switch parts and read it a second time. Got it? Go.

As students read, monitor the room so that you can move on to the next step as soon as they are finished.

STEP 5 **What do you notice/think?** *Now that you've read the story twice, look back at it. With your partner, take turns picking out a line and describe what it makes you think about or imagine. This story seems pretty simple at first but becomes more puzzling as you begin to explore. What's going on here?*

STEP 6 **Sharing.** *What did you notice or think when you talked about this story with your partner?* Call on or ask for volunteers. Be sure to elicit some conversation about the ending if students don't bring it up on their own. There can be multiple interpretations, all of which can be valuable as long as students can use the text to defend their conclusions.

Variation ▶ **Spread it out:** This lesson is set up for students to read and discuss two very short stories in one period. But splitting this lesson between two days would be just as effective.

Shoptalk ▶ You can use this lesson with any text that alternates between narration and dialogue—a pretty common format in literature, if you think about it. This lesson may challenge your kids a bit. We know that direct teacher modeling is rare in school, but student read- or think-alouds are almost unheard of. So, if you think your kids may find this activity extra challenging, be sure to model your own read-alouds and think-alouds for them first (Lessons 3.2, pages 22–24, and 3.4, pages 29–31.)

There's No Place Like It

Dean Christianson

The President was rushed to the Arizona desert to greet the arrival of the huge alien spacecraft.

"Peace," said the President.

"Thank you," said the very human-looking alien. "We've been on a million-year universal tour. We're excited about returning home."

"Please, visit. Then, good journey."

"No, you misunderstand," said the alien. "We *are* home."

Death in the Afternoon

Priscilla Mintling

"Come out from behind the tree, Louie, so I can spray your brains all over."

"You don't have the guts to pull the trigger."

"I've got more guts than you're gonna have brains."

"You've got peanuts for brains, Tony."

Bang!

"...and another!"

Bang!

"Louis! Tony! Supper!"

"Comin', Mom!"

Reading comprehension research shows that effective readers employ a finite set of thinking strategies as they make meaning from text: monitoring comprehension, connecting, visualizing, questioning, inferring, determining importance, and synthesizing. In this chapter, we offer one lesson for each strategy, in that order.

LESSON 4.1   Text Annotation

Have you ever watched your students numbly run their eyes across a page of text, and you can tell there is absolutely no comprehension happening at all? Scary, huh? But, to be honest, the same thing has probably happened to us, while reading something hard or boring, or at the end of a long day, when we are falling asleep with a novel in our lap.

But skillful, proficient readers (like us, usually) bring their full attention to reading, demanding clarity of the text as they go. They don't let their mind wander; they are actively thinking, processing the ideas as they read. One tool that powerful readers use to support this kind of thinking is text annotation, the practice of stopping to think and jot notes as they read.

There are a million ways to mark up text, using handwritten codes, symbols, or highlighting tools. And now there are digital programettes that allow you to stick your personal Post-it notes on any document in the whole Internet. Pretty cool.

But the most basic and important annotation of all is simply *writing words in the margin* that capture your thinking as you go, leaving tracks of your thinking right in the text. While our end goal is for kids to find their own stop-and-think spots, for this initial lesson, we provide a puzzling text with four preselected stopping places.

TEXT ▶ "Afterthoughts," by Sara Holbrook

"The Boy They Didn't Take Pictures Of," by Dave Eggers

TIME ▶ 50 Minutes

GROUPING SEQUENCE ▶ Whole class, pairs, whole class

USED IN TEXT SETS ▶ 4, 5

PREPARATION

For modeling your own annotation in Step 2, be ready to project the Holbrook poem or another short text of your preference. Have copies of the Eggers story ready to hand out, and predetermine partners.

STEP 1   **Explain annotation.** *Have you ever heard that expression, "getting lost in a book"? What does that mean? Has that ever happened to you?* Students will probably volunteer that this happens when they are reading a favorite YA author or series. *So sometimes we can read a work of literature straight through and understand it fine, first time. If the story is easy enough and interesting enough, we can kind of fall into it, like you get lost in a good novel.*

◀ **Steps** & **Teaching Language**

But other times, when we want to read harder texts, we can't just magically "get lost" in it—we need to be very active and intentional to make sure we understand what we read. Or we might get lost in a whole other way!

One way skillful readers enhance their understanding is by annotating the text, *which just means jotting notes in the margin that help them think about the story. You can use a journal, or a bookmark, or Post-it notes for this, and when you have your own copy, as we do today, you can write right on the story.*

STEP 2 **Model how to annotate text.** *Let me show you what I mean.* Project the Holbrook poem. Read aloud, stopping once in the middle and again at the end, and jot some notes that reflect your thinking about the piece, reading them aloud as you write. Basically, the first half of the poem talks about kinds of thoughts we keep bottled up inside, while the second part is about the benefits of expressing and working with our thoughts, whatever they are.

STEP 3 **Show thinking chart.** Next, show kids this list and point out which ones you just did (you don't need to try to do all of them, just a couple is fine). This chart will also be used in some later lessons.

THINGS TO THINK ABOUT WHILE READING

- What I understand right now (what's happening, who's who)
- Personal experiences that I am reminded of
- Visual or sensory images I am experiencing as I read
- Questions or wonderings that pop into my head
- Predictions about what might happen next
- Parts that seem especially important, interesting, or well written
- What I think the purpose or message is

You'll recognize that these topics are restatements of the seven comprehension strategies featured in Chapter 2 (pages 6–17): monitoring, connecting, visualizing, questioning, inferring, determining importance, and synthesizing.

STEP 4 **Introduce the story and discuss the title.** *Now it's your turn to try annotating. Today, we are going to read and annotate a story by Dave Eggers called "The Boy They Wouldn't Take Pictures Of." That's kind of a weird title for a story, isn't it? What do you think it might be about?*

Let kids speculate about the possible content of the story for two or three minutes. Already, you are helping them to think about the upcoming piece.

STEP 5 **Distribute the story and give instructions for reading and annotation.** *OK, here comes your copy of the story. The idea is* not *to read the whole thing through, but to stop and jot your thinking during your first "cold" reading. There are four stopping places marked along the way.*

Now you're going to record your thinking just like I did with the Holbrook poem. When you hit a stopping place, pull out of the text and jot some notes in the margin about what you are thinking at that moment. You'll probably write a few phrases or a couple sentences at each stopping place. I'll leave the "Things to Think About While Reading" chart up in case you need help.

I'm going to give you about five minutes for this, so you should have plenty of time to record some thoughtful notes. When you're done, you will be sharing these with a partner. Then later I'll collect them so I can see your thinking also. If you finish before other people, go back and reread the story and revise your notes. OK? Go.

STEP 6 **Monitor, circulate, assist.** Watch time carefully—you may need to shorten or extend it based on students' response.

STEP 7 **Pairs compare notes.** *Now get with your partner and take turns sharing what you wrote at each stopping place.* (This step essentially follows the format of Lesson 3.5, Partner Think-Alouds (page 33). Allow about three minutes for this.

STEP 8 **Pairs create one-sentence theme statements.** *So, "The Boy They Wouldn't Take Pictures Of" is basically three stories within a story, leading to a walloping ending, right? But what's the point? What is Eggers getting at? What's the message, the moral, the theme? Get back with your partner and come up with a one-sentence statement of the story's theme. It must be supported by details in the text itself.* Allow three minutes.

STEP 9 **Whole-class discussion.** Invite pairs to read aloud their statements about the story theme. Invite contrary opinions, encourage debate, and invoke the "take-it-back-to-the-text" rule. If your kids don't think of them, offer these interesting ideas raised by past classes.

The fact is, we do discriminate against ugly people.

We all think there is something terribly wrong with us.

If you suspect that people don't like you, you are probably right.

You can get so paranoid that you start making things up.

We are all alone in the world.

It's a mistake to let coincidences get you worried.

Variation ▶ **Naming and monitoring strategy use:** In Step 6, kids can categorize their own annotations, using the "Things to Think About While Reading" chart. If you do this often, it can help students to notice if they are over-relying on one or two strategies, and need to broaden their thinking repertoire as they approach text. For example, if a young reader is always connecting the text to her own life experiences (as is often the case), but very rarely visualizing or determining importance, that gives us a great point to raise in an individual reading conference—or in a whole class mini-lesson, if this particular problem is widespread.

Shoptalk ▶ For adult readers, annotation is a way of life when it comes to any purpose beyond personal entertainment. And "college readiness" definitely means students can annotate in ways that far exceed grabbing a highlighter and turning page after page yellow. If you're using a textbook, pass out sticky notes and have students place and write on them, just the way they marked stop and think spots in the short story. And when you do give students photocopies that they can write on, leave some extra space in the side margins for the note taking. Ideally, by the end of the year, your students will not ask if something needs to be annotated; they will just automatically do it.

Afterthoughts

Sara Holbrook

Thoughts love.
They look.
Eye-brood
    or smile.
Thoughts blurt,
race-rush,
    or wait a while.

Thoughts trapped inside,
may blame
    and boil.
Review. React.
    Relate. Recoil.
Thoughts expressed
    may find a way
to take a stand,
    find solutions,
lend a hand.

Thoughts
that can't find words
  exist,
    resist,
      insist
        unheard.

The Boy They Didn't Take Pictures Of

Dave Eggers

The boy, Charles, was part of a family of seven—four children, two parents, a grandmother they called Pippy. He was not the oldest and not the youngest but was eleven when he noticed something: everywhere in the house were pictures of all of the members of the family, together and alone, but nowhere was there a picture of Charles. He said nothing about it, because he made himself believe that it was not true, that somewhere—some upstairs bathroom or basement hallway—he would be proven wrong, he would find a picture of himself. ●

Did he ever investigate this closely? Never, of course. When he was fourteen, he spent a good deal of time at the house of a friend named Alex. Alex's mother, named Scarlet and looking that way, liked to take pictures of Alex's friends; she had a wall where she displayed them all. But as the months went by, and Charles's time at Alex's house implied that he should be on the wall too, nothing of the kind happened. Scarlet smiled at him, spoke to him kindly, but never asked him to sit on the fence in the front yard, where all the other boys posed. Again Charles said nothing because he figured it was an oversight only, one that, if pointed out, would make him seem gauche or needy or strange. ●

Many years later, now in his twenties, Charles dated a woman, Reah, who kept pictures on her shelves. Small gold and seashelled frames held photos of her friends and sisters and even her ex-boyfriends— who were now her good friends and (how nice!) called often. But after nine months together, there were no pictures of Charles on the shelves. Reah had never even taken his photo, or asked a stranger to take their picture together. Again, Charles said nothing. ●

But with each successive slight, from childhood till the present, with each odd instance of his seemingly lifelong invisibility, he wondered: Was he ugly? He wasn't, he knew this, but nor was he handsome. Aha! He did have an unshapely nose, and an incongruous chin, and some scars from acne that potholed his cheeks. But was that it? Did the people he knew simply prefer the more photogenic of their friends and family? He knew this was too simple, too crude, too enraging and wretched to be doubted for a moment. ●

Connections and Disconnections

LESSON 4.2

TEXT ▶ "Ambush," by Roger Woodward

TIME ▶ 20 Minutes

GROUPING SEQUENCE ▶ Individuals, recurrent pairs, whole class

The number one determinant of comprehension is prior knowledge—embodied in the connections we can make between a given text and our own life experience, schema, or knowledge base. Cognitive research says we can only add new knowledge by somehow connecting it to our existing knowledge. Sometimes that means busting up our paradigms, divesting ourselves of misconceptions, or rewiring our mental circuits. But we can only begin where we are, with our prior knowledge. So we are always encouraging students to seek out connections with what they are reading.

But kids don't always get a good connection. In the comic strip "Zits," teen reader Jeremy encounters this line from Chapter 2 of *The Scarlet Letter*: "On the breast of her gown, in fine red cloth, surrounded with an elaborate embroidery and fantastic flourishes of gold thread, appeared the letter A." Does Jeremy make any connections between Hester's dilemma and John Proctor's in *The Crucible?* Does he immediately hark back to what he studied in American history about the early Puritan colonies? Of course not! The letter A makes Jeremy think of tattoos, an "A" tattoo on Heather's breast, peeping out from a bikini top, maybe one made out of leather . . .

Now that's a distracting and unhelpful connection. Let's show kids how to make consistently valuable, relevant connections.

PREPARATION

Prepare copies and establish partners.

STEP 1 **Kids read and mark down their connections.** *Connecting your reading with your life experience is one way to make sense out of a text. But not every connection is relevant. Let's do a little experiment. Read this story and mark down two or three personal connections in the margin. What do certain words or lines remind you of or make you think about? Underline those parts and jot down a quick note so that you can explain your connections to your partner and the rest of the class.*

STEP 2 **Pairs compare.** After partners discuss their notes for a minute, ask a few to share with the whole class. Things that kids may connect with:

Neighborhood friendships/rivalries

Sneaking up on someone

Bicycles

◀ **Steps & Teaching Language**

COMMON CORE
STANDARDS SUPPORTED

- Read closely to determine what the text says explicitly; cite specific textual evidence. *(CCRA.R.1)*
- Determine central ideas or themes of a text. *(CCRA.R.2)*
- Participate effectively in a range of conversations and collaborations. *(CCRA.SL.1)*

Squirt gun/Super Soaker fights

Baseball

Getting injured, stitches, concussions, etc.

Fireworks

Run-ins with police

Getting someone else in trouble

STEP 3 **Read for theme.** *Now please reread the story carefully and think about the main message the author is trying to get across. Jot down the theme of the story at the bottom.*

STEP 4 **Pairs discuss themes.** Give students a minute or two, then have them share with the whole class. Kids may focus on issues like:

"The other side of the tracks" in neighborhoods

Privileged kids and poor kids

How getting revenge rarely "works"

The Vietnam war, the draft, who went to war

The roots of violence/warfare in childhood play

Pleasing and fooling our mothers

STEP 5 **Recheck connections.** *Remember when I said this was an experiment? Now that we've determined this story's theme, go back and review your connections. Put a check by the ones that helped you understand the story, and put an X by the ones that turned out not to help so much.*

STEP 6 **Pairs discuss useful connections.** *When you compare your coding, talk with your partner about why certain connections helped and others didn't.* Have pairs share some of the helpful connections with the whole class.

STEP 7 **Discuss distractors.** *What were some of the distracting or unhelpful connections from the story that you marked with an X? Why didn't they help?* Have some partners share.

STEP 8 **Apply.** Challenge kids to return to their regular reading, being on the watch for useful versus unhelpful connections, and have them report in a few days.

Variation ▶

Model your own disconnections: A way to enhance this strategy is to share a distracting connection of your own, showing students the text and pointing out the distractor. If you can't think of one you've recently experienced, read some short texts and one will pop right up, trust us. Smokey testifies: *I was reading this sci-fi story about an alien planet located in the constellation Libra. And the* *first thing I connected to was, wow, my sister is a Libra. And I started thinking about her and whether she actually fits the mold of that particular sign, and I just lost track of the text. My sister didn't have anything to do with the book, and neither did astrological signs; that whole line of thinking just distracted me from understanding the story.*

The authors of the Common Core Standards appear to not be big fans of comprehension strategy instruction (see page 9 of their Publishers' Criteria for a whiff of that repugnance). They seem to think that we teach *connecting*, for example, just for connecting's sake. So kids can tally up zillions of connections, and we can throw a cookie party for the Best Connector in the room. (If you happen to be teaching logic, tell your kids this is called a *straw man argument*). What we do see is teachers very thoughtfully showing kids how to use their background knowledge *when it enhances understanding*—and how to promptly discard connections that don't help.

◀ **Shoptalk**

Ambush

Roger Woodward

Here comes Joey Bacon, clanking up the hill on his rusty old Schwinn. A perfect target for my brand-new squirt gun. I scramble up the big green bench beside our tall stockade fence, and take up a sniper's position between two slats.

Joey slowly pedals into range. Red haired, sallow, freckled. He lives on the only farm left in our neighborhood. There are cows in his driveway. None of us has ever played there. But sometimes, Joey will join our work-up baseball games on the vacant lot. He can hit a little, not much of an arm.

From my hidden perch, I watch the enemy approach. Almost, almost, almost, fire! I arc the stream of water just ahead of my target, leading him like a quarterback leads a receiver. Joey rides directly into my perfectly descending stream.

"Hey! What?" He yells, and puts his bike down, wiping water from his eyes.

I'm done hiding now, laughing over the top of the fence. "Gotcha!" I taunt. Joey gives me a considered look, and picks up a rock from the shoulder of the road.

The last thing I remember thinking is how pitiful his throws from right field had always been. I come to in the car, my weeping mother driving with one hand while holding a blood-soaked dishtowel to my forehead. Eighteen stitches and a mild concussion. My dad never could get the blood out of the car seats.

Three weeks later, the local sheriff rings our doorbell. When my mother answers, I linger just behind her, eavesdropping.

"Hi, Carol. I'm just checking around with some parents today. Seems like we got some kid who's selling fireworks at the park, the big kind, y'know, M-80s, cherry bombs. I'd sure like to take him off the street, whoever it is."

Officer Sullivan smiles at me. As one of the local Good Kids, I'm not a suspect. "I'm not worried about Roger getting tangled up with that stuff. But if you hear anything, either of you." Gently checking the scar that I will carry for the rest of my life, I lean out from behind my mother and suggest: "Maybe Joey Bacon?"

Seven years later, another man in uniform pays a visit to our neighborhood. He rings the Bacons' doorbell and tells Joey's mom that her son died in an ambush near Khe Sanh. If I remember correctly, I was drinking a beer in my freshman dorm at the time.

LESSON 4.3 Drawing Text Details

Great literature evokes powerful visual images in your mind. That is, unless you have been playing Grand Theft Auto since the day you were born. Because today's kids have had vivid, extravagant images supplied for them throughout their lives, many of them need lessons in "remedial visualization." In other words, they need to practice *making their own mental images* when they read, listen, or view.

TEXT ▶ "Ascent," by Michael Salinger

TIME ▶ 30 Minutes

GROUPING SEQUENCE ▶ Individuals, groups of four, whole class

USED IN TEXT SETS ▶ 1, 7

PREPARATION

Practice reading the poem aloud. Make copies of the poem for each student as well as a projectable version. This lesson works best if you offer large drawing paper (legal or bigger is good) and an assortment of multicolored pencils and markers. Plan how to create groups of four for sharing at Step 4.

STEP 1 Hand out the poem and read it aloud. *Follow along with me as I read this poem called "Ascent" by Michael Salinger. Try to make a picture in your head of what is being described in this very visual poem.* Read "Ascent" aloud, slowly and with drama.

STEP 2 Give drawing instructions. *Now, draw what this poem is making you see. You can draw this in any style you want—stick figures, cartoon, diagram, whatever. Don't go all art-phobic about this. The goal isn't to get your drawing into an art gallery, it is to help you visualize what the poet is trying to show you.*

You might pick out just one section to focus on, or you can try to pull the whole thing together in one drawing, or even make a quick series of cartoons. You can label things with words if you like. Be sure to keep checking back into the poem for details to include.

This is a silent activity, so work quietly by yourself for a while—later we'll get into groups to discuss the poem. Ready? I'll give you about five minutes for the drawing. Raise your hand if you need help.

STEP 3 Circulate and assist. You'll probably have to referee the sharing of markers at first, unless you have provided plenty for everyone. As you circulate, give reassurance to kids who aren't confident of their drawing skills, and redirect students who are simply copying someone else instead of thinking about the poem.

STEP 4 Share drawings. *Now get into your groups of four. You are going to pass your drawings around and look at each one for about thirty seconds. I will tell you the timing for this.*

◀ **Steps & Teaching Language**

As you look at each drawing, think about which details from the poem your partners have highlighted. Keep your copy of the poem right in front of you. We are going to do this silently, and then we'll talk out loud in a minute. Ready? Go.

STEP 5 **Create a poem interpretation.** *Now that we have worked hard to figure out the events and details of this rock climbing poem, the question is: What's it really about? What's the author's purpose or message or theme?* If anyone in the room happens to be a climber, solicit their expertise and help with the technical vocabulary.

Still in your groups of four, talk for a few minutes about this and prepare a one- or two-sentence "gist statement" about the main meaning, the big takeaway from "Ascent." Take five minutes and be sure to write down your group interpretation.

STEP 6 **Share with the whole group.** Invite groups to read their poem interpretations aloud, with comments and discussion in between. To close the conversation, ask kids to list any questions or uncertainties they still have about the poem. You could frame this along these lines: "If you could talk to Michael Salinger about this poem, what question would you ask?"

STEP 7 **Ask the poet.** Like many poems and stories, this piece may leave readers hungering for more certainty about their interpretation. Most of the time, we simply have to live with this reality. But in these digital days, not always. We emailed Michael Salinger, who lives in Cleveland and who has competed in many national poetry slam events. We shared with him our own questions about the rock-climbing terminology and the origins of the poem—the same things our students asked. Here is his response. You can project it and/or read aloud to your students.

Hi guys,

I'm glad you asked. "Belay Off" is a term used by the person who is providing the safety line for a climber. When you begin a climb with a belayer—you click the line onto the harness with a carabiner and announce "On Belay" and the person holding the other end of the line responds "Belay On!" Conversely when a climber unhooks from the safety harness they shout out "Off Belay" and the person who had up til then been their safety system acknowledges this by responding "Belay Off." There are various reasons a person might go off belay. They may be on a safe ledge where they are resting, they may have reached the summit of their climb, or as I envisioned in this piece they have gone as far as their line will allow.

Since my son is a rock climber I felt that this was a perfect metaphor for a poem to be given to him on his graduation from college. I researched climbing terms and equipment to include in the piece and I hoped to recreate the tension of clinging to the side of a rock. I thought about this piece for several weeks before writing it—then out of nowhere the line "they tell you to never look down" just came to me and the poem just flowed from there. The term "Belay Off" was a revision added after the rest of the poem had been written, as bookends to the piece.

Michael Salinger

STEP 8 Discuss. *Did Salinger's email answer everyone's questions about the poem? What questions do you still have?* If you like, you can use the poet's message to open a discussion about the mix of conscious intention and deep inspiration that goes into the creation of any artwork.

Doing research to enhance literary understanding: Because this poem uses some technical language about rock climbing, students might want to look up these terms in a dictionary or online in order to understand the poem better. If smartphone use is allowed in your school, you could encourage kids to quickly look up some of these terms as they read. The best source we've found is

www.rockclimbing.com/Articles/Introduction_to_Climbing/Climbing _Dictionary_528.html.

Looking up words raises the interesting dilemma of breaking one's concentration to go off researching, versus simply reading on and trying to infer as much meaning as possible from context. Obviously, on the Big State Test there will be no chance of looking anything up—but in real life, curious readers do reach out when they care enough to get the words right.

Gallery walk: At Step 4, instead of having kids share their drawings in a small group, set up a whole-class gallery walk. Have students hang up their drawings at evenly spaced intervals throughout the room, so everyone can quietly circulate through the postings. Have kids bring a few Post-it notes with them and as they view each drawing, leave comments or reactions for the "artist" to read later. You'll want kids to visit only four or five drawings, not the whole circuit, which would take way too long and get old quickly.

◀ *Variations*

Drawing the details can really help students unlock difficult texts. For example, "Sinners at the Hands of an Angry God" can be a pretty rigorous and dry piece for American lit students, but once you get them actually drawing Jonathan Edwards' hell images, it's a whole 'nother story! After all their detailed depictions of perdition are posted, it's much easier to talk about how the Puritans viewed their world and how Edwards used specific imagery to control his flock.

◀ *Shoptalk*

Ascent

Michael Salinger

Belay off
They tell you to never look down
The average climbing rope is 50 meters long
And rated by the number of falls
It can withstand
Because
It is expected that you are going to lose your grip
And these ropes are designed to stretch
Up to 6.5%
Absorbing your body's weight
As it accelerates
Thirty two point one eight feet
Per second per second
Spring-backing you to a stop
Rather than snapping you in half
But with a carabiner click
You've unhooked yourself
Belay off
And up you scale
Chalk absorbs hand sweat
But not your fingertip pain
Trigger loaded cams
Sway at your waist
Like a cluster of colored pendulums
Picked one by one
Inserted into fissures and cracks
Then left behind
As if they were antique keys
Poking from an attic's trunk
And you look up
Because you've been warned to never look down
Feeling for imperfections in the rock
Facilitating enough friction
That you may cling to its face
As you surmount this obstacle
One hand
One foot
At a time
Simply
    Because
        It is there
And once you've reached the summit
Before you spy your next climb
Go ahead
Look down
See how far you've come
Belay off

Reading with Questions in Mind

LESSON 4.4

TEXT ▸ "Noel," by Michael Plemmons

TIME ▸ 50 Minutes

GROUPING SEQUENCE ▸ Whole class, individuals, pairs, individuals, pairs, whole class

USED IN TEXT SETS ▸ 1, 4, 6

One of the things we've all struggled with is how to move the conversation about text from teacher-driven to student-driven. Easier said than done, right? We've observed plenty of student groups where the kids come with their notes and their books, and then have complete discussions with the novel face down on the table. Really?! It's enough to make us move the kids back into rows, tell 'em to open *To Kill a Mockingbird* to page 193, and start *explicitly* pointing out all the details that would have supported their assertions that the Ewells were low class and lived in a dump. However—reality check—who's doing the work now? Rather than regressing, it's time to retrench and teach the kids how to keep the focus on the text via the questions they pose.

PREPARATION

Make a copy of "Noel" for each student. Use our projectable version of the story to share your notes/annotation/questions as you think aloud. Determine how pairs will form for their question discussion.

On the Web

◀ **Steps** & **Teaching Language**

STEP 1 **Pass out the story and introduce the strategy.** *One of the ways to read so that you stay engaged with the text is to be constantly thinking of questions, questions that you'll later use when you talk about the story with other people. However, some questions work better than others. The questions that you want to think up are ones that are intriguing or puzzling or can make others look at the story from different angles. Another quality of good questions is that you need to go back and use the text to defend your answer.*

STEP 2 **Read the title and first paragraph aloud as you think aloud and annotate, and students copy your examples.** *Before you start writing your own questions, I'm going to show you how I do it. Be sure to jot down the example questions I share with you.*

As you read, stop and pose some open-ended, text-based questions. Write them down so that students can see the projection and copy your examples. Here are some questions you might think of:

- Why is the story called "Noel"? What might it mean beyond the obvious definition?

- Even though there are holiday decorations, why doesn't this setting seem very welcoming?

- What do Mrs. Hathaway and Mrs. Overton do? Who seems to be in charge?

- Why do these two women care so much about these kids' looks and talents?

- Why are the kids here with them? What is the relationship between the kids and those women?

STEP 3 **Analyze the questions.** *Take a look at the questions I just wrote down. What do you notice about them? Turn to your partner and jot down some ideas.* Take a minute for pair share, and then list their suggestions. They might make these observations:

- Open ended

- Based on things in the story but you've got to think about how to answer, not just fill-in-the-blank

- Might have to read further before being able to answer

- Relate to character motivation/details and setting

- Predictions

- Make you read between the lines

- Make connections to text and background knowledge

- Use imagination

- Ask for details

I'm glad you noticed that my questions are doing a lot of different things. The one goal they all have in common is they dig into the story and ask the reader to really think about what the details mean and how they interrelate.

STEP 4 **Give directions for individual work.** *Now I want you to finish reading this story individually. As you read, stop and write some discussion questions. To write good ones, look back at the examples I gave you for the first paragraph and at the list we put together.* Keep this list on the board for reference or keep it projected. *Any questions? Start reading at the second paragraph. When you're done, you should have at least six new questions spread out through the rest of the story.*

STEP 5 **Monitor individual work.** As students work, roam the room. Pay particular attention to their question notation. Remind them to jot questions as they read rather than waiting until the end and going back.

STEP 6 **Question elimination.** *Now that you've finished reading, we're going to take a minute to review your questions before getting with your partner. First, I want you to reread all the questions (mine too) and cross out any that can be easily answered. For example, you might be reading a story and jot down, "Why did Jacob suddenly quit veterinary school?" It seems like an important question about character motivation, one that might take some inferences to answer. But then a couple of pages later, you find out that his parents were suddenly killed and now he doesn't have the money for tuition. That question has been definitively answered; as it stands it's not going to create a lot of discussion. If you find any questions like that, cross them out.* Allow a minute for this.

STEP 7 **Question ranking.** *With the questions you've got left, I want you to rank your three most interesting questions, the questions that would be most intriguing to discuss with your partner. Rank those 1, 2, 3, with number 1 being the absolute best question.*

STEP 8 **Partners meet and discuss.** *Meet with your partner to talk about your questions. Take turns asking a question and letting your partner share some ideas before you add your opinions and thoughts. Remember to always support your opinions with text details. Your opinions aren't valid unless you can logically point to the text for support. When it's your turn, use one of your numbered questions. Continue your discussion until I call time.*

STEP 9 **Monitor pair discussion.** As you observe, remind pairs to switch off after each question. Students frequently make the mistake of letting one partner ask all their questions at once. In a short-short story, this poses problems because sometimes both partners' questions can be similar. Call time before pairs are out of questions.

STEP 10 **Pairs analyze questions.** *Before we share in a large group, I want you and your partner to review your questions and pick out the one that created the very best discussion. Then look back at the list we brainstormed earlier and figure out what made it work so well.*

STEP 11 **Pairs share out.** Call on a few pairs to volunteer their best question and explain what made it work.

- **Longer text, larger groups:** When students are skilled at writing good questions and you adapt this lesson to longer pieces, increase the size of the group to three or four. ◀ *Variations*

- **Fine-tune question types:** As students master questions and understand certain craft elements, model those questions for students first and then instruct the kids to include those types of questions in their own discussion planning. Here are a couple of example questions from the second paragraph of "Noel" that are related to word choice.

   Why is Mrs. Overton described as "poker-faced"? Why say that instead of "serious?"

   Melinda squeaked with joy. Why didn't she yell or jump up and down?

In a textbook, the classic question placement is *after* the reading selection. But kids can practice reading with a question in mind if you pick a good open-ended question from that textbook list beforehand and give it to them when they begin reading—or at an appropriate spot a few paragraphs into the story. ◀ *Shoptalk*

Noel

Michael Plemmons

Mrs. Hathaway brought the children downstairs single file and seated them on straight-back chairs around the reception room, boy-girl-boy-girl, seventeen in all. In the corner stood a robust Christmas tree bedecked with candy canes and tinsel tresses. The air was thick with the scent of pine and furniture polish as a phantom choir sang "Noel" to the strains of a vinyl disc orchestra. Mrs. Hathaway was still fussing over their appearance, fixing the boys' neckties and correcting the girls' posture, when the first couple arrived. In hushed tones they spoke with Mrs. Overton at the front desk. "We were thinking about a girl," said the woman. Mrs. Overton smiled broadly and made a sweeping motion with her hand. "We have a wonderful selection of girls," she said. At this the girls came to attention in their places, each freckle blooming on rosy cheeks. And as Mrs. Hathaway presented them, each one stood and curtsied on cue. "Christa is a lovely child, age eight . . . Melinda has a beautiful singing voice for carols . . . Stephanie has an exceptionally sweet temperament. . . ."

The clients turned to Mrs. Overton and quietly indicated their choice. She nodded, poker-faced, and prepared the papers. Money changed hands. The girls eyed each other nervously as Mrs. Overton recited the rental stipulations: "You understand that this is only a 48-hour agreement. The girl must be returned by noon on the day after Christmas or late charges will be assessed at ten dollars per hour and you will forfeit the insurance deposit." When everything was in order she looked over at Mrs. Hathaway and said, "Melinda, please." A little squeak of joy escaped into the room as Melinda jumped up and rushed to join her hosts for the holiday. The other girls watched her go, their hope renewing as another pair of patrons entered the room from the foyer.

Throughout the afternoon they came two by two, childless on Christmas Eve. They were high-rise dwellers and they were pensioners from South Side bungalows. A few were first-timers, uneasy, unable to meet the children's eyes. (The repeat customers, who each year made up a majority of the business, had reserved their "Kristmas Kid" by name, weeks in advance, and had come by in the morning for express pick-up.) Most of those now arriving to browse among the leftovers were last minute shoppers.

The girls were in great demand, especially the youngest candidates in curls. Dimples and bangs, once again, were very popular. And for the boys, missing teeth and cowlicks were favorite features. Considering the irregular inventory, business was good. Of the original lot, only two rather plain-looking lads remained at six o'clock, closing time. Both bore the stigma of a pubescent mustache.

Mrs. Overton finished her filing while Mrs. Hathaway affixed the "Closed" sign on the door, unplugged the Christmas lights, and drew the window shades all around. The boys sat silent, watchful.

Said Mrs. Overton, "I told you about those two pre-teens, didn't I?"

"Yes, ma'am, you did."

"Then why did you bring them down with the others?"

"Well, I was hoping, I guess." Mrs. Hathaway glanced at her rejected charges. They gazed guiltily into their laps. "It did no harm to give them at least a chance."

Mrs. Overton regarded her for a moment, then answered calmly. "I suppose not." She was pleased with the day's proceeds, too pleased to argue over a minor transgression. Anyway, she did not want to discourage a certain degree of compassion, believing it was one of the qualities that made Mrs. Hathaway an effective matron.

Outside it was beginning to snow. Before leaving, Mrs. Overton wrapped herself in a muffler and donned a woolen cap. "I'll see you day after tomorrow then."

"Goodnight, ma'am," said Mrs. Hathaway, then turning to the boys. "Come along."

As they slowly ascended the stairs, one of the boys emitted a peculiar nasal sound, a congested sentiment perhaps.

"Quiet, child," said Mrs. Hathaway.

LESSON 4.5

TEXT ▶ Assorted Six-Word Memoirs

TIME ▶ 20 Minutes

GROUPING SEQUENCE ▶ Whole class, pairs, whole class

USED IN TEXT SET ▶ 7

Inferring Meaning

When we were collecting literary selections for this book, we wanted really short stories and poems, so students could read and discuss them in class. And there's no shorter genre than Six-Word Memoirs! Have you run across the books that offer hundreds of these? Or visited one of the websites where you can write and publish your own? Gotta warn you, it's pretty addictive.

Props go out to *Smith* magazine for repopularizing this mini-genre. The idea is to pack a whole life, or at least a major event, into just six words. The classic original is tenuously attributed to Ernest Hemingway:

For sale. Baby shoes. Never worn.

See? You really can make up a whole story to go with those six words, which is the point.

As kids move into more and more complex text through the school year, they must hone their ability to infer—to take clues from a text and combine these with their background knowledge to make reasonable guesses, hypotheses, and predictions about what an author means. In this lesson, we start supersimple, inviting kids to make inferences about six words at a time. Later, students can graduate to longer, more complex texts—from this book, from your anthology, or from the Common Core exemplars.

PREPARATION

Establish partners. Have sample memoirs ready to project or hand out.

Steps & Teaching Language ▶

STEP 1 **Explain inferring.** *We are always talking about how smart readers think. And one thing they do is* make inferences. *That's a fancy word for something we do all the time. If we smell pizza in the school hall this morning, we might infer that the cooks are making pizza for lunch today. Without walking down there to check, or looking it up in the bulletin, we can infer from the clue—the smell—that pizza is on the menu today. When we are reading, we do the same thing. We are always combining our background knowledge with what the author offers in the text. It's never just the author telling us—when we read, we make the story together with the writer.*

STEP 2 **Model inferring.** *So I thought it would be fun to practice inferring today with some really weird super-short texts. I've brought some six-word stories with me today. Here's a famous one by Ernest Hemingway.* Read aloud. *Now watch me try to infer what it means.*

Of course, do this in your own words, but maybe you'll say something like this: When I read this, I think someone was expecting a baby, but for some reason the baby never wore the shoes. Maybe the baby was never born, or died, or there was a miscarriage. Or maybe the father bought the shoes but the mother ran away or divorced him so he never saw the baby. Or it could be that some friend just gave the mom these shoes at a baby shower and the mother thought they were ugly and put them up for sale (and the baby was fine). But mostly, this just sounds sad and wistful, whatever happened.

See how simple? Get with your partner, and let's do several more, one at a time. I'll stop and give you time to try to blend the clues in the text with your own background knowledge and make sense of each "story."

STEP 3 **Kids infer from memoirs.** Here are a few samples to prime the pump. Improve our list by making up your own (and kids will get to write their own shortly). Pick a handful and have pairs talk through each one.

Homework: odd-numbered problems. 97. Zzzzzzz.

Moving again. Goodbye, strangers. Hello strangers.

Leap! Catch football. Crunch. Goodbye scholarship.

One-horse town? Ride it out!

Mistaken verdict. Life sentence. I'm appealing.

Expensive restaurant. Bad service. Twitter revenge.

Unmarked vehicle. Realization came too late.

I seem shy to some, apparently.

Done with dishes, wild to roam.

Bleached blonde. Everyone knew. Never cared.

Actually, I never had a mother.

Cleaning my room, stomping, stomping, stomping.

Root of evil? Money. Spend wisely!

Have volunteer pairs share their thinking after each memoir. Then invite people with a "different inference" to join in.

- **Kids write Six-Word Memoirs:** Have students write their own mini-memoirs, summing up their life (so far) or depicting a major event. To provide an audience, have everyone copy their six-worder anonymously onto an index card and place it in a hat. Then let each class member draw one at random and read aloud. If it feels right, let kids guess whose memoir each one is. Or have kids write six-word synopses about characters in a novel you are studying. For example:

  Uncle rules. Mother betrays. Son waffles. (Hamlet)

◄ Variations

COMMON CORE STANDARDS SUPPORTED

- Read closely to determine what the text says explicitly and to make logical inferences from it; cite specific textual evidence when writing or speaking to support conclusions drawn from the text. *(CCRA.R.1)*

- Interpret words and phrases as they are used in a text, including determining figurative meanings, and analyze how specific word choices shape meaning or tone. *(CCRA.R.4)*

- Participate effectively in a range of conversations and collaborations. *(CCRA.SL.1)*

On the Web

- **Go quotable:** This inferring practice also works well with famous quotations. Among our favorites to use with kids:

  > *The louder he spoke of his honor, the faster we counted our spoons.* (Ralph Waldo Emerson)

  > *Education is when you read the fine print. Experience is what you get if you don't.* (Pete Seeger)

- **Character inferences:** Studying Six-Word Memoirs is all about making inferences, and this short-short genre is a great way to introduce or reinforce this skill. While nonfiction tends to be more "face value," most fiction requires tons of inferring. Authors of stories and novels don't like to spell things out; they want readers to imagine and create based on the clues they've given them. And, in fiction, the majority of inferences have to do with character personality and motivation: Why did the character do that? What was he thinking? How does he feel about another character? How do you know? Once students know that making character inferences is normal and necessary when reading fiction, you can introduce the trickier kinds of inferences readers make, such as when a narrator is unreliable or when a character is using irony or sarcasm.

- Writing Six-Word Memoirs is a great way to reflect on characters found in your textbook or curricular selections. Copy the characters you wish to review onto slips of paper and have students choose from "the hat." Tell kids to keep their characters a secret while they are writing their memoirs. Then have them get into groups of four. In turn, each member reads his memoir and the others guess who it is—while defending their guesses with textual evidence, of course. Afterwards, each group picks the best memoir for the rest of the class to hear and guess.

Six-Word Memoir for Boo Radley in *To Kill a Mockingbird*:

> Waited a lifetime for that moment.

LESSON 4.6 Tweet the Text

Twitter is all the rage these days, though it does attract significant opprobrium from the-sky-is-falling school of culture columnists (and a few English teachers), who think that its 140-character limit is rotting the discursive capacities of addicted tweeters everywhere. Though it seemed like this gadget's usefulness would have stalled at pointless prattle—really, who cares what's on someone's mind around the clock?—it has evolved as a way to organize political protests, microblog, provide news updates, and publish really, really short stories.

The great thing about a tweet is that it can *never* be longer than 140 characters, and that includes the spaces! This mode forces kids to execute tight, concise writing and make every word do triple duty.

TEXT ▶ "The Sweet Perfume of Good-Bye," by M. E. Kerr

TIME ▶ 50 Minutes

GROUPING SEQUENCE ▶ Pairs, individuals, pairs, whole class

PREPARATION

Photocopy "The Sweet Perfume of Good-Bye" for each student. Determine how kids will form partners for pre- and postreading sharing.

STEP 1 Introduce the idea of smell. *What are some odors, good and bad, that you can almost automatically imagine smelling? If I just think for a second, I can imagine the aroma of pizza, Brut aftershave, and an overripe litter box. Take a moment and think about what smells come up for you. Now turn to your partner and share.* Ignore any giggling. After a minute of pair share, take a few examples and move on to Step 2.

STEP 2 Explain synthesizing with a tweet. *Think about those smells again. What if none of those items you talked about had any fragrance at all? How would that make you feel? What would you miss?*

Pass out the story. *The main character in this story is Caroline. She is a scientist from Earth doing research on a distant planet called Farfire, and part of her job is to keep her Twitter followers apprised of her discoveries. Take a look at the text and notice where there is extra space between the paragraphs. These are the places where Caroline sends a tweet. As you read, I want you to stop at those spots, put yourself in Caroline's shoes, and write her tweet based on what she has discovered and experienced. I'll model the first one for you.*

STEP 3 Model tweeting the text. Read the story aloud up to the first space and then stop. First think aloud and then write your tweet. Maybe something like this: *What has Caroline learned so far? It looks like Farfire has lots of things Earth does: roses, lemons, grass. The big difference is that nothing gives off an aroma. The only exception is when someone is dying, and that aroma is incredibly pleasant. What would Caroline tweet?*

◀ **Steps** & **Teaching Language**

Farfire resembles Earth, but nothing has an odor on this planet except for death. People smell intoxicating just before they die. Odd.

That's 134 characters including the spaces. Any questions on how to continue on your own? Just remember that your tweets are always from Caroline's perspective. It's important that you stop and tweet at the points indicated rather than reading the whole story and going back. Remember that people tweet in real time, reacting to whatever they have just encountered. The energy of Twitter is its spontaneity. If you read and then go back, you will have lost this.

STEP 4 **Kids tweet through the story.** Give students time to read the rest of the story and tweet where the spaces indicate.

STEP 5 **Pairs compare tweets.** Move students into their pairs to compare and discuss their tweets. Encourage them also to discuss and try to clarify any parts of the story that confused them.

STEP 6 **Whole-class discussion.** Bring the class back together and ask for pairs to share their sweetest tweet. Be sure to share the tweets from the story's end. These should be dramatic and also a clear indication whether students completely grasped the main character's final predicament.

Variations ▶

Off-stage story events: A *big* focus of the CCSS is that kids always support their opinions and ideas with the text. However, that doesn't mean fun and imagination are off limits. If you've ever watched *Late Night with Jimmy Fallon*, you might have seen a segment called #latenighthashtags. The day before the segment Jimmy releases a topic for viewers to tweet responses. Here are a few examples:

> #WorstFamilyTrip
>
> #ThatsMyMom
>
> #MyCrazyFamily
>
> #WorstXmasGifts

Viewers respond and Jimmy reads the funniest ones out of the thousands (no lie) he receives. Here's one for #WorstFamilyTrip:

> My family made me sleep in what they called "the nest"—blankets in a pile on the floor of a hotel room.

You can find all of these segments at www.latenightwithjimmyfallon.com/blogs /twitter-hashtag-game/.

All of the posted segments are pretty funny, but—WARNING, WARNING, WILL ROBINSON!—some of the tweets and improvised comments are edgy, so please do not roll this video for your sixth graders unless you have a retirement plan in place.

Besides getting you sucked into old Jimmy Fallon bits, this twitter subgenre is also a great way to get kids to think more deeply about characters, point of view, and plot events. After reading a story or poem, have the kids choose a character, inanimate object, emotion—whatever the text has to offer. Or, if you want greater variety (kids generally home in on the most prominent character), brainstorm the character possibilities ahead of time, write them on slips of paper, and have students choose at random out of the hat. Once everyone has a character, next offer a hashtag topic just like Jimmy Fallon and invite them to respond in a tweet as that character. The catch is that the tweet must be original; it cannot refer to an event in the story. However, the imagined event must be logically supported with existing text in the story—even though the event wasn't in the story, it totally could have been.

You can just have the kids do a quick share and text defense with the usual partners followed by hearing some volunteers in the large group. Or, you can make the sharing a bit more physical and elaborate via the on-your-feet sharing elaborated in Lesson 9.1, Literary Networking (pages 187–195.)

And if you decide to use this strategy a second time, have the kids brainstorm possible #hashtag topics that would work with the text and characters under study.

Language arts textbooks are always trying to get kids to write *summaries*. Well, tweeting provides a playful way to work on summarization. Maybe we should be thinking of tweets as *precis*? French educators have long believed that a key discipline is for students to constantly practice creating brutally concise summaries of poems, books, and plays.

◀ **Shoptalk**

We just tried our hand at it:

> In future dystopia, chosen teens battle to death in a government reality show that distracts citizens from their suffering and exploitation. (*The Hunger Games*)

> Redneck boy and runaway slave float down the Mississippi, encountering humanity's follies on shore, and each others' souls on their raft. (*Huckleberry Finn*)

Feel free to use these as examples, as well as your own. Your kids can tweet any other text in this book, in your curriculum, or the textbook.

The Sweet Perfume of Good-Bye

M. E. Kerr

Here nothing smells.

Almost nothing smells.

The roses are red beyond belief but give off no aroma. The lemons are as yellow as the sun, but there is no lemony fragrance, just a semblance of bitterness as you bite into one. The fresh-cut bright green grass where my lovers sit does not even smell, as it did summer mornings when I was on Earth and could smell it from my room while the boy cut our lawn.

I called them "my lovers" with a little smile. That is my sense of humor emerging (though I am thought to be a humorless young scientist). They do not make love to me, of course. They are mine only in the fact that I am studying them.

Here the only perfume is the sweet perfume of good-bye that comes on a person one hour before death. I cannot describe it accurately, even though I am a stickler for accuracy. Like our lilies? A little, but more rare and tantalizing, and people rush to be near whoever is dying, keeping a respectful distance (scores of them behind me as I write this), but still lingering nearby for a faint whiff.

Carlo, the boy, is dying. He has just begun to give off this haunting, beautiful scent. His girlfriend, Marny, is ecstatic as she breathes it in. They sit on the grass near me, having their last conversation.

I can hear them. It is love talk of the passionate variety.

The great advantage of being thought to be crazy is that I can sit near them and they ignore me. Let her be, they say. The poor thing they say. We have so much and she has nothing but her mixed-up brain, they say.

It is important for you to know that there is no murder here, no suicide, no wars, no illness. The only way you can die is naturally, when your time comes, and no one knows when that will be.

Carlo is my age, seventeen.

I have a certain freak value here.

They ask me to be on late-night television talk shows of the kooky variety.

They pretend to treat me with respect, but no matter who the host is, there is always the slanted smile, the wink I am not supposed to see, the same questions.

"So what is Earth like?"

"Filled with the most magnificent fragrances!" I respond.

"Is everyone there an hour away from death then?" Ha! Ha! from the studio audience, but I persist. "No, listen! Our flowers smell. Our food smells. The very air smells. Not always good. We have bad smells too."

"So you spend all your time on Earth mesmerized by these odors, ah? How do you get anything done on Earth? How did your people ever build that fantastic spaceship you supposedly came here in, if you have all these odors to distract you?"

"We take our scents for granted, you see."

"Of course! Of course! And does your spaceship smell?"

The audience is bent double with laughter, and it is just as well in this phase of the interview, for I am not to disclose anything about the mission, not even in jest, not even here in this report.

I am to concentrate on Farfire.

That is what they call this place.

I was chosen because of my practical nature, my keen ability to be objective and unemotional. I am my father's daughter. Doctor Orr remarks on it often, telling me that I am rational and unstirrable beyond my years.

"Tell me, Caroline—is that your Earth name or your Farfire name—Caroline?"

"It is my Earth name. I am not from Farfire, so I have no Farfire name."

"Caroline's not too unlike a Farfire name, though, is it?"

"There is a lot of similarity between Earth and Farfire."

"Yes, well tell me, Caroline, do you have death on Earth too?"

"Of course we have death."

"Of course you have death." His tone mocks me again. "Except when you Earth folks die, there is no odor." Big wink to the studio audience.

"Not a good one, no."

"What's a bad odor, pray tell?" and there is more laughter.

"I can't describe it. Burnt rubber. Dead flowers. Feces. Those are bad odors on Earth."

"Feces smell on Earth?"

"Yes, they do," and the audience is in convulsions again.

"Well, Earth must not be all that lovely. You must be glad to be on Farfire, hah?"

I was, in the beginning. I truly was. Anticipating it, before I left, with pleasure. Challenged when I arrived. All of it new. But I did not calculate this part of it, being taken for a laughable freak, the way on Earth we treat those who say they've seen flying saucers or been to Mars.

"You'll not be there long," Father reassured me. "The moment you hear three beeps in your earpiece, use your minimike to assure Doctor Orr you're going directly to the field where you were dropped. He'll get you home safely in about two years, just in time for your nineteenth birthday!" Father was excited. "There's no telling what you'll learn about your Farfire teenage counterparts!"

"But will I blend in?" I ask him. "Will they take me captive? Will I be in any danger?"

"They will treat you as interlopers have been treated from time immemorial."

"How is that?"

"They will find some way to trivialize you. They will not believe you. It's all to your advantage."

"Caroline, Marny and I saw you on television," Carlo calls over to me. If anything could ruffle me, it would be that exquisite fragrance, almost making me homesick, it's so voluptuous. "We want to ask you a question." His lop-sided smile reminds me of the talk show hosts. "How," says Carlo, "do you know someone's dying on your Earth, if there is no perfume?"

I try to tell him, but his eyes glaze over as I start to describe traffic accidents, war, heart disease, all of it, and Marny giggles into her hands.

"How," Carlo interrupts me as though he is bored with my ranting and raving, "do you handle death then? Death sounds like something horrible."

"How," I come back with a testiness that surprises me, "do you handle the idea that in about forty-five minutes you won't ever be with Marny again?"

He laughs gaily. "We will have been together for as long as we were intended to be together. What more can anyone want?"

Marny asks, "On Earth, do people die at the same time?"

"No, but . . ." I have no ready answer. "But we don't like death."

"What sense does that make?" Carlo says. "Everyone must die. It can't go on forever."

In a while they prepare for his funeral.
They sing:

> *My! My! My! I smell good-bye!*
> *I know you've got to go*
> *So one last kiss*
> *The scent is bliss!*
> *Good-bye, the scent's to die!*

They all wear white and dance.
Marny can't stop smiling with joy.

There is nothing ever said about God here.
After the funeral I ask Marny if there is religion, God, what?
"All of that is after death," she says.
"But what exactly do you believe happens after death?"
"We don't know," she says, and her mouth tips in a grin. "I suppose on Earth you do?"
"We have certain beliefs," I say. "We have concepts. There is a concept of heaven, and a concept of hell. Now, heaven is . . ." and even as I talk, Marny wanders off from me, yawning, calling over her shoulder that she'd really like to hear all about it . . . some other time.

I have never been treated so rudely. That is the part that is so hard to bear: me, Caroline Aylesworth, winner of so many, many honors in science my book-shelves cannot hold all the gold statuettes, my walls with no room left for framed certificates. Not even *listened* to here on Farfire!

I cannot say that I am in any way disappointed when I hear the three beeps, even though this tiny taste of Farfire *has* provoked considerable curiosity in me . . . and even though there is no way ever again to have that curiosity satisfied, for there is no returning here.

"Hello, Caroline!" I hear Doctor Orr's familiar voice. "Do you think you got a good sample?"

"Not a comprehensive one, by any means, but enough about Farfire to make a highly interesting report."

"Excellent! And you know how to find your way to the field?"

"Of course I do."

"I'm here now, waiting for you."

"Give me about an hour and fifteen minutes."

"Gladly," Doctor Orr answers. "My God, Caroline, I'm almost overwhelmed by this wonderful fragrance here!"

"A fragrance, Doctor Orr? Not on Farfire. You see—"

He interrupts me with a whoop of joy. "*Un*believable! Almost like lilies! It's come upon me suddenly! Caroline? It's so all pervasive! It's on *me!* My hands, my face—it's the sweetest perfume!"

Of course, I cannot get to him in time.

I sit down right where I am and make my entry.

I write, *I think I've lost my ride home.*

In the interest of accuracy, I cross out "I think."

Written Conversation

TEXT ▶ "Rose," by John Biguenet

TIME ▶ 50+ Minutes

GROUPING SEQUENCE ▶ Individuals, groups, whole class

USED IN TEXT SET ▶ 6

Dear Reader,

If you have read any of our other books, you have probably come across this strategy before—it is one of the very few we have repeated here. That's because we believe that letter writing is the most neglected tool in our teaching repertoires. We're talking about notes, memos, emails, all kinds of correspondence between teachers and students—but especially, between kids and kids.

Here's why written conversation is so valuable. You know how you can have whole-class discussion, say about Act 3 of *Romeo and Juliet*, and the same three kids raise their hands and talk while everybody else just sleeps? Been there. But what if instead you put kids in groups of three and have them write simultaneous notes to each other about the play? Then *everyone* is engaged—"talking," reading, and thinking at once. No one can sleep because they have letters to write and answer. This really works, especially when you announce at the outset: "I'll be collecting these." And no, you don't have to read every word or grade them. Just a quick skim and checkoff is all that's needed to ensure focus and legibility.

The rest of what you need to know is right in the lesson steps. Thanks for listening.

Sincerely,
Smokey and Nancy

PREPARATION

Project or hang up the "Things to Think About While Reading" chart (page 38). Have copies of the story ready, along with full-size sheets of paper for writing notes to each other. Form kids into groups of three. If you have uneven numbers, form a couple groups of four—but no pairs. There will be three passes of notes, no matter what size the groups are. (This will make sense shortly.)

Steps & ▶
Teaching
Language

STEP 1 **Invite students to read the story.** *Today, we are going to read a short story by John Biguenet called "Rose." After you've read it, we'll have a discussion—but it will be a little different from other discussions we've had. You'll see in a few minutes.*

While you read the story, enter the text thinking and pay attention to your responses. Stop, think, and react, right? If it helps, refer to our chart of

"Things to Think About While Reading." When you have finished the story, you are going to want to read it again, because there are some tiny details that become very important once you've read it the first time. OK? Enjoy!

Allow sufficient time for reading.

STEP 2 **Set up the activity.** Reconvene the class. *Interesting story, right? In a minute we are going to have a written discussion about it, instead of the usual out-loud one. Basically, you'll each write a short note to your group about the story, and then you'll pass these "letters" around the group and answer them in writing. We'll swap notes three times, and I will give you the timing as we go. Just think of this as legalized note-passing in class.*

Groups of three, pull your seats together so you can easily pass papers and talk to each other later, when the time comes. Next, each person please grab a piece of paper and put your first name in the upper left-hand margin. This is called your "check-in." Every time a paper is passed to you, you put your name right below wherever the last person stopped writing. That way, we can easily see who wrote what.

Finally, there are three rules for written conversations:

1. Use your best handwriting so people will be able to read your ideas.

2. Use all the time for writing. I'm only going to give you a minute or two to write each note, but keep that pen moving the whole time with comments, connections, questions, arguments about the story—until I tell you to stop and pass.

3. No talking! This is a silent activity. You'll get to talk out loud later.

OK. Write until I call time. Remember, it's only for a minute. Write a note to your buddies about your thoughts, reactions, questions, interpretations, or feelings about the story, "Rose."

STEP 3 **Writing time and monitoring.** As students write, don't look at the clock. That "one minute" thing was just to reduce kids' anxiety. Keep time by walking and watching kids write. When most students have filled a quarter of a page, or written at least several lines, then it is time to pass. We often go well beyond the one-minute promise, allowing two or even three minutes of writing, as long as the class is showing some momentum and stamina.

STEP 4 **First pass of papers.** *Pass your papers to the next person, going to the left around the group.* When everyone has received a letter, say: *Now read the note on the page, and just beneath it, write an answer to your buddy. You can tell them your reaction, make a comment, ask questions, share a connection you've made, agree or disagree, or raise a whole new idea about "Rose." Just keep the conversation going!*

STEP 5 **More writing time.** Walk the room, looking over shoulders to provide help and to time the next pass. Reiterate the instructions if needed—especially about "no talking" while passing. *Remember, we are having a silent discussion here!*

STEP 6 **Second pass.** *Pass again, please, to your left. Look! Now you have two letters to read. So I am going to give you a little extra time to read and respond. You can answer one letter, or the other letter, or maybe you can find a way to respond to both. Just keep that conversation going. I'll give you a couple of minutes for this.*

STEP 7 **Letters return to owners.** *Now pass the papers so everyone gets back the one they started. Read the whole thing over and enjoy the conversation that* you *started. You won't write an answer this time.*

STEP 8 **Groups talk out loud.** As soon as kids finish reading and start talking—and they will—say: *Please feel free to continue the conversation out loud for a few minutes. Use your letters however they help you. What's your understanding or interpretation of this story? Why do you think John Biguenet wrote this? In other words, what's the author's theme or purpose?*

STEP 9 **Whole-class discussion.** Now you can gather all thirty kids and enjoy wide participation, not just the usual handful of Horshaks (Arnold Horshak, the nerdy hand-waver in TV's *Welcome Back, Kotter*, circa 1975–1979, played by Ron Palillo, who passed away when this book was going to press, God love him).

Let's convene as a whole class and see where this silent discussion took us. Will each group please share one highlight, one thread of their discussion? Something you spent time on, something that sparked lively discussion, maybe something you debated or argued about. Or maybe you discovered some key details that unlocked the story for you in some way. Who'd like to share?

Having rehearsed their thinking in writing, kids—even the usually shy ones—should be ready and willing to share.

STEP 10 **Debrief the process.** Don't forget that you have two things to discuss—the story and the process the kids have just used. It is important to reflect upon the activity itself, because you want this write-around tool to enter your kids' repertoires for repeated use. *How'd you like this note writing? What worked for you and what made it hard? How could we make it better next time?*

- **Start with a shorter story:** "Rose" is a great piece of work, but it is a little on the long side for in-class reading. At minimum, that means you must have instructions ready for kids who finish fast. Alternatively, if your kids will actually do homework, you could assign the story overnight. Or, you might want to do your first written conversation with a shorter piece that minimizes reading rate disparities. Your call.

- **Prompt kids during reading:** Are you concerned that your kids won't remember enough to write about after they have read the story? If so, make a handout of the "Things to Think About While Reading" chart, and have them use it for quick note taking as they read. Make sure they don't think you want them to fill every box. Say: *Just use the one that fits when you have a thought, question, or reaction—and jot a few words to label it. Then right back to the story.*

- **Making the transition to talk:** At Step 8, when groups go out-loud for the first time, you may choose to offer them a specific prompt rather than having them just carry on with ideas from their written discussion. Something like:

  - Exactly what do you think happened to the boy?
  - Why didn't the wife tell the husband about the photos?
  - What can you infer about the husband's character or personality?
  - What time period do you think this story is set in?
  - How does the title connect with certain story details? What might these details represent that goes beyond their literal meanings?

  Send kids back into their now warmed-up groups to discuss and find evidence in the text that illuminates these questions. Or you can shift directly to whole-class discussion.

- **Nonfiction connections:** At the core of this story is the idea of "age progressions," special forensic photographs that can show what a person might look like in the future. Typically, these photo constructions have been used by police to determine what a kidnapped child might look like three, five, or ten years after being abducted. Today, a decade after the story was written, you can take any person's picture and go on a website like www.age-me.com and have the image age-progressed right before your eyes.

Assuming your school allows access to such a site, you could have your students plug in their own photographs and see what they will look like as they age. Be careful you don't get tangled in family searches for lost children. Also, truth in advertising: professional forensic artists scoff at these free age-progression websites and charge up to $250 for a professional version.

Shoptalk ▶ Written conversation is a great way to have a discussion on *any* text—from your textbook, the curriculum guide, or something you've found on your own. Students can write about their responses to their reading, just as we have modeled here, or you can supply a more focused prompt as long as it is debate-friendly and multifaceted. The best part about watching students in the midst of a written conversation is their almost automatic rereading of the text. As they write, students constantly look back for proof or for new ideas to write about. And as the note exchange goes on, they have to be rereading their partners' comments as well. Written conversations in which kids take on the roles of characters in a story—especially characters who are in conflict with one another—can provide opportunities for kids to pinpoint what the characters believe and why they are acting as they are.

Rose

John Biguenet

"It must have been, I think she said, two years after the kidnapping, when your wife first came by." The voice on the phone sounded young. "What was that, '83, '84?"

"Kidnapping?"

"Yeah, she told me all about it, how it was for the private detective you hired after the police gave up."

"You mean the picture?"

"Right, the age progression."

"You could do it back then?"

"It was a pain in the ass. You had to write your own code. But, yeah, once we had the algorithms for stuff like teeth displacement of the lips, cartilage development in the nose and ears, stuff like that, all you had to do was add fat-to-tissue ratios by age, and you wound up with a fairly decent picture of what the face probably looked like. I mean, after you tried a couple different haircuts and cleaned up the image—the printers were a joke in those days."

"And you kept updating Kevin's..." He hesitated as he tried to remember the term. "Kevin's age progression?"

"Every year, like clockwork, on October twentieth. Of course, the new ones, it's no comparison. On-screen, we're 3-D now; the whole head can rotate. And if you've got a tape of the kid talking or singing, there's even a program to age the voice and sync it with the lips. You sort of teach it to talk, and then it can say anything you want, the head."

The voice was waiting for him to say something.

"I mean, we thought it was cool, Mr. Grierson, the way you didn't lose hope you'd find your boy one day. Even after all these years."

He hung up while the man was still talking. On the kitchen table, the photo album Emily had used to bind the pictures, the age progressions, lay open to one that had the logo and phone number of Crescent CompuGraphics printed along its border. His son looked fifteen, maybe sixteen, in the picture.

He had found the red album the night before, after his wife's funeral. Indulging his grief after the desolate service and the miserly reception of chips and soft drinks at her sister's, he had sunk to his knees before Emily's hope chest at the foot of their bed, fingering the silk negligee bruised brown with age, inhaling the distant scent of gardenias on the bodice of an old evening gown, burying his arms in all the tenderly folded velvet and satin. It was his burrowing hand that discovered the album at the bottom of the trunk.

At first, he did not know who it was, the face growing younger and younger with each page. But soon enough, he began to suspect. And then, on the very last leaf of the red binder, he recognized the combed hair and fragile smile of the little boy who returned his gaze from a school photograph.

As he thought of Emily secretly thumbing through the age progressions, each year on Kevin's birthday adding a new portrait on top of the one from the year before, he felt the nausea rising in his throat and took a deep breath. It's just another kind of memory, he told himself, defending her.

He, for example, still could not forget the green clock on the kitchen wall that had first reminded him his son should be home from school already. Nor could he forget the pitiless clack of the dead bolt as he had unlocked the door to see if the boy was dawdling down the sidewalk. And he would always remember stepping onto the front porch and catching, just at the periphery of his vision, the first glimpse of the pulsing red light, like a flower bobbing in and out of shadow.

In fact, turning his head in that small moment of uncertainty, he took the light to be just that: a red rose tantalized by the afternoon's late sun but already hatched with the low shadows of the molting elms that lined the street. And he remembered that as he turned toward the flashing light, lifting his eyes over the roses trellised along the fence—the hybrid, Blue Girl that would not survive the season, twined among the thick canes and velvet blossoms of the Don Juan—and even as he started down the wooden steps toward the front gate, slowly, deliberately, as if the people running toward the house, shouting his name, had nothing to do with him, he continued to think rose, rose, rose.

LESSON 5.2 Thirty-Second Look

Tone is such a subtle thing. If an author's good, precise word choices become organic. We read, we feel, we visualize, we empathize, we're moved, we're absorbed. Generally, we readers don't stop every few lines and admire the word choices: "Huh, I would have pictured something totally different if the author had described that character as skinny versus anorexic." Through tone, the author "cops an attitude" and hopes the reader cops it as well.

Ever read *The Art of Racing in the Rain* by Garth Stein? The story is written from the perspective of Enzo, a dog who wishes he were human (kind of like Pinocchio). This speech is from early in the novel. Read it and tell us what attitude the author wants us to cop about Enzo.

> *Here's why I will be a good person. Because I listen. I cannot talk, so I listen very well. I never deflect the course of the conversation with a comment of my own. People, if you pay attention to them, change the direction of one another's conversations constantly. It's like having a passenger in your car who suddenly grabs the steering wheel and turns you down a side street. For instance, if we met at a party and I wanted to tell you a story about the time I needed to get a soccer ball in my neighbor's yard but his dog chased me and I had to jump into a swimming pool to escape, and I began telling the story, you, hearing the words "soccer" and "neighbor" in the same sentence, might interrupt and mention that your childhood neighbor was Pelé, the famous soccer player, and I might be courteous and say, Didn't he play for the Cosmos of New York? Did you grow up in New York? And you might reply that, no, you grew up in Brazil on the streets of Três Corações with Pelé, and I might say, I thought you were from Tennessee, and you might say not originally, and then go on to outline your genealogy at length. So my initial conversational gambit—that I had a funny story about being chased by my neighbor's dog— would be totally lost, and only because you had to tell me all about Pelé. Learn to* listen! *I beg of you. Pretend you are a dog like me and listen to other people rather than steal their stories.*

Don't you just love that dog? What wisdom! Plus Enzo uses dog analogies: sitting in a car, chasing a ball, total dog perspective. And Enzo's vocabulary shows he listens and remembers (Nancy's cat Scully will *never* use the word "deflect" in her memoir, and she's been living with Nancy for fourteen years!). Excellent, you get an A on tone detection.

Unfortunately, trying to teach kids about tone can be a little deflating because it requires serious reduction and dissection. When we study tone, the story can no longer wash over us. We're getting into how the sausage is made, not a pretty picture—unless you are planning to make sausage yourself. Then

TEXT ▶ *Mining Village,* by Stevan Dohanos

TIME ▶ 30 Minutes

GROUPING SEQUENCE ▶ Individuals, pairs, whole class

USED IN TEXT SET ▶ 6

you *want* to see how it's made, and that's what we want to capitalize on. Studying tone is essential for learning how to become a better writer.

This lesson introduces tone with an image.

Steps & ▶ Teaching Language

STEP 1 **Prepare for note taking.** *Get out a sheet of loose-leaf paper. Today we're going to "read" an image for thirty seconds. As you concentrate on the painting, I want you to try to memorize as many details as possible. When the time is up, I will remove the image and give you a quiz.*

STEP 2 **Project the painting for thirty seconds.** After time is up, remove the image.

STEP 3 **Memory note taking.** *Now I want you to write down everything you remember related to the prompts I give you.*

Give these prompts one at a time. As you move through the prompts, you might write key words on the board or project them, but do not give students the entire list at once.

- *How many people are in the piece?*
- *How would you describe them?*
- *How is each one dressed?*
- *What do people do for a living?*
- *What kind of setting is depicted? Where do these people live?*
- *What colors do you remember in the setting?*
- *What kind of feelings do you get from the setting: tidy, chaotic, calm? Those are just examples.*
- *What is this piece about?*
- *What's the overall feeling you got looking at this piece?*

STEP 4 **Pair share.** Pairs meet and spend a couple of minutes comparing what they jotted down.

Pay particular attention to details one person remembered that the other didn't. That's why we always work together. Different people notice different things and bring different ideas to the table. Listening to what others think expands our own thinking.

STEP 5 **Project the image again.** *Using the image and your notes, I want you to think about the story this piece is telling and the impression the artist is trying to give the viewer about the story. What artistic choices did the painter make to shape the depiction?*

COMMON CORE STANDARDS SUPPORTED

- Read closely to determine what the text says explicitly and to make logical inferences from it. *(CCRA.R.1)*
- Analyze how specific choices shape meaning or tone. *(CCRA.R.4)*
- Integrate and evaluate content presented in diverse formats, including visually and quantitatively, as well as in words. *(CCRA.R.7)*
- Participate effectively in a range of conversations and collaborations. *(CCRA.SL.6)*

STEP 6 **Share out.** Ask pairs to share their "stories" and explain what details led them to those conclusions. Students should mention details such as:

Smokestacks against blue sky

Schoolboy is clean while miners are dirty

Miners look tired

School looks a little tattered but happy (flower cut-outs in windows)

Ground looks beaten, dead tree

A sameness—houses look the same, miners look the same

Sense of generational tradition

Not a bad life—necessities of life met, working for a living

Everyone looks safe

There may be environmental dangers around

Maybe predictable or boring but a calm town

STEP 6 **Conclusion.** *What does the artist want us to think about coal mining? Who do you think the audience was for this painting? Authors work the same way as visual artists but with words. The words they use are chosen with care so that they make exactly the intended impression on the reader. A good writer does this so skillfully that we don't even notice; we're just scooped up by the story. However, for us to become better readers and writers, it's important that from time to time we stop and ask, "What's going on here? What did the writer just do that made me think that?" Now that you know what tone is, this is something we'll be revisiting for the rest of the year.*

- **Chamber of Commerce brochure:** Have pairs write an ad inviting people to become residents of this community, emphasizing the positives. Or write a complaining letter to the editor of the local paper about how the mining industry, with its pollution and job dangers, is threatening the town's health.

- **Examine the photographs on your community's website:** Have students look up their own town's website and study the photographs. What impressions do these photographs give of your town, particularly to those who might be thinking about visiting? What tonal elements are present to give this impression?

- **Contrasting tone:** Whereas some viewers think this mural portrays a neutral tone about West Virginia coal mining, photographs taken of community members following the April 5, 2010, explosion that left twenty-nine West Virginia coal miners dead portray a stark contrast that you might want to discuss with your students.

◀ *Variations*

Montcoal Mine Disaster

http://sharrett.blogspot.com/2010/04/montcoal-mine-disaster.html

W. Va. Coal Country After 29 Miners Die in Blast

http://www.washingtonpost.com/wp-dyn/content/gallery
/2010/04/06/GA2010040600590.html

Mining Town Waits for Word on Missing Miners After Blast

By David A. Fahrenthold, Washington Post Staff Writer, Wednesday,
April 7, 2010

http://www.washingtonpost.com/wp-dyn/content/story/2010/04/05
/ST2010040505519.html?sid=ST2010040505519

Shoptalk ▶ The study of tone is something that needs frequent visits. Every written thing has a tone, even an encyclopedia entry. Whenever tone is going to be important to understanding a piece, try introducing the discussion with an image.

In literature, we refer to feelings/impressions we get from a piece as tone, but in the nonfiction world it is often referred to as "author's attitude." Many traditional standardized reading tests (and, very likely, any newer ones) have items that ask, "What is the author's attitude toward this subject/this topic?" Any way you cut it, tone is determined by word choice. Once the kids get a feeling for how word choice reveals tone or attitude, challenge them to find examples from their own reading and share with the class.

Stevan Dohanos, *Mining Village,* 1937 (study for mural, Huntington, West Virginia, forestry service building). Smithsonian American Art Museum, Washington, DC / Art Resource, NY.

LESSON 5.3 Follow-Up Questions

If you want to see some good follow-up questions in action, watch Jon Stewart's interviews on *The Daily Show*. Go load the dryer if actors are promoting their movies, but sit up and pay attention when his guests are political figures. Stewart asks a question and then he listens; he listens because his next question is going to zero in on the contradictions of the previous answer. Stewart won't let a guest wiggle off the hook or change the subject. He asks for details. He asks for history. He demands that his guests defend their assertions with facts versus hearsay or talking points. Stewart insists on burrowing deep into a topic.

Unfortunately, you're not going to be able to show many of these interviews to your kids because it's likely that some webpage banner ad for condoms will suddenly crawl by, midinterview. However, you can watch some of Stewart's interviews for your own edification: http://www.thedailyshow.com/extended-interviews.

When it comes to literature discussion, we want our students to be as dogged as Stewart but without the killer instinct. In conversation, when a student's opinion is vague or unsupported, we want our kids to be interested, to listen, to pursue the ideas bubbling under the surface. Very often kids have great insight, but it just doesn't come out right at first because they haven't had enough extended practice in academic discussion. And the other kids in the discussion aren't used to being the ones asking the follow-up/clarification questions because that's always been the job of the teacher. Refining discussion takes practice, explicit demonstration, and coaching, but it's definitely worth the time investment.

TEXT ▶ "Deportation at Breakfast," by Larry Fondation

TIME ▶ 50 Minutes

GROUPING SEQUENCE ▶ Individuals, whole class, pairs, whole class

PREPARATION

Make a copy of "Deportation at Breakfast" for each student. Determine the method of projection so you can show your follow-up question notes when you model the strategy. Determine how pairs will form for their question discussion.

◀ **Steps & Teaching Language**

STEP 1 **Pass out the story and review deep questions.** *We are always talking about how to make our literature discussions more fun and interesting.* (If you've previously taught Lesson 4.4, Reading with Questions in Mind, you could view the class lists made then.) *Let me just ask you, what kinds of questions make for a really good conversation in a small group? Go ahead and shout some out, and I'll write them down here.* Kids will probably volunteer many of these; fill in others yourself if you like.

- Open ended

- Based on things in the story but you've got to think about how to answer, not just fill-in-the-blank

- Might have to read further before being able to answer

- Relate to character motivation/details and setting

- Predictions

- Make you read between the lines

- Make connections to text and background knowledge

- Use imagination

- Ask for details

STEP 2 **Pass out stories and give directions.** *This story is called "Deportation at Breakfast." When you read this story, remember to jot down interesting discussion questions as you go. Don't wait until you've finished reading and then go back. By the time you are finished with this story, you should have seven or eight good questions. Get started now because as soon as everyone's finished we're going to begin discussion.*

STEP 3 **Monitor reading.** Gently nudge students to follow the directions to write questions as they read.

STEP 4 **Model asking follow-up questions.** *Today we're going to refine your discussion skills by practicing follow-up questions. These are questions you ask after your partner has already given a comment or answer. The goal with these questions is to get your partner to talk in more detail and also to go back to the text and defend their opinions with specific details. Now I need a volunteer.* Have a student stand next to you as you project your note taking. *Thanks. Be sure to bring your story with you.*

OK everyone, as you see me ask follow-ups, I want you to pay attention to how I try to listen very carefully to what my partner has to say, but I write down only the questions I ask.

Take a look at the first paragraph of the story. Here's my original question (the question should be already be written on your copy in the margin). What kind of impression do you get from the story's opening description of the restaurant? The student might answer *"casual, cheap."*

However he or she answers, respond with this next question: *What in that first paragraph makes you think that? I want you to think about your answer while I jot down this question.* Write the question on your copy of the story underneath the original question. Then ask for the answer. The student should point out some text details.

Listen carefully and then ask a second follow-up question. *From the details you just mentioned, do you think the narrator is a regular or a first-time customer? Why? Remember, don't answer until I've written the question down.*

Continue the modeling with another question or two. There are two key points to remember. One, the next question is always based on the partner's previous response. Two, the partner can't answer a follow-up question until after you've written it down; this second step automatically builds in wait time.

After the last question, if there are any ideas you wanted to add, go ahead. The point to remember here is that the person asking the questions never shares his ideas until he has really listened to what his partner has to say.

STEP 5 **Debrief the modeling.** *OK, I want you to give my temporary partner a big round of applause because it's tough to get up in front of the class and then get grilled by me! Thank you, _____.*

In a moment you're going to work on follow-up questions with your own partners, but first let's see what you noticed. Turn to your partner and try to make a quick list of characteristics of good follow-up questions. Give pairs a minute to talk. Then have partners share their "good follow-up question characteristics" with the whole class.

Great. You noticed that good follow-up questions really extend a discussion. There are a couple other things I want to make sure you noticed before we get started. What did I do after I asked each question? Yes, I wouldn't let my partner answer the question until I finished writing it down. This seems trivial, but it's actually pretty important. When I make my partner wait to answer, I'm actually giving what's called wait time, time to think. That way they can explain their thoughts more clearly and in more detail.

What was the other thing I made sure I did? Yes, I wrote my follow-up questions in order underneath the original question. One other thing you should have noticed was that I didn't add my own thoughts about the questions until I had thoroughly interviewed my partner. That is SUPER important. When it's your job to ask questions it's your job to mainly listen.

OK, everybody clear on how to ask questions when it's your turn? Don't forget to take turns asking questions. Go.

STEP 6 **Monitor the pair discussions.** Coach the questioners to make their partners wait to answer; no answering while they're still jotting a follow-up. Step in if you see one person asking all the questions.

If they are following the instructions correctly, don't expect students to get through all of their questions. The goal of this exercise is to slow down discussion and make it more thorough. Watch the time, and when you want to move on, instruct pairs to jump to the end of the story and discuss some of their final questions if they haven't already gotten there.

STEP 7 **Pairs prepare to share with the class.** *As I was monitoring, I heard a lot of good questions and a lot of really interesting discussion. Take a look back at your question strings. Which set of questions produced the best discussion? What did you talk about? Look over your stories with your partner and find something interesting to share with the rest of us. Be sure to talk it over so that both of you are prepared to share.*

STEP 8 **Share out.** Call for volunteers or call on students at random since you told them to be prepared. Be sure to discuss the end of the story after Javier has been removed.

Variations ▶ **Connecting nonfiction with allegory:** Did you notice that by the end of the story the narrator was behind the counter cooking people's breakfasts? Might this story be about something bigger than just an independent diner that has lost its help or maybe its owner? In certain states, strict laws have made life very uncertain for immigrants. In response, they have moved away, creating costly labor shortages:

> **The Law of Unintended Consequences:**
> **Georgia's Immigration Law Backfires**
>
> To forgo a repeat of last year, when labor shortages triggered an esti-mated $140 million in agricultural losses, as crops rotted in the fields, officials in Georgia are now dispatching prisoners to the state's farms to help harvest fruit and vegetables.
>
> *Forbes,* May 17, 2012

If you wanted to extend the exploration of the central idea of this story, students might research the positive economic impact and important contributions immigrants make to the United States.

Shoptalk ▶ Knowing how to listen and ask good follow-up questions is the foundation of any kind of peer-led discussion. Also, asking follow-ups can rein in loquacious members and get thoughts from the quieter students out on the table. Often, the members who usually dominate discussions find the ideas of others inter-esting once they begin to ask follow-ups. We always tell students if you ask good follow-up questions, you'll have gotten your classmates to think about every-thing you were thinking, without you having to tell them anything! Also, hope-fully, your members will bring up some ideas that you *hadn't* thought of.

While the stories we use for modeling are short, the pieces in your textbook often are not. You can't emphasize enough to your kids that getting into the habit of jotting notes *as they go along* saves time later on. Rather than having to reread a twenty-page story later, they'll be able to skim the reading because their notes will help them remember what's important.

Deportation at Breakfast

Larry Fondation

The signs on the windows lured me inside. For a dollar I could get two eggs, toast, and potatoes. The place looked better than most—family-run and clean. The signs were hand-lettered and neat. The paper had yellowed some, but the black letters remained bold. A green-and-white awning was perched over the door, where the name "Clara's" was stenciled.

Inside, the place had an appealing and old-fashioned look. The air smelled fresh and homey, not greasy. The menu was printed on a chalkboard. It was short and to the point. It listed the kinds of toast you could choose from. One entry was erased from the middle of the list. By deduction, I figured it was rye. I didn't want rye toast anyway.

Because I was alone, I sat at the counter, leaving the empty tables free for other customers that might come in. At the time, business was quiet. Only two tables were occupied, and I was alone at the counter. But it was still early—not yet seven-thirty.

Behind the counter was a short man with dark black hair, a mustache, and a youthful beard, one that never grew much past stubble. He was dressed immaculately, all in chef's white—pants, shirt, and apron, but no hat. He had a thick accent. The name "Javier" was stitched on his shirt.

I ordered coffee, and asked for a minute to choose between the breakfast special for a dollar and the cheese omelette for $1.59. I selected the omelette.

The coffee was hot, strong, and fresh. I spread my newspaper on the counter and sipped at the mug as Javier went to the grill to cook my meal.

The eggs were spread out on the griddle, the bread plunged inside the toaster, when the authorities came in. They grabbed Javier quickly and without a word, forcing his hands behind his back. He, too, said nothing. He did not resist, and they shoved him out the door and into their waiting car.

On the grill, my eggs bubbled. I looked around for another employee—maybe out back somewhere, or in the washroom. I leaned over the counter and called for someone. No one answered. I looked behind me toward the tables. Two elderly men sat at one, two elderly women at the other. The two women were talking. The men were reading the paper. They seemed not to have noticed Javier's exit.

I could smell my eggs starting to burn. I wasn't quite sure what to do about it. I thought about Javier and stared at my eggs. After some hesitation, I got up from my red swivel stool and went behind the counter. I grabbed a spare apron, then picked up the spatula and turned my eggs. My toast had popped up, but it was not browned, so I put it down again. While I was cooking, the two elderly women came to the counter and asked to pay. I asked what they had had. They seemed surprised that I didn't remember. I checked the prices on the chalkboard and rang up their order. They paid slowly, fishing through large purses, and went out, leaving me a dollar tip. I took my eggs off the grill and slid them onto a clean plate. My toast had come up. I buttered it and put it on my plate beside my egg. I put the plate at my spot at the counter, right next to my newspaper.

As I began to come back from behind the counter to my stool, six new customers came through the door. "Can we pull some tables together?" they asked. "We're all one party." I told them yes. Then they ordered six coffees, two decaffeinated.

I thought of telling them I didn't work there. But perhaps they were hungry. I poured their coffee. Their order was simple: six breakfast specials, all with scrambled eggs and wheat toast. I got busy at the grill.

Then the elderly men came to pay. More new customers began arriving. By eight-thirty, I had my hands full. With this kind of business, I couldn't understand why Javier hadn't hired a waitress. Maybe I'd take out a help-wanted ad in the paper tomorrow. I had never been in the restaurant business. There was no way I could run this place alone.

LESSON 5.4 # Save the Last Word for Me

As we heighten our students' awareness of text, one goal is for them to "locate and lift" elements that are intriguing, important, or noteworthy. When we spoon-feed kids these text highlights, at best they act mildly interested. Just as often, though, they tune us out or simply try to figure out what might be on the essay test. No habits of mind and reading are internalized.

But when we ask kids to seek those special lines or passages *themselves*, they're usually much more engaged. And then, whenever we listen in on groups, we *always* hear kids talking about the same passages we would have pointed out ourselves in the first place. Big duh.

But there's a common problem. In small-group meetings, the text picker often blurts out his thinking right at the beginning. The other kids in the group listen and nod. When the picker finally ends with, "Anybody got anything to add?" the rest of the members unanimously shake their heads. "Nope, you've said it all." Even if another student might have had a different idea or interpretation, she's reluctant to share because the "right" answer has already been presented.

To get more conversational mileage out of good text liftings, to get some real discussion going, we must show students how to "save the last word."

PREPARATION

Make a copy of "Stingray" for each student. Determine how groups of four will form.

STEP 1 **Instructions for reading.** *As you read this poem, please stop along the way and do two things: Underline words or phrases that seem important, surprising, interesting, thought provoking, or puzzling. Then, before continuing to read, jot down some notes on what you were thinking. Try to imagine that you are having a conversation with the text inside your head. Your notes are your side of the conversation. Be sure to pick out three or four lines from each page of the poem.*

STEP 2 **Monitor reading.** If you notice some students finishing sooner than others, just nudge them to reread the poem and see what else they notice.

STEP 3 **Form groups of four.** *Move with your group and number off one through four. Number ones, I want you to turn to your group, and point out the first line you underlined so that the others can find it. Go ahead and read it aloud. Good. Now everyone look back at me.*

◀ **Steps** & **Teaching Language**

TEXT ▶ "Stingray," by Michael Salinger

TIME ▶ 50 Minutes

GROUPING SEQUENCE ▶ Whole class, individuals, groups of four, whole class

USED IN TEXT SET ▶ 6

STEP 4 **Initial instructions for Save the Last Word for Me.** *Sometimes when I watch groups discuss literature, I notice that the person who initiated the discussion often reads the passage and then automatically goes ahead and explains it. Then everyone nods in agreement and it's on to the next passage. However, I think your groups have a lot more discussion in you and many more great ideas and observations to share.*

So, number ones, I want you to do something different this time. Instead of explaining the line you just read aloud to your group, I want you to turn to them and say, "Save the last word for me." Then wait until everyone else in the group says something about the line or what it makes them think about. Only after everyone else in your group has weighed in can you add your own explanation. Now go ahead and try it. When you have finished discussing the first passage, stop talking and look back at me.

STEP 5 **Reflect and plan turn taking.** *Nicely done. It was pretty impressive how much everyone had to say when the person who chose the line talked last. I want you to continue to use Save the Last Word. Be sure to move the discussion around the group, letting members take turns reading their lines aloud. That means the twos go next, then the threes, and so on. Once everyone has read a line, the ones will start a new round.*

STEP 6 **Monitor.** Listen in on discussions, and notice where groups are getting bogged down. Step in to remind members to offer up only one Save the Last Word item and then let the next member take a turn. Also watch who is talking/answering the most in a group. When you see a dominant member, intervene. Tell the talker that until you call time, their job is to listen carefully to what the others have to say before adding their comments.

STEP 7 **Sharing.** Reconvene the large group when you notice the group discussions winding down. Ask each group to share one interesting line and the ideas it generated.

STEP 8 **Refinement of discussion.** *Before we finish up, let's take a moment to reflect on the process. I bet you noticed that it was a lot harder to think of something new to say when you were the last person to add an idea for Save the Last Word, so let's plan a strategy for how to expand the responses.*

Let's assume that the first person who responds usually says why they think the Save the Last Word person picked that passage. OK, there are still three or four other people in the group who have to come up with something else that's valid and original and interesting. What are some other ways you could respond?

Have the groups brainstorm ways members can expand their comments when the most obvious ideas have already been taken. Make a master list and then refer to it the next time you use this strategy in class.

Ways to Respond to a Line

- Explain why the line/word was important

- Explain what surprised you about the line/word

- Explain what you pictured when you read that part

- Connect that line/word with another

- Add on to what someone else has said

- Ask a question

Using questions: We admire the educational organization called Facing History and Ourselves, about which we'll say more in Chapter 10 (pages 223–278). It has a nice variation of "Save the Last Word" on its most useful website (www.facinghistory.org/resources/strategies/save-last-word-me).

◀ ***Variations***

Ask students to think about three "probing" questions the text raises for them. (A "probing" question is interpretive and evaluative. It can be discussed and has no clearly defined "right" answer, as opposed to clarifying questions, which are typically factual in nature.) Students answer the question on the back of an index card. When they meet in small groups, students select one of their questions for the other students to discuss.

STLWFM is one of our absolute favorite discussion strategies. It works for any kind of reading—poetry, fiction, nonfiction—and it always expands the conversation in ways that wouldn't have occurred otherwise. The structure naturally compels talkative kids to quietly wait for their turn sometimes, offers reticent kids designated spaces to speak out, and helps everyone to balance airtime in small groups. As the CCSS encourage us to sponsor far more kid-kid talk in our classrooms, this is a go-to structure for orderly, engaged conversation.

◀ ***Shoptalk***

Stingray

Michael Salinger

The young man believed
he had hooked an angel
shark
line ripping from his bait casting reel
drag click whizzing away like
a New Year's Eve noisemaker
attached to an electric drill
the rest of the anglers
at his end of the pier
grabbing their gear
clearing way
to watch this fight
big fish
big fish

big fish on
passes
      tide steady
down 600 foot fishing pier
as tackle lay abandoned
on weather cured planks
so that the owners
could catch this show

50 pound test line
stretching tight
guttural cat howling
like an out of tune violin
while the young man
rappels down a mountainside
back leaning with all his weight
gaining three feet
giving up
two
towed from one rough hewn railing
to the other
for three tortuous quarters of an hour
before we even see
the fish

rolling near the surface
like a king sized sheet
flashing by
in a washing machine
filled with dark green ink
the white underside
of a 150 lb. sting ray
slicing by for a fraction of eternity
then diving as if sucked down a drain
fiberglass composite rod
broomstick thick
arches downward
toward the moon's reflected
static scribbled across the waves
twenty feet below the pier
a catapult
the instant before sword
slices rope
and our guy is hanging tight
and time stops
        and solidifies
like the briny residue of sea spray
crystallizing in the corner of one's mouth
while we wait
seconds tick tick ticking away
each of us expecting
the line to snap

but he's hanging tight
when most would have cut it loose by now
a sting ray is a garbage fish after all
not fit for food
too expensive on a taxidermist's bench
but it's a matter of principle now
and finally
the rod slowly unbends
like an arching dinosaur's neck
the fish breaks the surface
and surrenders
a giant three pronged gaffing hook

attached to tire swing thick rope
pulls the fish up
dripping
like a Volkswagen being lifted
from a farm pond by crane
three men haul it over the railing
drop it on the deck
slick white belly up
blood spatter illuminated by mercury vapor
softball size mouth full of pointed teeth
gasping in the terrible air

and

the first baby was a surprise
like a black dinner plate
gliding out from under a rug
but four more followed
each
mindful of the stinger
gingerly
tossed back into the sea
by astonished fishermen
then the mother is heaved over
smacking the water spread eagle flat
with the sound of
tree split by lightning cracking
predator attracting blood
billowing wake trailing her escape
her offspring
fish born out of water
fly in formation
oblivious to the sacrifice

LESSON 5.5 Literature Circles

Have you ever been a member of an adult book club? A group of friends that gathers periodically to discuss a chosen book (and maybe eat snacks, drink wine, and gossip just a bit)? If so, you've been in the grown-up equivalent of the school activity called "literature circles."

Between us, we have written two whole books about the many variations and benefits of lit circles, book clubs, and/or reading groups. Whatever the particular version, the consistent purpose is bringing an authentic, real-life literacy practice into the classroom without letting it get turned into some kind of mechanical, small-group worksheet. We've been lucky to work with thousands of teachers around the country in fine-tuning this structure with their kids.

One common misconception about small, peer-led reading discussion groups is that they are only suitable for whole novels. *Au contraire!* We can— indeed, we must—have students practice lit circling with shorter works first, before they launch into the extended discussion of whole books. This lesson provides just that practice. We have chosen a longer and quite delectable Don Zancanella short story, and allocated parts of two days for this work.

TEXT ▶ "The Chimpanzees of Wyoming," by Don Zancanella

TIME ▶ Two class periods

GROUPING SEQUENCE ▶ Whole class, groups, whole class; repeat sequence

USED IN TEXT SET ▶ 8

PREPARATION

Copy the story in two sections as indicated. Predetermine groups of three to five, with four being optimal. Be ready to explain ways students can capture their responses while reading, in Step 1. Figure out how the reading will be done. We prefer to have kids doing the reading in class so we can personally guide and support them—and make sure everyone gets done on time. But if you cannot allocate that much time, the reading can be done as homework. In that case, you'll only need class time for the lesson start-up (ten minutes), the first and second book club meetings (twenty minutes each), and a closing whole-class roundup (another ten)—about one hour total.

STEP 1 **Explain note taking and assign the first section.** *OK, guys. Over the next couple of days we are going to read this story and discuss it in a format called literature circles. Has anybody done that before? It's pretty simple. You read the story on your own, being on the lookout for questions or topics that would be interesting to talk about with a small group of your classmates.*

If we were reading this story in our textbook, we'd have to use Post-it notes to capture our responses, because we can't mark it up, right? But here, you have your own copy of the story, so you can write away, right on the page. What kinds of things could you be watching for, that might be interesting to talk about in a book club?

◀ **Steps &
Teaching
Language**

Invite students' suggestions and list or project these. Many of them will probably overlap with items on your trusty "Things to Think About While Reading" chart (page 35). If key ones go unmentioned, reiterate them or point to the chart, which should be hanging prominently in your room.

And then, I happen to know that you'll be encountering some information about a very interesting time period in American history, and there may be some historical details well worth talking over. So, I think you'll be able to mark plenty of discussion-worthy topics as you read this first half of the story.

Hand out part 1 of the story. *Happy reading, everyone.* Allow necessary in-class or at-home reading and writing time.

STEP 2 **Next day: convene first meeting.** Have kids gather in their groups of four, making sure they are arranged for good hearing, eye contact, and engagement. In other words, "eye to eye, knee to knee, ear to ear." Make sure everyone has their annotated copy of the story in hand, ready to go.

OK, guys, you'll start your book club discussions in just a minute. But first I want to make sure that you all have several interesting topics to discuss when you meet. So right now, everyone look through your notes you've made in the margins and pick out the one most interesting thing that you'd like to discuss with your group. Go ahead, find it and then put a star by that item. Allow about thirty seconds for this.

Everybody found their best item? Good. Now it's time to jump into discussion. Each of you take a turn at presenting your item. However, try not to rush. Go back and look at the story. Try to get all your ideas out there and ask some questions to get others to do the same. See how deep you can take a topic before you move on to a new discussion item.

STEP 3 **Monitor and assist.** As you visit groups, just listen. Resist the urge to intervene or steer kids toward "correct" interpretations. In lit circles, it's students' responsibility to run their own discussion. You can use your observations later, to create mini-lessons that make the next meetings even more effective. If you find a group that's totally stuck, "donate" a rich, open-ended question to get them going, and then walk away.

STEP 4 **Groups list themes and predict conclusion.** At the end of today's meeting, while kids are still sitting in groups, have them meet for one more minute to make specific predictions about (1) where they think the plot of the story is going and (2) what they think the author's purpose, message, or theme is going to be. They should write these predictions down, and then have one person from each group report back to the whole class on its prognostications. This will be a great opportunity for you to ask, "What in the book made you think that?"

Hand out the second half of the story and assign reading and note taking for tomorrow. Don't be surprised if kids insist on reading the ending right on the spot, no matter what bell might be ringing.

STEP 5 **Commence the second meeting.** Same rules as the first lit circle meeting session. If kids think they first need to identify the one most interesting discussion topic from their notes, you can repeat that step. Usually, this is unnecessary, because kids are into the story and a whole lot happens in the second half. After about half the meeting time has elapsed, interrupt groups and add this instruction:

In about ten minutes, we are going to get together to talk about this story. We want to focus on the really big ideas: what's the point, the message, the takeaway? Why did Zancanella go to the trouble to write this story? What points is he making about people, animals, war, humanity, faith, idealism, the opening of the West, or any other theme you see here? Be ready to address those topics when we come back.

STEP 6 **Class discussion.** Invite an open and wide-ranging discussion of the book, but keep pushing on the "so what?" question—what does it all add up to? What is this story saying, teaching, showing? You may wish to keep a list of big themes or strands of thinking, so the kids can keep track and build on these. To us, the story is a great example of a literary text with multiple, interweaving themes.

STEP 7 **Debrief the lit circle process.** Take time at the end to have students reflect on this unique discussion structure. *What worked well? What could we do differently next time? Are we ready to apply this kind of reading and discussion to a whole novel?*

- **Setting the story stage:** If your kids need some help jumping into the story and the time period, do a quick lesson with the first paragraph. You can do a simple read-aloud, or a think-aloud, as kids follow along, and then invite discussion about what's going on here. This clever opener introduces the story, provides a backstory for the narrator, and sets us up to enter the immediate post–Civil War era when almost any young man you meet would have recently fought in either gray or blue.

- **Capturing reading responses:** Many teachers have come to equate literature circles with handouts called "role sheets," introduced in Smokey's 1994 book *Literature Circles: Voice and Choice in the Student-Centered Classroom.* These sheets give each kid in a book club a different reading and discussion task: question asker, passage reader, vocabulary enricher, illustrator, etc. We no longer use or recommend these tools, because much better ones are now available, plus the role sheets were never designed for anything but temporary, introductory

◀ **Variations**

use. In our 2006 book *Mini-Lessons for Literature Circles*, we describe five other, better ways for kids to capture their responses while reading: annotating with Post-its (as used here), bookmarks, journals, drawings (see page 47 in this book), and text coding.

- **Evoking inquiry:** Another step ahead with lit circles has been the realization that requiring kids to put on a skit or make a poster after reading a book can be inauthentic in the extreme. What do real readers do? Make dioramas? Or do they close the book with more questions than they started? Such as:

  - Did this kind of show really happen? Were apes and other exotic animals used for entertainment in the West?

  - What is the real temperament of chimpanzees? The ones in the story are very sweet, but didn't I just read about one that mauled a woman's face? How close to human are they?

  - I never heard of a gold rush in Wyoming—what was it like compared to the one in California?

  - Those Civil War battles referred to in the story—what were they like? Did some of the soldiers have what we now call PTSD?

  - In these times, how much tension was there between ex-soldiers of the Confederacy versus the North?

  - Is it historically true what the narrator says, that violence begets violence?

  - The author says that ex-soldiers from both North and South have been *galvanized*. That's an unusual word with many meanings. Which of them make sense in this context?

  - What does Zancanella mean in this line: "We bleed grace from our everlasting souls."

  Let each group pick an inquiry question of their own, or from this list, and give them one class period to research that topic. Everyone reports back by summarizing their findings on a note card to be posted, giving a thirty-second oral report, or making a three-slide presentation.

Shoptalk ▶ When you are teaching whole-class novels, or longer stories from the textbook, lit circles are a natural way to enhance student engagement and responsibility. Envision it: when four-member book clubs are meeting around the room, then six or seven kids are "on stage," talking at once. And the other members, three of them in each circle, experience significant positive social pressure to listen thoughtfully and respond. This doesn't mean we teachers disappear in lit circles. We can intersperse our own questions and comments before or after kids' meetings. And when we go to sit in on a book club, we can deeply assess kids' thinking and interaction.

The lit circle structure is appropriate for the discussion of kid-accessible text. It is not well suited to the hardest, densest, most alien works. If the kids are struggling so hard to comprehend that you have to explain virtually everything to them, then it's time to pick another title. Nancy will never forget the time she inherited the freshman English unit on *Lord of the Flies* from a previous teacher. Whereas her older kids always loved the novel's dark themes and twisted view of humanity—and what's with that rotting pig's head?—the fourteen-year-olds hit one brick wall after another. Nancy knew it was time to return the novels to the closet when one really sweet little freshman boy said, "*Lord of the Flies* was really interesting once you explained it to us."

The Chimpanzees of Wyoming

Don Zancanella

The Frontier Index, *a newspaper published from a railroad car that moved west with the workers building the first transcontinental railroad, reported in their issue of June 10, 1868, that chimpanzees had recently provided an evening of theatrical entertainment at a saloon in Laramie City, Wyoming Territory. No further mention of the animals appeared in the historical record until the following fragments from the journal of their keeper, Samual Coffey, were discovered by Coffey's great-granddaughter.*

Wyoming Territory, 1868

June 9

Left Laramie City at sunrise. A rough, disorderly settlement—just what one would expect to find at the farthest edge of civilization. To our advantage, the residents had money to spend and were starved for entertainment. Our performances were well attended, and when I passed the hat, it came back overflowing.

For the first few hours today, I followed the new railroad tracks. They are truly marvelous, the bright steel rails like two lines of quicksilver drawn across the undulating plains. Although I had hoped to see the encampment where the actual laying of the track is occurring, I turned north, following the trail as I had been advised. I feel compelled to continue toward South Pass City without delay, for I have been warned about foul weather and hostile Indians so often that I expect to see bolts of lightning and flying arrows over the crest of every hill.

The apes are traveling well, if a bit subdued. Whenever I stop, I open their cage, but they seem stunned by the immense openness of the landscape and will come forth only with great coaxing. During the afternoon they slept, lulled by the rocking of the wagon. We are all three pleased with our new outfit—two sorrel mules and a small buckboard wagon. My only worry about the apes is the rough diet our journey has forced upon them. Fresh fruits and vegetables, which they prefer above all, have become increasingly unavailable since Omaha. Tonight, their dinner consisted of potatoes and an oat porridge which I spoon-fed to them like babes.

June 10

A day spent plodding over an unbroken plain. I am bone-tired. One of the mules chomped me on the shoulder as I unharnessed her for the night. They are both ill-tempered but strong.

June 11

Forded the North Platte today. Had been told that it could be easily crossed by mid-June, but it took all my courage and ingenuity to get the team and wagon across't. I released the apes from confinement so that, if the wagon overturned, they would have a fighting chance. To my surprise, the Duchess plunged in immediately and swam to the far shore. I knew the beasts could swim, but not with such ease and grace. For his part, the Duke lolled about in the back of the wagon as if it were an emperor's chaise, dipping his long hand into the current from time to time to bring up a cool draught. I saw no human nor any sign of one for the entire day. Nonetheless, I have convinced myself that Indians are lurking just out of sight. The apes were exhilarated by the river crossing. They screeched and chattered all through a sunny June afternoon.

June 12

If yesterday was lonely, today was a social whirl. A party of five men overtook us just before midday. First came the usual questions and excitement about the apes, and then speculation about prospects for gold in South Pass. They had all heard fantastic tales of riches but the letters I received from my brother have all been much more cautious in their optimism. I never thought I would view a brace of hairy apes as my financial security, but I find myself comforted by the knowledge that if Brother Andrew's claim fails to prove out, I can continue my work as—I don't believe I've ever called myself such before—an entertainer.

Later, during the afternoon, we passed a party of three men, one of whom had gotten a sizable knot on his head from being thrown by his pony. I offered to let him ride in the wagon for a spell, but as he was climbing in, he caught a glimpse of the Duke (who bared his teeth). He recoiled in such horror that he tumbled over a thistle bush. He said he'd rather crawl than ride with monsters. Then, just at dusk, I saw a small band of Indians riding single file along a ridge parallel to the trail. I began to tremble and wished I'd convinced the injured fellow to ride along, but presently the Indians appeared to lose interest in us and turned away to the north.

June 13

The Indians I saw yesterday reappeared this morning but not to cause any harm. There were six, all on horseback, and they paralleled my path for half a mile before veering closer. They only wanted to see the apes.

—Do they speak? one inquired, in English.

—No sir.

—What do they eat?

—About anything a man will eat, though they are partial to fruits and grains.

—Are they for sale?

I hadn't given the possibility any consideration and had to gather my thoughts.

—Eighty dollars, I said.

He frowned and shook his head. Before they left I allowed each of them to stroke the Duchess's arm. From their friendly demeanor, I take them to be Shoshone.

June 14

The apes appear lethargic and low-spirited. I suspect it is because their rations are so meager and inappropriate to their nature.

June 15

Last night we climbed on Russell Creek with three other parties, all gold seekers headed for S.P. An air of festivity prevailed, with everyone throwing a portion of their provisions toward a grand feast. Afterward, the Duke and Duchess performed. The evening's playbill:

acrobatics (tumbling and balancing)

husband and wife spat

mother and ill-mannered child

It was a lively performance despite their poor health. I purposely did not include "Romeo and Juliet" because all who were present may become part of my audience in S.P. and I want them to be eager for more. (I have also begun to train the Duke to ride one of the mules—I see great possibility.)

Bought 1 peck carrots and 20 turnips from a man from Dayton, Ohio. The apes ate with gusto.

June 16

Rain all day. The apes seem to enjoy it, or perhaps it is their improved diet. As for me, I am wet and miserable. My slicker is one issued me during my military service. It was the only item fit to take with me when I was discharged, and now it is in damn poor shape too.

June 17

We reach South Pass City. In my anticipation I had imagined it to be a metropolis, a city of gold, but it is little more than a single muddy street flanked by log huts and hastily constructed lean-tos. Slops are emptied onto the road, and skinny dogs snapped at the mules as we proceeded through town. But I am delighted to have a warm bed and a tight (or only slightly leaky) roof under which to sleep.

Andrew is astonished by the apes and laughs wildly every time he looks at them. I had explained in my last letter that they would be accompanying me, but he says he never received it and wouldn't have believed it if he had. I explained how the apes had been left in a field beside Mother's house when the owner of a one-horse circus was shot dead in a barroom. How I coaxed them into the barn with a pan of molasses and saw in their eyes a pleading that I could not ignore.

Good news about Andrew's claim. It is northeast of town and has been paying out as much as $12 a day. He says the mules are a godsend. Then he asked what salary the Duke and Duchess would take for hard-rock mining. And laughed uproariously.

Five of us sleep in the one-room cabin. Brother Andrew, his partner, Tim Haggarty, the apes, and myself. The apes are well-mannered and nest like spoons on a cowhide rug beside the stove.

June 18

To the claim with Brother A. It is in a narrow, rocky draw, surrounded by pine and juniper. The two main seams run along one side of the draw for a stretch of more than 40 feet, and then split into several smaller veins which turn back into the hillside. The bedrock is sandstone and granite. Gold mining will be an entirely new enterprise for me so I asked many questions. Gold, I find, comes not in thumb-size nuggets but embedded in quartz that must be pulverized in a noisy, steam-powered machine called a stamp mill. The resulting rock dust is then washed with quicksilver, to which the tiny fragments of ore adhere. But though the process was unfamiliar, the work itself is as backbreaking as I had expected—digging rock and hauling rock, the fortune hunter's lot.

Inquired of the owner of the Republican Tavern about the possibility of the apes performing there on Saturday evening and Sunday afternoon. As luck would have it, he is something of an amateur naturalist and knew as soon as he laid eyes on the Duke and Duchess that they are chimpanzees, species *Pan troglodytes*. Not only will he sponsor our performance, but he agreed to pay us a portion of the net proceeds, sure to be quite beyond what the passing of the hat generally obtains. A welcome offer, as I have today only $5.11 in ready money, a large part of my savings having been spent on the mules and wagon in Laramie City.

During the day when I work the claim, I will tether the apes nearby, in the shade of a juniper perhaps, so they may have some freedom of movement and fresh air.

June 19

This morning, as I was loading the wagon, two hard cases (pretty drunk it seemed and this at 7 o'clock) approached and began taunting the apes. The Duke screeched at one of them—a barrel-chested fellow with a yellow beard. In retaliation he took a length of cordwood from the stack by the fence and said, "I'll break his goddam noggin if he comes at me."

At that very instant, Andrew came out the door brandishing his shotgun.

"You be on your way," said he.

The ruffians backed off, but the taller one said, "I was at Chancellorsville. You can't scare me."

Not a one of us spoke for a long moment, but finally they did move up the street. I could have told him that I was at Chancellorsville too, but he was drunk and would not have appreciated the coincidence.

Since I have owned the apes, I have made a study of the responses they provoke from onlookers. Some laugh wildly, as if these man-shaped creatures are a joke, a caricature of human form and behavior. Others approach with childlike curiosity, asking question after question, as if the strangeness they see might be dispelled by words. Still others are terrified, thinking them furry demons, hunchbacked goblins with toothy grins.

June 21

The vein Andrew and Haggarty have been digging for nigh on thirty days turned out to be blind. That is, it disappeared into the hillside more abruptly than anticipated. They concluded that it will not be worth our trouble to mine it out further, and so we start on the second major ledge tomorrow, hoping it will pay out. At this rate, our labors will not even cover our expenses. But miners are like poker players. They continue because all their hardships can be redeemed by a single run of luck.

Last night I dreamed of Chancellorsville. As usual it is raining heavily and I am lost in the woods. As I walk, I begin to notice that wounded men, dying men, are somehow entangled in the branches of the trees. I will not recount the dream in more detail because I fear writing it down will hasten its return.

June 22

There is a certain nobility about the apes. They are exceedingly kind to one another, and their eyes sometimes reveal a melancholy thoughtfulness. This is the tenth month in which they have been in my possession, and I have begun to view them as more than mere beasts. Indeed, they often seem at least half human. Even those who see them as curiosities are moved by their portrayal of Romeo and Juliet—when the Duchess cradles her dying mate in her arms and then lays herself down beside him.

June 23

Tonight we played the Republican. The evening's playbill:

acrobatics

husband and wife spat

dancing

Romeo and Juliet

Although the applause was gratifying, the hat was not well filled. Miners, I begin to see, are a penurious lot. Thus, the small share of the evening's drink receipts given us by the owner is a welcome supplement. Our earnings for the evening: $6.23.

As I gazed out across the audience, every third soul seemed to bear some mark of warfare—a missing limb or scar or clotted eye. Hardly a man in South Pass City did not fight in some great battle—at Chancellorsville or Chickamauga or Antietam or Lookout Mt. Andrew and I started off in the same unit, two knot-headed farm boys from Missouri. Then we were separated and I did not lay eyes on him for two and a half years.

Occasionally, a fight interrupts at one of the mining camps over old animosities, Blue and Gray. But mostly we seem to do our best to forget. Some of the men from the South we call "galvanized Yankees" because they have so quickly and completely shed their former allegiances. But we have all been galvanized.

June 25

The apes have been stolen. Early this morning, I tethered them at the claim, just as planned. When I returned to visit before midday, they had vanished. Andrew insisted they must have escaped, but I know they could not have untied the ropes. If they chewed through them, fragments would have been left behind. Still, we searched up and down the surrounding hill until nightfall but to no avail. Tonight

I discovered that the two men who harassed the Duke and Duchess on the street on Tuesday have left town. I am convinced they have robbed me. I will set out to hunt them down tomorrow. Andrew cannot accompany me because he does not have complete faith in his partner, Haggerty, and fears losing his claim. So I will go alone.

June 26

Followed the trail south, but a party heading in the opposite direction said I was the first soul they'd met all day. Turned back. I am riding a small gray mare belonging to the stable smithy, having left the larger of the two mules at the livery as collateral. I carry a carbine rifle belonging to Andrew which I hope I will not have to use.

Late this afternoon, went a little way north toward the Wind River Mountains following a recommendation from Andrew, based upon intelligence gathered from other miners. I should have listened to him in the beginning. It has been unseasonably cold and I am sore with rheumatism. I do not believe I am cut out for tracking desperadoes.

June 27

Early today I found the remains of a recently used camp. I do not have evidence that it was the thieves but see no other option than to follow this trail farther.

Whenever I sit beside a fire in the darkness. I am carried back to the nights before battle when we would stay up until dawn, made sleepless by fear and excitement. Then the thunder of the cannons would commence and the horses would start to stomp and moan and I would wish for my mother and father, using the prayers I learned as a boy. I think I am somewhat like a father to the apes. 1 know they are not Christian and cannot pray, but I hope they are now remembering me and can take some comfort in those memories.

How does a beast think? What causes it happiness and what causes it pain?

June 28

At last today I am on the trail of the thieves. Early this morning, I encountered two trappers coming down from the high country. Yes, they said, they had indeed seen the very robbers, one on horseback and the other driving a buckboard wagon on which was lashed a large crate covered with tarpaulins. "Pigs," the trappers were told when they inquired about the nature of the cargo. They estimate I am only a few hours behind. It occurs to me that I do not know which army the man with the yellow beard fought with at Chancellorsville.

Now, as I write by the firelight and wait for the morning when I can take up my pursuit, my heart swells with compassion for the apes. Perhaps they are being beaten, or starved, or even if not, they must be terrified to travel all day in darkness, hearing only strange voices. They have the minds of small children and cannot understand.

June 29

Tonight I am almost too tired to write. Just after sunrise, I glimpsed the outlaws on a high plateau, perhaps a mile distant. Certain I could overtake their slow wagon, I spurred the little gray onward but lost them where the trail forked into two wooded canyons. Searched them both from end to end and then explored the steep ridge between the canyons on foot. Came near to a bear but did not shoot because I did not want to disclose my position. Only with luck did I find my way back to my horse. Tonight I build no fire and make these marks by the light of the moon.

June 30

It is with great sadness that I write these lines. Today, I arose at first light and rode hard. Presently, I heard a single gunshot and, following the sound, spied the smoke from a campfire rising from a copse of willows by the south fork of the creek. I urged the gray to a gallop, holding the rifle in one hand, ready to fire. But they had escaped, leaving the Duke shot dead. The Duchess sat beside him on the ground, holding his hand to her face and softly keening.

What I took for a campfire was their little wagon set ablaze. I reason that they intended to shoot them both and burn the bodies but heard me coming and only finished half the job.

What unnatural evil is it in men that one would do such a deed? What motive had they for stealing the apes, and what enmity for me or for them that they would in cold blood murder a husband before his very wife? I wept to see her there and then gathered her in my arms.

July 1

Today, we buried him. All night, she slept beside his body. At first I did not know how I would bring her back. She does not ride and walking would take several days and we haven't the food to last. Then I hit upon the idea of a travois of the kind I have seen Indians use. I was able to build a rude version, the Duchess seated upon a pallet of pine boughs and two long poles lashed to the saddle. It is clumsy but faster than walking. From time to time she becomes agitated and peers back in the direction from which we have come.

July 2

Late today we reached South Pass City. Andrew is outraged at the murder of the Duke and wants to mount a posse, but I am not in favor. You have been robbed of your livelihood, says he. I do not believe the courts will provide adequate redress, I tell him. Also, violence begets violence. During our dispute, the Duchess throws herself at him, teeth bared, and it requires all my strength to wrestle her away. Her fangs closed only on the fabric of his shirt or he would have been badly injured.

I pity mankind. We have contracted a disease of the spirit. It robs us of our compassion. It is a contagious madness. It is worse than typhoid. It compels us to murder the innocent. We bleed the grace from our everlasting souls.

July 4

Independence Day here is a great cutting loose. Drunken miners shoot off their pistols on Main Street and explode whole cases of dynamite in the nearby mining camps. Windows shatter and horses bolt. I was awakened at dawn by an ungodly explosion that sounded as if it were in the next shack. The Duchess shrieked and cowered on her rug. I dressed and took her into the hills near Andrew's claim, away from the cacophony.

The day was warm and I napped for a time. Then fed us both a holiday picnic—tinned apricots, barley sausages, and biscuits baked by the Swede who lives in the house behind Andrew's. When we finished, we sat in the sun, and the Duchess began to frolic on a patch of grass. Presently, she executed a pirouette that is part of a dance that she often performed with the Duke. A second time she did it, now looking expectantly at me. I responded with the Duke's step, a hop and a bow, as best I could, and she followed suit. Together, we perform a little minuet on the hillside. When we are finished, we drink the juice from the apricot tin. I notice that the shooting has ceased and all that remains is the faint smell of gunpowder passing now and then on the air.

When we want students to dig deeper into stories, novels, poems, or drama, we need multistep lessons that don't just require closer readings, but build energy and genuine curiosity for multiple visits to the text.

LESSON 6.1 Denotation/Connotation

It seems like those literary terms—*denotation* and *connotation*—come up on tests a lot more than we wish. Why can't reading tests just ask kids about word choice and imagery? Between the two of us, we've heard hundreds of young adult and adult authors speak about their craft and writing process. Never has a single one talked about denotation and connotation. They talk about word choice. This quick lesson is about precise word choice, but we're using the customary school language as well.

TEXT ▶ "Chameleon Schlemieleon," by Patric S. Tray

TIME ▶ 20 Minutes

GROUPING SEQUENCE ▶ Whole class, pairs, whole class; sequence repeats

PREPARATION

Determine how students will form partners for postreading sharing. Notice that the first three lesson steps simply involve doing the same thinking on three different words. The dictionary definitions are on the website.

On the Web

STEP 1 **Discuss word choice: *intelligent.*** *Everyone is going to need a sheet of paper.* As you talk about the following words, write the words, definitions, or notes on the board as you discuss them. *Copy this word down:* intelligent. *What does that word mean to you? What do you picture when you see or hear this word? Jot down some notes.* Take responses. *How are your responses different from this dictionary definition*? Show the dictionary definition and read aloud:

◀ **Steps** & **Teaching Language**

• *Having good understanding or a high mental capacity; quick to comprehend.*

• *Displaying or characterized by quickness of understanding, sound thought, or good judgment.*

• *Having the faculty of reasoning and understanding.*

What's different between what you wrote and the dictionary definition? Turn to your partner and compare your notes to the definition. Ask for volunteers to share their findings with the class. Students should notice they focused on what they pictured and what the word made them

- Read closely to determine what the text says explicitly and to make logical inferences from it; cite specific textual evidence when writing or speaking to support conclusions drawn from the text. *(CCRA.R.1)*

- Interpret words and phrases as they are used in a text, including determining connotative meanings, and analyze how specific word choices shape meaning or tone. *(CCRA.R.4)*

- Participate effectively in a range of conversations and collaborations. *(CCRA.SL.1)*

think of: connotations versus denotation. *All of the images you just mentioned reflected the word's connotations. When asked, no one recited a dictionary definition.*

STEP 2 **Discuss word choice: *genius.*** *Copy this word down:* genius. *What does that word mean to you? What do you picture when you see or hear this word? How is what you picture different from what you pictured for the word* intelligent? *Jot down some notes.* Take responses. *Compare what you wrote to this dictionary definition. What do you notice?* Show the dictionary definition and read aloud:

- *An exceptional natural capacity of intellect, especially as shown in creative and original work in science, art, music, etc.*

- *A person who has an extraordinarily high intelligence rating on a psychological test; has an IQ score in the top 2 percent of the population.*

What's different between what you wrote and the dictionary definition? Turn to your partner and compare your notes to the definition. Share out.

STEP 3 **Discuss word choice: *algebra.*** *Try this one. Copy this word down:* algebra. *What does that word mean to you? What do you picture when you see or hear this word? How might it relate to the other two words we just discussed? Jot down some notes.* Take responses. *Compare what you wrote to this dictionary definition. What do you notice?* Show the dictionary definition and read aloud:

- *The branch of mathematics that deals with general statements of relations, utilizing letters and other symbols to represent specific sets of numbers, values, vectors, etc. in the description of such relations.*

What's different between what you wrote and the dictionary definition? Turn to your partner and compare your notes to the definition. Share out.

STEP 4 **Define denotation and connotation.** Write the word *connotation* on the board. *I want you to write this word next to each set of notes. Write it by your notes for* intelligent, genius, *and* algebra. *If a connotation is what a word makes us think about and picture, what do you think a denotation is? Turn to your partner. There's a clue in the letter "d."*

Take ideas. If kids are still off, say: *Let me give you another clue* [point to dictionary definitions]*; these definitions here would be considered denotations. Turn back to your partner and see if you can figure out the difference between connotation and denotation.*

Take ideas. *Yes, you figured it out. A denotation is how the dictionary defines a word. What's important to remember here? When authors write, their word choices are mostly controlled by connotation. Authors actively think about what readers will feel or picture when they come across a specific word.*

STEP 5 **Discuss word choice: brainiac.** *Let's try one more. Copy this word down:* brainiac. *What does that word mean to you? What do you picture when you see or hear this word? How does it relate to* intelligent *and* genius? *Jot down some notes.*

Take responses. *Compare what you wrote to this dictionary definition. What do you notice?* Show the dictionary definition and read aloud: *A highly intelligent person.*

What's different between what you wrote and the dictionary definition? Turn to your partner and compare your notes to the definition. Share out. Isn't it interesting that the dictionary definition kind of equated it with intelligent *but you pictured something far more specific?*

STEP 6 **Project the story and give directions.** *Today you are going to read a really short story. As a matter of fact, this story is so short that you will be able to reread it a few times in a matter of minutes. As you read the story, I want you to pay particular attention to connotation. When a story is this short, the author has to make his word choices especially precise. Each word has to get across the perfect connotation so that the reader leaves with what the author intended. As you read and reread this story, jot down the words that you think were very deliberate choices on the part of the author. Then jot down what you picture, the connotation. Don't be tempted to copy every word. Pick the five or six best ones. Go.*

STEP 7 **Pair share.** *Turn to your partner and compare the words you picked. Talk about why the author chose those words rather than others that might have similar denotations, or dictionary definitions.*

STEP 8 **Share out.** Ask for volunteers or call on some students. You might want to point out some for discussion. *Why* nerd *instead of* genius? *Why* algebra *instead of* world history? *Why* clique *instead of* click? *Why* calculations *instead of* plan?

- **Story emulation:** Use this story as a mentor text. Have students write original fifty-five-word stories about other events using the exact same format. Emphasize that you want them to choose their words carefully. They need to think deeply about connotation.

- **Verbal irony:** This story is also an excellent example of verbal irony. If you want to extend the study a few more moments, you might touch on this literary device as well. Hey, it's in the CCSS under Language Standards. *Verbal irony is a play on words intended for the reader. Very often verbal irony ends up having an opposite or very different meaning than a word or phrase's denotation. Take a look at the phrase "hoping to clique." What does this character want to happen at his new school? By the end of the story, how has the*

◀ **Variations**

opposite happened? Have pairs reread the story, this time looking for other phrases that really have opposite meanings. They should point out

- The title of the story, "Chameleon Schlemieleon"
- "Doubting my calculations"
- "I failed"

Shoptalk ▶ Textbooks and many novel lesson plans focus on the authors' use of connotative language. And you can teach this craft element with almost any piece of literature. Almost. There are some works that intentionally use very spare, even denatured language. One example is Lois Lowry's *The Giver,* which we talk about teaching in Chapter 11. When Smokey read the book for the first time, he remembers being disappointed in the prose, thinking, "The writing sure isn't anything special." But once the Giver offers Jonas the power to see the world in all its color and sensory detail, the book's language becomes far more lush and connotative. Pretty skillful craft on Lowry's part, and a great teaching tool for us.

The deliberate use of connotative language is directly connected to tone (fiction) or author's point of view or purpose (nonfiction). If you *really* want your students to examine journalistic bias in writing that is supposedly objective, collect some articles about the same political candidate from conservative and liberal publications. One great example was when John Edwards was running in the presidential primaries (for the moment let's ignore his later revealed sexual indiscretions). While a local conservative paper described him as an "ambulance chaser," the local liberal paper described him as a trial lawyer specializing in medical malpractice. What's the connotation associated with each phrase? How does it slant the *objective* reporting?

Loaded language can be found in literature as well. When was the last time you read *Anthem* by Ayn Rand or Patrick Henry's "Give Me Liberty or Give Me Death" speech? As readers, students need to recognize that the use of connotation and loaded language is intended to sway a reader's thinking.

Chameleon Schlemieleon

Patric S. Tray

The Brainiac. The Nerd. Not anymore.

A midsemester move to a new school.

A chance for a new identity.

Algebra. First day. First period. Sitting in the back with the cool people hoping to clique, I finish my exam long before anyone else.

Doubting my calculations, the teacher grades it aloud: 100.

I've failed.

Setting the Scene

We love that scene in *Bridget Jones's Diary* where Bridget attends what she thinks will be a costume party dressed as a Playboy bunny. Instead, the setting turns out to be a formal afternoon garden party (if you don't remember the scene, you'll find the video excerpt in a Google snap). The incongruity of her costume and the setting provide humor, yet also encourage the audience to sympathize with poor Bridget as she deals with a very uncomfortable situation. For students to start noticing character details like these, we have to help them realize how setting influences plot and character.

> ### PREPARATION
>
> Prepare a projectable image of *Wanderer in the Storm*. If you plug the title and artist's name into Google Images, you'll get an assortment of reproductions to choose from. Once you have the image, determine how you will allow students to view the entire image first and then one quadrant at a time. This is very easy to execute with a series of PowerPoint slides, using the cropping tool to create the four sections. Two different ways to address quadrant examples are illustrated at the end of this lesson. Choose the one that best suits your students.
>
> Determine how students will form partners for sharing.

Steps & Teaching Language ▶

STEP 1 **Examine common settings.** *What settings do you commonly find yourselves in during the week?* Have students quickly brainstorm with their partners and then take some responses. They will probably be pretty general: home, school, sports team, church, car. Pick one and ask them to think about all the settings within a big setting. For example, if the big setting is school, the smaller settings include each different class, the hallway, the cafeteria. *How do these different settings at school affect your behavior throughout the day? Are you the same person in the first hour that you are in PE, gym, the cafeteria?* Have students talk with their partners about how setting influences their behavior and then take a few comments in the large group.

STEP 2 **Connect setting with character motivation.** *In a way, setting is almost like another person or, in the case of a story, another character. Do you ever notice that you're a louder, more outgoing person with some friends than with others? Setting can do the same thing to a person. Ever been to a sports event where people are really involved in the game? They jump up, scream, pound the air with their fists. Now imagine if the same person were listening to the game on his headphones and acted the exact same way on a public bus. It just wouldn't fit. People would think he was crazy.*

STEP 3 **Prepare for note taking.** *When you're reading a story, it's really important to pay attention to the setting. Lots of times that is the part of a story that we kind of ignore, but we shouldn't. Besides just helping us imagine where the story takes place, the setting directly affects the character and the plot. If it weren't for a particular setting, the characters and events would turn out differently. Since setting is so visual, we're going to practice looking at setting using a painting. Get out a piece of notebook paper and fold it so that when you open it up, it forms quadrants.* Be sure to demonstrate the folding and have the kids follow along.

STEP 4 **Project the full image.** *I want you to take a look at this painting for just a minute and see what you notice about the setting. Don't write anything down. Just look.* Show the full painting for about thirty seconds.

STEP 5 **View by quadrants.** *Now we're going to look closely at the painting one section at a time. As you view each section, write down every detail you notice in the corresponding section of your paper. Include people, clothing, objects, buildings, colors, shapes, and feelings. Just try to jot down everything you see. If you still have time on a painting section after you've jotted some notes, don't give up looking. Keep studying that quadrant of the picture and see if you can find a detail you previously overlooked.* Show each quadrant of the painting for about a full minute as students jot notes on the details.

STEP 6 **Project the full image again.** Students will be surprised by how different and more detailed the painting looks now compared to when they viewed it the first time.

STEP 7 **Pairs discuss.** *OK, now turn to your partner and discuss your thinking about the image, using your notes as a guide. Try to notice the similarities and differences in what you and your partner saw and recorded.* After about three minutes of pair share, return to each quadrant projection and ask for pairs to come up and point out some of the things one of them noticed but the other didn't.

STEP 8 **Pose questions.** *Now that we've really looked at these setting details, I want you to talk with your partner about three questions.* (You might project these questions on the board as you present them and then return to the picture.)

- *What story does the setting tell?*
- *How is the man influenced by the setting?*
- *How would the story and the character change if the exact same man was walking around your neighborhood on a hot, sunny summer day?*

STEP 9 **Share out.** End by hearing from partners about those three questions. *From now on, when you start to read a piece of literature, remember to think about the setting. Stop and try to picture a painting that depicts the*

COMMON CORE STANDARDS SUPPORTED

- Read closely to determine what the text says explicitly and to make logical inferences from it; cite specific textual evidence when writing or speaking to support conclusions drawn from the text. *(CCRA.R.1)*

- Integrate and evaluate content presented in diverse media and formats, including visually, as well as in words. *(CCRA.R.7)*

- Participate effectively in a range of conversations and collaborations. *(CCRA.SL.1)*

setting and the characters in the setting. Always remember that the set-ting is a silent character, never speaking but always influencing the other characters and the plot events.

Variations ▶

Smartphone photos: Depending on your school's phone policy, you might tell the kids to get out their phones and browse their personal photos for one that includes them and an interesting (and school-appropriate) setting. Let them share photos with their partners and talk about what was going on and how the setting influenced the events captured on film. Be sure to ask the kids whether the setting directly influenced their decision to take the picture. Most will answer yes, which just emphasizes once again what an important role setting plays.

Shoptalk ▶

As we well know from teaching writing, the best authors show rather than tell. And often, the simplest way to introduce a literary element to students is to begin by "reading" an artwork. What an artist does with paint and brushes, an author does with words. So we are always on the lookout for art images or photographs that can help us introduce craft techniques.

- If you live near an art museum, go there and take notes or even photos of the pieces that would work in your classroom. Most museums will allow you to take photos as long as you can figure out how to shut off your flash. When you are noting or photographing paintings, always remember to copy down the information on the plaque. That will make it very easy to look the piece up later on the museum website or Google Images.

- Browse museum websites and save the images that suit your purposes. Though you can do this from the comfort of your home computer, the downside is that most museum online collections are voluminous. If you don't know what you're looking for, this can take hours.

- Flip through all those old basal textbooks you have lying around. Most major publishers have blanket deals with certain museums and often have tons of artworks that usually get ignored by teacher and student alike, probably because they just seem to be there to pretty up the page rather than being integral to a literature lesson. These books can be a great source; under each piece you will find the title, artist, and museum in which it resides. Then you can Google with that information to find an image or go straight to the museum website.

Carl Julius von Leypold, *Wanderer in the Storm*, 1835, http://www.metmuseum.org/toah/works-of-art/2008.7. Image copyright © The Metropolitan Museum of Art. Image source: Art Resource, NY.

Quadrants shown separately

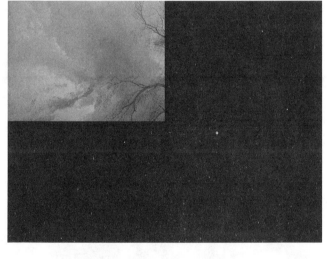

Quadrants with rest of painting blacked out

Two-Column Notes

TEXT ▶ "Forwarding Order Expired," by John M. Daniel

TIME ▶ 20 Minutes

GROUPING SEQUENCE ▶ Individuals, pairs, whole class; sequence repeats

USED IN TEXT SET ▶ 1

Who doesn't like to make lists? They help you remember your chores, errands, and goals. Plus, you can check off items as you accomplish them—what a good feeling. Have you ever gotten to the grocery store and realized you left the list back home? You probably did OK working from memory, but for Nancy, that story always ends the same: "Once I get home with six bags of food, I realize I forgot the two most important items I went shopping for in the first place."

When we make a list, we are often mentally categorizing the entries, whether we realize it or not. Even though we don't consciously plan it, our grocery lists are probably organized by the store's floor plan, recipe requirements, or food type. When kids read, they've got to organize information too, but they've also got to expand on it, and two-column notes are a great way to make this happen. Most commonly, two-column notes are used when students can't write in the assigned text.

Typically the left-hand column is reserved for text quotes chosen by the reader, while the right-hand column contains the reader's thoughts/reactions/questions pertaining to the text. However, since this book encourages you to provide consumable copies for the kids, we also show you a variation that invites students to explore their personal connections in ways that enhance understanding and inference.

On the Web

> ### PREPARATION
>
> Make one copy of "Forwarding Order Expired" and the two-column notes sheet (available on the book's website) for each student. Determine how students will form partners for sharing.

Steps & ▶ Teaching Language

STEP 1 Pass out the two-column notes sheet and give directions. *In a few minutes we'll be reading a really short story that is packed with meaning. To figure it out, you first need to do some thinking about yourselves by making some lists in response to the prompts in the left-hand column. The sheet asks you to think about being ages you haven't reached yet. To put yourself in the place of someone older, you might try imagining how your parents or other adults in your life might answer.* Model your own reflection and advice for elementary school so that everyone knows how to fill out the chart. *Any questions? Go ahead and fill out the chart right now so we can talk about it in a couple of minutes.*

STEP 2 Monitor work. As students fill in their notes, encourage them to give answers with specific rather than vague word choices. Nudge the ones who are done lickety-split to go back and see what they can add.

STEP 3   **Share and compare.** *Now get together with your partner and compare your notes. Be sure to discuss the advice you gave to each age. Talk about how you came up with it and why you felt that was the most important thing to say.* Give pairs a couple of minutes to discuss and have a few kids share what they talked about, particularly the advice.

STEP 4   **Pass out the story and give directions.** *When I told you this story was short, I wasn't kidding. As you read, compare the character's feelings with your own feelings about being different ages. When you finish, think about what point the author is trying to make. What's the theme? Mark the lines that led you to the theme.*

It will take only a minute or so for the kids to read the story.

STEP 5   **Share and report out.** *Get back with your partner to discuss the story. How did your own thoughts on aging compare with that of the character's? What point was the author trying to make with regard to human nature?* Give students a minute or two for discussion and then end with the class sharing ideas about the theme and author's point about human nature.

- **YouTube Connection:** If you want the kids to pursue the theme of talking to one's self at different ages a little bit more, tell them to go home and look up this YouTube video: "A Conversation with My 12 Year Old Self: 20th Anniversary Edition." Filmmaker and actor Jeremiah McDonald, obviously a ham since early childhood, had the foresight to videotape himself when he was twelve "talking" to his future older self. Choosing a different path than the wistfulness and poignancy of "Forwarding Order Expired," this short video exhibits irony, sarcasm, and snarkiness thanks to its clever editing. The video is short, under four minutes. Unfortunately, there are a few swear words, so if you are thinking about showing it at school, *preview it first.* Used as a set, the story and video provide an interesting way to compare two texts on the same subject but with very different tone and theme.

- **Two-Column Notes for Post-Reading Thinking:** The two-column note sheet in this lesson focuses on prereading connections, but this tool is also great for postreading thinking. Below is an analysis of Tom Robinson's choices after his false conviction for the rape of Mayella Ewell. Tom had a choice: wait for the appeal Atticus was sure of securing or try to escape from prison. For the white community of Maycomb, Tom's decision to "run" is foolhardy, an opinion many of my students initially hold as well. However, once we complete the two-column notes, the kids understand that there was no good choice for Tom. As a matter of fact, by the time we finish this

COMMON CORE STANDARDS SUPPORTED

- Read closely to determine what the text says explicitly and to make logical inferences from it; cite specific textual evidence when writing or speaking to support conclusions drawn from the text. *(CCRA.R.1)*

- Determine central ideas or themes of a text and analyze their development; summarize the key supporting details and ideas. *(CCRA.R.2)*

- Analyze how and why individuals develop over the course of a text. *(CCRA.R.3)*

- Participate effectively in a range of conversations and collaborations. *(CCRA.SL.1)*

◀ ***Variations***

chart, most of the kids may still not agree with Tom's choice, but they certainly understand it and empathize with him, particularly once they see that they can think of more reasons for him to try to escape than wait.

WAIT FOR APPEAL	TRY TO ESCAPE
• Atticus thought Tom might be able to win.	• Risk of death worth it—slight chance he might succeed.
• Tom was safer in jail.	• Saw an opportunity.
• Escape would fail.	• Tired of other people trying to give him chances.
• There was no jury, just judges.	• He thought he was going to lose anyway.
• Make history. Tom could be the first black man to win over a white man in a trial.	• Winning the appeal could return him to the same court for another trial.
• Atticus is a good lawyer and won't drop the case.	• No black man has ever won a case over a white man.
• Tom would have more time to live.	• He was scared.
• Tom might eventually be legit/free.	• Even if he won he would still be in danger from lynch mobs.
• Might be acquitted.	• Even if he won appeal, his family wouldn't be safe unless they moved, and he might not be able to get a job.
• Might have punishment reduced from execution to prison sentence.	• No rights even if he won.
	• He had to get out of a world run by white men.
	• He gave up (didn't believe in the system).

Shoptalk ▶ The many varieties of double-entry journals are a classic tool for holding kids' thinking. Other favorite column heads include:

What I noticed / What I wondered

Film detail / text connection

Video detail / text or personal connection

Character 1 details / Character 2 details (useful in comparing protagonist and antagonist)

Character's problem and solution / What I would have done

Words / Connotation

The author says / I say

Facts / Opinions

Reasons to believe / Reasons to doubt

WHICH AGE IS THE BEST?

Imagine that you are seventy years old. Based on your own experiences, goals, and future dreams, how might you fill out this chart at different points in your life? When you get to ages far older than you are now, think how your parents, relatives, and other adults in your life might answer.

Age and best memories	Advice you'd give someone that age so that person would really appreciate and enjoy that stage of life
Elementary school	
High school	
Midtwenties	
Midforties	

Forwarding Order Expired

John M. Daniel

At ten I received a letter from the
man I would become. "I've learned to
correspond across the years," it said.
"Enjoy your youth."

At forty, I received the boy's reply:
"I can't wait to be your age."

I wrote the next letter forward
thirty years. "I hope you're well."

My letter was returned unopened.

LESSON 6.4　Point-of-View Note Taking

Have you ever had this experience? There's a book that you just love to teach, that's very dear to you personally, but year in and year out, your kids just don't give a damn about it. Isn't that infuriating? Like, what's the matter with you people? "The Importance of Being Earnest" is so trenchant, so droll, so delicious!

This shocking lack of teen appreciation is primarily because today's students are defective. But a contributing cause may be that so much of the literature we assign was written for *adults from a different social class and era*. With these works, there's often a huge gap in worldviews between the long-dead middle-aged characters and the fourteen- or sixteen-year-olds trying to follow their monumentally uninteresting behavior.

Of course, this epiphany does not mean we should convert the whole curriculum to young adult literature, where every protagonist is an adolescent (though we do favor heaping doses of YA in a balanced diet of reading). The answer is to explicitly show kids how to decenter and put themselves in the minds of grown-up writers writing about grown-ups. Enter Dave Eggers, who has written the perfect story for this task.

TEXT ▸ "Accident," by Dave Eggers

TIME ▸ 20 Minutes

GROUPING SEQUENCE ▸ Individuals, pairs, whole class, pairs, whole class

USED IN TEXT SET ▸ 7

> ### PREPARATION
>
> Have copies of the story ready for everyone and determine how pairs will be formed. If possible, grab a photo of two boxers in a clinch (as described in the story) and have it ready to project later on. Try Google Images for "boxers in clinch."

STEP 1　First reading. *I brought you an interesting story by Dave Eggers today. Just read the story through one time. Enjoy!*

STEP 2　Short general response. Invite students to share some initial reactions to the story. Probably these will gather around "that old man seems crazy, pathetic, and weird." Keep it short.

STEP 3　Explain point-of-view note taking. *So this was a story told from the older driver's point of view, right? You hear all about what's going on in his head, but not the kids in the Camaro. Now you're going to read the story a second time with a partner. I want you to jot down some things that the kids in their car might* think, say, *or* do *at different points in the story.*

Notice there are stopping points marked in the story (after violent, sighs, heart, *and at the end). With your partner, take turns reading each section aloud. After each one, decide what the kids in the car might think, do, or say at that moment. Write it down, word for word, in the margin. Ready? Go.*

◄ **Steps** & **Teaching Language**

STEP 4 **Monitor.** Circulate, observe, help where needed.

STEP 5 **General discussion.** Invite volunteer partners to share their point-of-view notes on how the Camaro passengers might have reacted at each of the four stopping points in the story.

STEP 6 **Pairs study narrator's point of view.** *Now that we have explored the kids' point of view, let's try to dig deeper into the older driver's—the narrator's—perspective. We see everything he says and does, and we hear what he is thinking, right on the surface. What's up with him anyway? Here are three focusing questions to choose from. With your partner, pick any one you like and go back to the story to develop your interpretation.*

1. *When he drives away from the accident, what kind of life will the narrator be going back to? Family, home, job, problems?*

2. *Some readers think that the narrator actually caused the accident on purpose. Why would he do that, and what evidence is there in the story to support that idea? Or maybe the accident was actually the teenagers' fault, but for some reason he blames himself?*

3. *(If possible, project an image of this kind of classic boxing scene.) What do you make of this image of fighters clinging to each other? It seems a little far-fetched at first. Here's an image of what Eggers seems to be conjuring up. How good a fit is this metaphor with the actual events of the story?*

You'll have to do some serious inferring here, adding your own back-ground knowledge to the clues in the text. I'll give you five minutes. Be sure and jot down your findings so you can report later. Mark any details on the text that you are using to make your case. If you are done exploring one question, pick another and keep working.

STEP 7 **General discussion.** Invite volunteer groups to share their thoughts about the focusing questions.

Variations ▶

- **Focus on inferences:** This story can obviously be used for a simple *inferring* lesson, by having students draw inferences from the quite evident behavior, statements, and actions of all the characters.

  Teens: seemingly calm, patient, not scary, becoming puzzled

  Narrator: isolated, sad, lonely (why?), depressed, maybe suicidal

- **Second-person narration:** "Accident" is also a great example of second-person narration, which "implicates" the reader as a co-experiencer of the story. Have kids try writing a one-paragraph narrative in "normal" first person:

  "This morning I was running late for school and then I couldn't find my homework . . . "

Then have them rewrite it in second person:

> "You are running late for school this morning and then you can't find your homework . . . "

Pretty interesting what it takes to do this, and how the story becomes quite different.

Whenever a text has strong, single-character narration, the reader must always ask, "How reliable is this speaker? How is this character's personality, background, and perspective coloring the narration? Is it truthful?" Reexamining a story, poem, or novel chapter from a different character's point of view will give the kids better insight into *all* of the characters as well as other literary elements at play. For what it's worth, we think the narrator in "Accident" is pretty damaged/unreliable: "so lonely always."

◀ *Shoptalk*

Accident

Dave Eggers

You all get out of your cars. You are alone in yours, and there are three teenagers in theirs. The accident was your fault and you walk over to tell them this. Walking over to their car, an old and restored Camaro which you have ruined, it occurs to you that if the three teenagers are angry teenagers, this encounter could be very unpleasant. You pulled in to an intersection, obstructing them, and their car hit yours. They have every right to be upset, or livid, or even violent. ●

As you approach, you see that their driver's side door won't open. The driver pushes against it, and you are reminded of scenes where drivers are stuck in submerged cars. Soon they all exit through the passenger side door and walk around the Camaro, inspecting the damage. "Just bought this today," the driver says. He is eighteen, blond, average in all ways. "Today?" you ask. You are a bad person, you think. You also think: What an odd car for a teenager to buy in the twenty-first century. "Yeah, today," he says, then sighs. ●

You tell him that you are sorry. That you are so, so sorry. That it was your fault and that you will cover all costs. You exchange insurance information, and you find yourself, minute by minute, ever more thankful that none of these teenagers has punched you, or even made a remark about your being drunk, which you are not. You become more friendly with all of them, and you realize that you are much more connected to them, particularly to the driver, than would be possible in any other way. You have done him and his friends some psychic harm, and you jeopardized their health, and now you are so close you feel like you share a heart. ●

He knows your name and you know his, and you almost killed him and because you got so close but didn't, you want to fall on him, weeping, because you are so lonely, so lonely always, and all contact is contact, and all contact makes us so grateful we want to cry and dance and cry and cry. In a moment of clarity you finally understand why boxers, who want so badly to hurt each other, can rest their heads on the shoulders of their opponent, can lean against one another like tired lovers, so thankful for a moment of rest. ●

LESSON 6.5 Seeing a Character

Remember when people used to actually take pictures on film and then drop the roll off at Fotomat? (Yeah, we're both *that* old.) Nancy had a friend who always made sure she was the one to pick up the photos and go through them before anyone else. As she looked them over, she pulled the pictures she didn't like, particularly of herself, ripped them into pieces, and threw them away. Nowadays, with the advent of digital photography, social networking, and Google, no one is safe. Your chances of ripping up a bad photo before anyone can see it have vanished. You can pull an incriminating photo off your Facebook page, but once it hits the ether, that photo might have eternal life, just like a vampire.

But think about it. What are all of these photos doing? They are visually characterizing us. Those images, along with our Facebook updates and our unwary blogs, paint our picture via direct characterization—what a character says or does. And then add other people's commentary about us, on our wall or their own Facebook pages, and now we've added indirect characterization as well. Yep, in case you didn't realize it, you are the protagonist in your own personal never-ending drama, and your characterization constantly changes with the latest postings.

Even though you might be slightly superannuated like us (and enjoy reminiscing about pictures you could actually hold in your hand), your students live in a different world, and posting the latest photos is part of their daily routine. Those photos get studied, so why not get the kids to start thinking about literary characterization in a visual way as well?

TEXT ▸ *Untitled*, painting by James Henry Moser

TIME ▸ 15 Minutes

GROUPING SEQUENCE ▸ Whole class, pairs, whole class

PREPARATION

Obtain a projectable copy of this painting (google "Henry Moser Untitled"). Make one photocopy of the Venn diagram (available on the book's website) for each student. Determine how pairs will form for quick sharing.

On the Web

STEP 1 **Pass out the Venn diagram and have kids label it.** *Please mark the left-hand circle "Child 1" and the right-hand circle "Child 2." For the moment, just leave the intersecting part unlabeled.*

STEP 2 **Project the painting.** *I want you to look carefully at the two children in this painting. What can you tell about them? Don't just think about what they look like physically. Look carefully at their facial expressions, their body language, and what they're doing. Jot down as many details as you can about each child. Use the left-hand circle labeled "Child 1" for the subject on the left and use the right-hand circle. . . who can finish the sentence? You got it. Leave the center part of the diagram blank for the time being.*

◀ **Steps** & **Teaching Language**

Give students a couple of minutes to observe and jot details. Move on to the next step as you see the note taking begin to stall.

STEP 3 **Pair share.** *Looks like everyone has a lot of good observations. Go ahead and compare what you noticed with your partner. See if you missed anything. If you did, add it.*

STEP 4 **Adding inferences.** *For this next part, you'll keep working with your partner. Using the painting and all of your notes, I want the two of you to figure something out: What are these kids like? What kind of people are they? What can you tell about their personalities? Talk together and jot down some ideas about each child in the circles you've been using. For the time being I still want you to keep that center area blank.*

STEP 5 **Discuss relationships.** *Now it's time to use the middle area. Once again, using the painting and* all *of your notes, I want you to figure out what kind of relationship these two kids have. Talk it over with your partner. Try to create a bit of a story versus just a word or two. It doesn't count if you just write down "friends." You need to go way deeper and be able to logically defend your inferences with details from the painting.*

STEP 6 **Share out.** Ask pairs to share their inferences about each child as well as the relationship between them. Finish in this way: *You really noticed a lot of details and created some pretty good stories about why these two children are together and how they relate to one another. In every story, authors do the same thing, but they use words instead of paint to get their characterization across. They depend on you—the readers—to paint a picture of each character in your mind.*

Variation ▶ **Author portraits:** Locate photos or paintings of famous authors (the one your kids are reading right now, for example) and have students do a "deep reading" of their faces and surroundings. What does an author's portrait tell us about his or her life and work? You'll obviously want to select the images that are dramatic and "telling." There are some especially fascinating pictures of Joseph Conrad, Ernest Hemingway, Mark Twain, Virginia Woolf, and William Faulkner. There's a whole book about author photos that contains some stellar examples: *Written Lives,* by Javier Marais. And the New York Public Library website offers access to its large gallery of author photos at http://digitalgallery.nypl.org.

Shoptalk ▶ Most middle and high school literature textbooks are jammed with classic art images from great museums. Don't let these be mere decorations! As we've demonstrated in several different lessons, you can use images to teach or review specific literary thinking and then segue to stories and poems. And when each kid already has a textbook, a copy of the image right in front of him, you don't even have to prepare a projection. (However, if you want to project a big, high-resolution version, look at the caption, go on the web, and grab it.) As this lesson and Lesson 6.2 show, you can do "close readings of images," just as we do with text. Focus kids on different picture segments through masking or specific directions, provide for structured note taking, add ample think time, and give thoughtful prompts for discussion.

As with the coal mining painting featured in Chapter 5, it's interesting to look at the history behind the painting. Did you know what the artist of this untitled piece is most famous for? Early in his career, James Henry Moser illustrated the stories of Uncle Remus. This "gig" offered him the financial support necessary to continue his career as a painter, a career that proved prolific and respected. Here's an interesting question to pose to your students: How does being hired/commissioned to create a piece of art or music narrow an artist's choices and shape the creative process?

James Henry Moser, *Untitled* (Two Children Playing Checkers), 1913. Smithsonian American Art Museum, Washington, DC / Art Resource, NY.

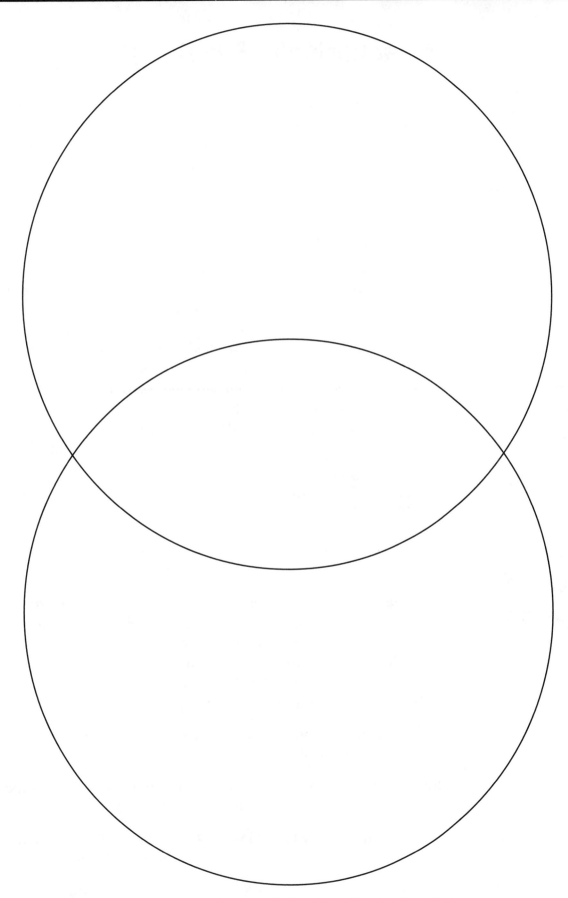

Metaphorically Speaking

TEXT ▶ "Fight #3," by Helen Phillips

"How Water Feels to the Fishes," by Dave Eggers

TIME ▶ 50 Minutes

GROUPING SEQUENCE ▶ Individuals, pairs, whole class

USED IN TEXT SET ▶ 7

All the world's a stage,
And all the men and women merely players;
They have their exits and their entrances;
And one man in his time plays many parts,
His acts being seven ages. At first the infant,
Mewling and puking in the nurse's arms.

—William Shakespeare, As You Like It

Great authors, from the ancients to the postmodernists, have always trafficked heavily in metaphor. From the tiniest simile to the most elaborate allegory, comparison is a writer's go-to tool for making ideas strange and new and deep. But also, since time immemorial, school students have struggled to make sense of figurative language in literature. Sometimes they'll even deny that authors committed metaphor on purpose. "You gonna tell me that Nathaniel Hawthorne actually sat there and put color symbolism into *The Scarlet Letter*?"

This lesson introduces a story that's one big, extended, and artful metaphor, from Helen Phillips' debut novel, *And Yet They Were Happy*. Then in a variation, we offer another text that offers an even more extended use of figurative language.

> ### PREPARATION
> Have copies of the story ready and establish partners for pair sharing.

Steps & Teaching Language ▶

STEP 1 **First reading.** Have students read the Phillips story silently. No preliminaries.

STEP 2 **Second reading.** When they have finished, ask: *So is this story literally true? Did a strange man and woman invade a couple's apartment and fight for a couple of days and make a huge mess?* At least a few kids should see that this is not a "true story." *Please reread the story now, looking for specific details that show whether this story is literally true. Mark any lines that help you figure this out.*

STEP 3 **Monitor and assist.** You may need to reexplain the preceding instruction as you circulate.

STEP 4 **Pairs discuss.** *Now join with your partner and see what spots you marked in the story.* Allow two to three minutes.

STEP 5 **Discuss with whole class.** *What were some clues that suggested the story was not literally true?* Among the things kids may notice:

The invading couple simply "appears" in the apartment.

The apartment owners hide in the corner.

"They float upward and upward."

The plates and wineglasses refuse to serve the invaders.

"The jade plant withers."

"We roll ourselves into balls and roll ourselves into the closet."

The "invisible" man and woman disappear.

OK, so unless this is a science fiction story, it is not meant to be literally true. We are not supposed to believe the surface-level events actually occurred. Instead, Helen Phillips wrote this whole story as an extended metaphor, a comparison with something else. The invisible invading couple is one long metaphor—but for what? See if you can decode that metaphor in one phrase or sentence at the most. What does the invading couple mean? Talk with your partner.

STEP 6 **Monitor and assist.** Allow three to five minutes of work time.

STEP 7 **Regather.** Call the whole group back together to explore possible interpretations of the controlling metaphor of Fight #3. Previous classes have thought the "invisible invading couple" showed:

How you can sometimes feel like a completely different person

How fun it is to get crazy mad

How hard it can be to have a long-term relationship

How people can have cycles of loving and hating another person

How people can get out of control when they fight

How we can be horrified by things we do or say ourselves

How much anger people have inside, and how powerful it can be

How nice people can be capable of super-bad behavior

- **Ask the author:** Because this story is so deliciously symbolic, we had to ask Helen Phillips where the piece came from. She was gracious enough to send us this email (probably because we know her mom).

  I wrote Fight #3 shortly after I became engaged to my wonderful husband. As I prepared, emotionally and logistically, for the wedding, I found myself deeply frustrated by the dearth of representations of love in all its complexity. Even the greatest of relationships contain moments of darkness, don't they? I didn't want advice about flower arrangements; I wanted advice about how to maintain a marriage for decades, how to weather the stormy times, how to cultivate an infinite sense of gratitude for one's partner. I didn't feel like the radiant glowing bride; I felt like an explorer about to set out on a terrifying and potentially glorious adventure.

 **Variations**

On the Web

In my book And Yet They Were Happy, *I explore the idea of marriage by transfiguring it into many different (and often surreal) manifestations. Fight #3 is one such manifestation. In this piece, I was attempting to process the way tenderness and darkness can coexist. The first couple watches in horror as the invading doppelganger couple lays waste to the life and home they've carefully constructed together. Don't we all have moments when we can't believe how badly we're behaving? Don't we all sometimes come back to our partners, tail between our legs, and confess that we don't know what overcame us? True love doesn't mean always behaving perfectly; it means forgiving imperfect behavior in ourselves and in our partners. We each contain within ourselves the compassionate partner and the unreasonable partner, two sides of the same coin. This story is my effort to literalize the idea that each of us possesses multiple selves, all of which inevitably surface in our most intimate relationships.*

You could show this note to students after all the discussion is done. In one sense, kids would then know if they "got it right." But the much more fun debate topic: Who says the author knows what it is about? Writers do not always plan or even know what they are streaming onto the page, and readers are always pouring themselves into the text, to the point of nearly becoming coauthors.

- **Metaphor Mentor Text:** Dave Eggers' "What Water Feels Like to the Fishes" is pretty much a story both *made up of* and also *explicitly about* figurative language—similes and metaphors. Building from the oft-pondered question, What does water feel like to fish? Eggers creates a charming thought experiment in two short pages. This is a natural mentor text for having kids write their own metaphors.

Shoptalk ▶ Our literature textbooks are chock full of stories that use metaphor and symbolism. We ELA teachers love that stuff and apparently whoever oversees state textbook adoptions loves it too. Ever wonder why "The Road Not Taken" by Robert Frost is such a staple? However, metaphor, particularly extended metaphor, can throw kids quite a curve ball: "You mean the story isn't even really about that?" Young readers need repeated practice with parallel meaning, so they become vigilant for any extended metaphor that might lurk, like Rosencrantz and Guildenstern, in the wings. And rather than translating the metaphors for kids when selections get rough, guide them down their own path of figurative discovery with repeats of this lesson, substituting your own text.

Fight #3

Helen Phillips

Sometimes a strange man and woman appear in our apartment. They have a terrible marriage. They throw their snakeskin suitcases down in the living room, pop open the brass snaps, and pull out their foolish, expensive clothing. Soon their belongings are strewn over every surface. Clinging to each other, we hide in the corner. Meanwhile, they stride bitterly through the rooms. They fight in the morning and leave for work without apologies, their minds still fizzy with hate. They enjoy hatred, the crazy freedom of it, the delightful abandon, almost like shedding the pull of gravity, taking flight from the stupid safe green earth, no longer handcuffed by the idea of home. They whisper cruel things and leave and return and whisper other, crueler things, their tense jaws no longer serving to muzzle their tongues, words unleashed to punch and pinch. Hate untethers them; they float. They float upward, upward. They cook, but fail to use enough butter. The food turns out dry and unsatisfying. Our plates prefer to jump out of their hands and shatter rather than serve them another meal. Our wineglasses crack rather than enable them to drink. They're forced to buy packaged crackers and cookies; soon there are crumbs everywhere. The desk, the bathtub, the bed—no place is spared the niggling filth of crumbs. They never scrub anything. The counters become sticky with unattended spills, the couch is stained, the coffee table nicked. And still they detest each other. They say, You clean it up. No, you. No, you. No, you. No, you. Even our invincible jade plant withers. Terrified, we curl ourselves into balls and roll ourselves into the closet.

When we reemerge, our plates and wineglasses sit tidily in the cupboard. The jade plant is thriving. The invisible suitcases are gone. The invisible man and woman are gone. We sigh. We go to the bed, where there are no crumbs. For a while, we forget about them. But soon we will begin to prepare ourselves for the next time they come and invade us.

How the Water Feels to the Fishes

Dave Eggers

Like the fur of a chinchilla. Like the cleanest tooth. Yes, the fishes say, this is what it feels like. People always ask the fishes, "What does the water feel like to you?" and the fishes are always happy to oblige. Like feathers are to other feathers, they say. Like powder touching ash. When the fishes tell us these things, we begin to understand. We begin to think we know what the water feels like to the fishes. But it's not always like fur and ash—and the cleanest tooth. At night, they say, the water can be different. At night, when it's very cold, it can be like the tongue of a cat. At night, when it's very very cold, the water is like cracked glass. Or honey. Or forgiveness, they say, ha ha. When the fishes answer these questions—which they are happy to do—they also ask why. They are curious, fish are, and thus they ask, Why? Why do you want to know what the water feels like to the fishes? And we are never quite sure. The fishes press further. Do you breathe air? they ask. The answer, we say, is yes. Well then, they say, What does the air feel like to you? And we do not know. We think of air and we think of wind, but that's another thing. Wind is air in action, air on the move, and the fishes know this. Well then, they ask again, what does the air feel like? And we have to think about this. Air feels like air, we say, and the fishes laugh mirthlessly. Think! they say. Think, they say, now gentler. And we think and we guess that it feels like hair, thousands of hairs, swaying ever so slightly in breezes microscopic. The fishes laugh again. Do better, think harder, they say. It feels like language, we say, and they are impressed. Keep going, they say. It feels like blood, we say, and they say, No, no, that's not it. The air is like being wanted, we say, and they nod approvingly. The air is like getting older, they say, and they touch our arms gently.

LESSON 6.7 **Rereading Prose**

As students get into the upper grades, it is guaranteed that they will encounter more difficult literature. The Common Core is going to make sure of that. Plots will move from linear action to subtle characterization and detail. Climaxes will now occur when a character has an "aha" moment, not when he beats up a bully. We ELA teachers enjoy these more challenging and subtle texts, because we know how to pay attention to details, look for clues, and read between the lines. But our kids sometimes read these selections and conclude, "That story sucked! What's the point? Nothing happened!"

The *sine qua non* strategy for difficult literature is rereading. We know that. The kids know that. When quizzed about strategies to use when reading gets difficult, rereading is the number one strategy students will list themselves. However, in real life, kids fight rereading, and even when they try it, they still come back with the same report, "Yeah, I reread it, but that story still doesn't make any sense." They know they *should* reread, but they don't know how to break that act down into manageable, purposeful chunks.

TEXT ▶ "The Father," by Raymond Carver

TIME ▶ 50 Minutes

GROUPING SEQUENCE ▶ Whole class, individuals, pairs, whole class

> ### PREPARATION
>
> Make one copy of "The Father" and the Rereading Chart (page 135; available on the book's website) for each student. Determine how students will form partners for postreading sharing.

STEP 1 **Introduce reading like a detective.** *"The Father" by Raymond Carver is a story about some mysterious family secrets. But like a lot of literature we'll be encountering this year, it's pretty subtle. You've got to really pay attention to all the details in order to put the clues together. If you read the story through once or even twice but don't know what to look for, you might say, "What was the point? Nothing happened?" However, if you find the clues, you'll realize that something pretty big is happening.*

When you read stories like this, you've got to put yourself in the shoes of a detective. A detective gathers clues and then puts them together like a puzzle. He keeps looking for evidence and even returns to the scene of a crime numerous times in the hopes of noticing something he's missed. That's what you're going to do today. Pass out the story and the chart.

STEP 2 **Give instructions for note taking.** *Instead of trying to read this story looking for everything, I want you to examine the "crime scene," looking for only one kind of evidence at a time. Take your chart and fold it in thirds so that just the column that says "Setting" is visible. The first time you read this story, all I want you to do is look for setting clues and*

◀ **Steps & Teaching Language**

- Read closely to determine what the text says explicitly and to make logical inferences from it; cite specific textual evidence when writing or speaking to support conclusions drawn from the text. *(CCRA.R.1)*

- Determine central ideas or themes of a text. *(CCRA.R.2)*

- Analyze how and why individuals, events, or ideas develop and interact over the course of a text. *(CCRA.R.3)*

- Participate effectively in a range of conversations and collaborations. *(CCRA.SL.1)*

jot them down in that column as you read. The clues might be directly stated or just hints that will make you "read between the lines" to fill in the missing details. I'll model the first paragraph for you.

STEP 3 **Model the process.** Read the first paragraph aloud and then stop. As you think aloud, be sure to write your notes on the board or project them so that students can copy your setting details onto their charts. *Hmm, what have I learned about the setting from this first paragraph? OK, there's a baby in a newly painted basket beside the bed, blue ribbons, blue quilts. Mom, three sisters, and Grandma are there. Oh, and it mentions that the mother just got out of bed, so that sounds like morning. Where is this taking place? Given those details I'm guessing a house or apartment. It sounds like the baby is in the mother's bedroom since the author mentions the mother getting up. Also, apparently the room is big enough for five people to stand around the crib.* In the Setting column write:

House/apartment

Biggish bedroom—mother's

Morning

Everyone understand how I figured that stuff out even though the story never directly mentions any of the details I wrote down? I had to be a detective, look for clues, and then fill in the blanks. When a story makes you fill in the blanks from clues, it's asking you to make inferences. Any questions? Now I want you to read the rest of the story and look for more setting details. Remember, they might be directly stated or you might have to read between the lines. If you notice other stuff in the story, that's fine, but for right now I only want you to take notes on setting.

STEP 4 **Students read and take notes.** Give students time to read the rest of the story and jot notes on setting. Monitor the room as students read to make sure they are only filling in the Setting column and that they are adding to the list you started.

STEP 5 **Pairs, then whole class share.** Move students into their pairs to compare and discuss what they discovered about setting. Then bring the class back together and add to the list. When a student volunteers something, remember to always ask what text evidence led her to think that. Students should notice:

Kitchen with table and chairs (at least one).

Kitchen appears to be a separate room since there's the phrase "looked through to the kitchen."

Physically, Dad is separated from the rest of the family.

Setting is private—outsiders can't listen in or observe family.

STEP 6 **Explain how to complete other columns.** Repeat Steps 3–5 as you move through the Character Details and Plot Events columns. If you need a more detailed explanation of how to model these columns, jump down to the Shoptalk section. Otherwise, carry on; you've got it!

STEP 7 **Discussion.** After they've reread the story for the third time, invite kids to review their notes prior to talking about the ending. Then ask: *What is the secret between the father and his mother that is so tension filled that it appears they won't even speak of it? Do you think his wife knows? Why or why not?* Have pairs share first and then report out to the larger group. In conclusion, advise students that whenever they encounter a perplexing story/poem, they should break it down and look for discrete elements through multiple readings, rather than looking for everything on the first pass.

◀ *Variation*

Chart modifications: You can modify this rereading chart to suit the elements students need to focus on. Also, it doesn't need to be three columns. You might have students take two-column notes on setting and character. Then when it comes to plot events, they might instead annotate directly on the story. What else could you look for in a story and put in a column?

Tone words/phrases

Similes/metaphors

Dialogue details

Narration details

Symbolism clues

I'm confused/clarification questions (first column) and answers found on the second reading (second column)

◀ *Shoptalk*

We've mentioned the importance of teacher modeling several times in the book. However, we realize acutely that most of us were never trained to demonstrate our own thinking in real time, but mainly to talk about our knowledge. Two different things. This lesson has a lot of modeling. If you're still curious about how to hone this skill, read this fuller description of Step 6, with more examples of modeling.

Character Details

Hmm, what have I learned about the characters from this first paragraph? This family was expecting the new baby since the basket was newly painted. There are three little sisters, their mother, and a grandmother, but I'm not sure what side of the family the grandmother is on. The mother might still be recovering from childbirth since it says "was still not herself," or maybe she just needed some coffee. The baby seems very young (maybe home from the hospital only a day) because he just seems to lie there staring or blinking and helpless. Also, we know he's a boy because of the blue ribbons and quilts. The sisters seem excited about the baby since they are rubbing his chin and standing around the basket. I get the feeling from the girls that the baby hasn't been in the house long.

In the Character Details column write:

> Three little sisters—excited about new baby
>
> Mother—might be tired, overwhelmed
>
> Grandmother—who's side?
>
> Baby—boy, maybe just home from hospital a few days

Character details students should notice:

> Dad is sitting in the kitchen with his back to everyone.
>
> One of the sisters is named Phyllis.
>
> Grandmother is doting.
>
> Mother loves the new baby.
>
> Another sister is named Carol.
>
> Phyllis seems older because she says, "All babies have pretty eyes."
>
> Another sister is named Alice.
>
> The sisters want to know who the baby looks like while the adults (mother and grandmother) seem hesitant.
>
> There is some real tension between grandmother and father. Grandmother must be father's mother.

Plot Events

Hmm, what have I learned about the plot from this first paragraph? Seems like a lot of the plot details overlap with the character details. But if I just list what's happened so far in the story, here's what's going on. In the Plot Events column write:

> Mother, grandmother, and three little sisters are gathered around new baby.
>
> *Here's what's interesting about this first plot event: the father isn't in the room. Your job now is to observe the plot events that might explain why.*

Plot events students should notice:

> Dad can hear them playing with the baby but he isn't participating.
>
> First mother is reluctant to say who the baby looks like and then grandmother becomes hesitant as well, even though at first she mentions the grandfather.
>
> Kids are determined to figure out who the baby looks like.
>
> Kids realize father doesn't look like any relatives they know.
>
> When Phyllis starts crying, no adult comforts her. Instead, grandmother says "hush" and turns away.
>
> Dad—white face, no expression. Like he's just been reminded of something awful.
>
> There may be some tension between the grandmother and father. She won't look at him.

REREADING CHART

Text Title _____

Name _____

Date _____ Hour _____

SETTING DETAILS	CHARACTER DETAILS	PLOT EVENTS

The Father

Raymond Carver

The baby lay in a basket beside the bed, dressed in a white bonnet and sleeper. The basket had been newly painted and tied with ice-blue ribbons and padded with blue quilts. The three little sisters and the mother, who had just gotten out of bed and was still not herself, and the grandmother all stood around the baby, watching it stare and sometimes raise its fists to its mouth. He did not smile or laugh, but now and then he blinked his eyes and flicked his tongue back and forth through his lips when one of the girls rubbed his chin.

The father was in the kitchen and could hear them playing with the baby.

"Who do you love, baby?" Phyllis said and tickled his chin.

"He loves us all," Phyllis said, "but he really loves Daddy because Daddy's a boy too!"

The grandmother sat down on the edge of the bed and said, "Look at its little arm. So fat. And those little fingers! Just like its mother."

"Isn't he sweet?" the mother said. "So healthy, my little baby." And bending over, she kissed the baby on its forehead and touched the cover over its arm. "We love him too."

"But who does he look like, who does he look like?" Alice cried, and they all moved up closer around the basket to see who the baby looked like.

"He has pretty eyes," Carol said.

"All babies have pretty eyes," Phyllis said.

"He has his grandfather's lips," the grandmother said. "Look at those lips."

"I don't know . . ." the mother said. "I wouldn't say."

"The nose! The nose!" Alice cried.

"What about the nose?" the mother asked

"It looks like somebody's nose," the girl answered.

"No, I don't know," the mother said. "I don't think so."

"Those lips . . ." the grandmother murmured. "Those little fingers . . ." she said, uncovering the baby's hand and spreading out its fingers.

"Who does the baby look like?"

"He doesn't look like anybody," Phyllis said. And they moved even closer.

"I know! I know!" Carol said. "He looks like Daddy!" Then they looked closer at the baby.

"But who does Daddy look like?" Phyllis asked.

"Who does Daddy look like?" Alice repeated, and they all at once looked through to the kitchen where the father was sitting at the table with his back to them.

"Why, nobody!" Phyllis said and began to cry a little.

"Hush," the grandmother said and looked away and then back at the baby.

"Daddy doesn't look like anybody!" Alice said.

"But he has to look like somebody," Phyllis said, wiping her eyes with one of the ribbons. And all of them except the grandmother looked at the father, sitting at the table.

He had turned around in his chair and his face was white and without expression.

LESSON 6.8 Rereading Poetry

This lesson puts a new spin on old-school poetry lessons, in which teachers excitedly count off iambic pentameter for a crowd of napping adolescents. Then the bell rings, kids plug in their earphones, and head home listening to poetry disguised as songs.

Today's teenagers, like those of all past generations, aren't poetry averse; we just have to put them in the driver's seat. To help kids get comfortable with the sometimes puzzling tricks and compact nature of printed poetry, we invite them to discuss poems in the style usually reserved for literature circles—but first, they have to prepare for a lively, purposeful discussion.

TEXT ▶ "Ducks," by Michael Salinger

TIME ▶ 50 Minutes

GROUPING SEQUENCE ▶ Whole class, individuals, groups of four, individuals, groups of four, whole class

USED IN TEXT SET ▶ 2

PREPARATION

Make a copy of "Ducks" and "Poetry Discussion Notes" (available on the book's website) for each student. Determine how students will form groups of four for poem reading and discussion.

On the Web

STEP 1 **Pass out the poem and form groups.** *Lately we've been working on becoming more skillful in reading and discussing poetry and I've seen you grow quite a bit. I'm feeling confident that you are now ready take on even more responsibility for leading the discussion.*

STEP 2 **Read the poem aloud.** *To get started, I'm going to read this poem aloud to you just to introduce it. I want you to follow along and see what you notice.* Read with your customary verve and drama.

STEP 3 **Pass out "Poetry Discussion Notes."** *The sheet I just passed out lists several different ways you can dig into a poem in a discussion. When you combine all of those different items, you've really looked at it from several different angles. Many of the main headings are literary elements and discussion skills we've talked about before, so no big surprises here. Instead of me reading all of this to you, I want you to take a couple minutes to read it silently and mark any instructions that confuse you or raise questions. If you're done before I call time, read the instructions again.*

STEP 4 **Monitor silent reading.**

STEP 5 **Clarify directions and negotiate responsibilities.** *Now get together with your group of four. You probably noticed that there's quite a bit to do on that sheet. Rather than each person completing all of those notes, you'll be sharing the work. Each of you will be responsible for four items on the sheet. Your group can decide who is responsible for which topics. However, at least two people in each group have to cover a topic. So*

◀ **Steps & Teaching Language**

- Read closely to determine what the text says explicitly and to make logical inferences from it; cite specific textual evidence when writing or speaking to support conclusions drawn from the text. *(CCRA.R.1)*

- Determine central ideas or themes of a text. *(CCRA.R.2)*

- Analyze how and why ideas develop over the course of a text. *(CCRA.R.3)*

- Analyze how specific word choices shape meaning or tone. *(CCRA.R.4)*

- Participate effectively in a range of conversations and collaborations. *(CCRA.SL.1)*

- Determine or clarify the meaning of unknown and multiple-meaning words and phrases. *(CCRA.L.4)*

in other words, you can't have everyone drawing a picture and no one preparing some discussion on Poet's Craft. Any questions? Decide who's doing what and write those assignments down. Give students enough time and nudging to make sure they really know who is doing what.

STEP 6 **Students prepare individually.** *Now that you've decided on each person's responsibilities, take some individual time to get ready for discussion. As you reread the text, go ahead and write on the poem and in the margins. If you are one of the artists, a pencil or pen sketch is fine. I have some blank paper you can use. Raise your hand if you need a piece.* Give students some time to work alone with the poem.

STEP 7 **Groups reconvene and discuss the poem.** *Before you begin your discussion, take a look back at the "Poetry Discussion Notes" and decide what you want to start with and what you want to end with. Then you can fill in the other areas as you go. As different members bring up the items they prepared, remember to get other people involved in the discussion. Your job isn't to give a report. Your job is to get other members talking about how your topic is reflected in the poem.*

STEP 8 **Monitor the groups.** Listen in on conversations, coach when necessary, and watch for the moment when discussion seems to reach a lull. That's the time to pull everyone back together.

STEP 9 **Share out.** *Now it's time for us to hear what you talked about. What's one idea from your discussion that stood out?* Call at random or take some volunteers. And carry on from there.

Variations ▶ **Poetry pick:** Send students out on a mission to find poems they think would be interesting for their group to discuss. On the given day, each member brings in four copies of the poem they're recommending. The group reads through them and decides which one they want to study at length using "Poetry Discussion Notes."

Shoptalk ▶ The handout with this lesson would be easy to misuse. You could turn it into a worksheet, assign points to each section, and have kids fill it out for homework. We recognize this risk after our experience with the literature circle "role sheets" featured in some of our earlier work. Though intended to support student-led discussion (much like our "Poetry Discussion Notes"), these tools got loose on the web, they became detached from their original instructions, and much mischief ensued.

We like Stephanie Harvey and Anne Goudvis's idea of "thinksheets" rather than worksheets. A thinksheet is a tool you use to prepare your thinking for a genuine literacy event. Thus, we might have kids leave their poetry thinksheets behind when they come to discussion, so a natural conversation can emerge around their thinking, and not a serial read-aloud of everyone's notes.

Discussion Questions

(at least *three* per poem)

- As you read the poem, *what did you feel, think, notice,* or *wonder*?

- Be sure you have questions that focus on different parts of the poem (beginning, middle, end).

- Think about whom the poet is addressing. Who is the speaker?

- What parts do you understand? What parts are confusing?

- What feelings or emotions does this poem evoke?

- What message is the author trying to get across?

Create questions that come directly from your own reaction.

Important Lines (at least *three* per poem)

Those that catch your attention might be lines that seem especially important, interesting, puzzling, beautiful, strange, well-written, controversial, or striking in some other way.

Be ready to read these aloud and explain why they "jumped out."

Words (at least *three* per poem)

- Find words in the poem that are puzzling, unusual, pack a punch, create a picture, or are unfamiliar.

Circle them in the text.

- You may also run across familiar words that stand out somehow in the poem—words that are repeated a lot, used in an unusual way, or key to the meaning of the poem.

Write the words, definitions (if unfamiliar), and your ideas in your notes.

Poet's Craft

How has the poet used rhyming, metaphor, simile, alliteration, onomatopoeia, repetition, rhythm, or other poetic devices?

Jot down notes and be ready to explain.

Connections

(at least one or two per poem)

What does this poem remind you of? Does it make you think of another poem or novel you've read? An incident from your own life? Something in the news? A television program, movie, play?

Jot down one or two of your own specific connections and notes that explain them. Be ready to talk about your connections and tell your group the whole story.

Title

What does the title have to do with the poem?

Jot down your ideas.

Drawing (at least one per poem)

On a blank sheet of paper, sketch a full-page, detailed picture related to the poem. What do you visualize when you read this poem? This can be a drawing, cartoon, diagram—whatever. You can draw something that's specifically talked about in the poem, something from your own experience or feelings, or something the poem made you think about.

Be ready to show your drawing to your group and talk about it.

Ducks

Michael Salinger

White strips of rags
Dangle and wave attached to the tips of bamboo rods
Knuckle jointed
Fifteen feet long
One grasped in each sinewy hand
Of the Vietnamese duck man
As he steers this hungry flock
From one rice paddy to the next
Eating the insects that would wish
To snack on
Fresh green shoots
Quacking foul and boisterous as
Traffic in a Hanoi roundabout

The face of a clock
Reading quarter past ten
His arms soaring forward
As if outstretched wings
The birds nested in the center
Of the walking flock are of little concern
To the leather weathered skinned duck man
It is the outliers that he eyes
From beneath his straw *non la*
Those few who would rather snap at the muslin scraps
Than attend to the task at hand
Just as one is gently tapped back in at the right
Another attempts to escape to the left
Dreaming of pastures not within the constrictions
Of this day's curriculum

And every good tender of livestock knows
One never plays favorites
Although
How can he help but admire
Those who push at the edges
The ones
Who make him work
The hardest?

CHAPTER 7 — UP AND THINKING

We know that adolescents (like all other humans) need to wiggle, to move, to stretch. And yet we cling to school designs and procedures that criminalize physical movement. Not only is this motivationally self-defeating, it's also a cognitive downgrade to have kids sit still all day. Thinking can actually be enhanced if motion is introduced. Where do you stand? Place yourself on a continuum. Act this out. Change partners. Perform your thinking. Make us see your argument. Stand and deliver!

LESSON 7.1 Find an Expert

Some Common Core Standards authors mysteriously deny the centrality of background knowledge in comprehension. Weird, huh? We wonder how the standards writers believe that *they* comprehend tough text? Just by knowing a lot of words?

Anyway, this peculiar omission doesn't mean we repudiate thirty years of solid research. On the contrary, we make every possible effort to ensure that when our students face high-stakes texts or tests, they bring with them the broadest, richest possible background knowledge, and the discrimination to use it well.

With this next strategy, we see how students can often be experts on the very topics necessary for comprehending text. "Find an Expert" is a way for kids to reveal, and maybe revel in, their background knowledge in an energetic, conversational way.

TEXT ▶ "The Horror," by Dave Eggers

TIME ▶ 20 Minutes

GROUPING SEQUENCE ▶ Whole class, multiple partners, individuals, pairs, whole class

PREPARATION

Each student will need a copy of the "Find an Expert Who" form and "The Horror." Determine the "dance floor," the place where students will go to find new partners. Figure out how to have the kids quickly move some furniture around so there's some space. Use the projectable "Find an Expert" instructions for students to refer to as they work.

On the Web

STEP 1 **Introduction.** *Today we're going to read a really short story with some subtle themes. For you to catch them, we need to first think about some topics that will help and that I know we have experts on—right in this room!*

STEP 2 **Distribute "Find an Expert Who" sheets.** *In a moment we're going to find some experts, but first I want to model the steps.* Ask for a volunteer or draft a student.

◀ **Steps & Teaching Language**

On the Web

STEP 3 **Model the steps.** *The goal of this activity is for you to meet briefly with a series of different partners, each time discussing a different topic from this list.* (Project "Find an Expert" Steps.) *Partners find each other by waving their papers while they are standing here in the "dance floor" area. Don't worry if you have to stand in this area for a minute before finding a new partner. People will finish up at different rates. However, it's important that when you need a new partner, you* always *return to the "dance floor."*

Once you find your partner, leave the "dance floor" and continue your fact-gathering interview elsewhere in the room. Find a topic your partner knows something about and interview them, jotting down the details.

Find a topic your volunteer student partner is an expert on and continue. *First we're going to greet each other by name and then see what we are experts on. For example, my partner has seen a modern horror movie. Pay attention to the questions I ask.*

- *What was the title?*

- *What was it about?*

- *How did they try to make it scary?*

- *What's the scariest scene you remember?*

Notice that I jotted down notes while I interviewed? After my interview is finished, my partner signs my paper legibly and then it's her turn to interview me. After that second interview I sign her paper. When we're both done, we thank each other and move back to the "dance floor" for new partners.

When I look for a new partner, I need to find someone who can be interviewed on topics I don't have notes on yet. And we want this to move fast! Each interview pair should meet for one and a half to two minutes.

Any questions? OK, then let's hit the dance floor! Continue to find partners and interview them until I call time.

STEP 4 **Monitor and coach.** Let kids interview for six to eight minutes total. Urge kids to return to the "dance floor" when they need a new partner and insist they move back into the room for interviewing. Also, insist whenever possible that just two students pair up. Otherwise, you will see big clots of friends converging to discuss their personal agendas rather than uncovering experts.

STEP 5 **Call time.** Have everyone return to their seats and look over the expert information they have gathered. Then question the class for a couple of minutes:

Who found someone who's seen a horror/slasher movie? Show hands. *What are the techniques the director used to try to make it scary?*

Anybody find someone who saw a horror/slasher movie that mostly took place during the day? How did the director manage to make that scary?

Who found someone who knew someone who saw a ghost? What was their story?

STEP 6 **Pass out the story.** *Now that we've met some experts, we've got the background knowledge for reading this story. As you read, underline passages that relate back to some of the conversations you had. Also, when you get to the last two sentences, underline those. Underneath, jot down the point you think the character is trying to make. If you finish before we reconvene, read the story again and see what else you find.*

STEP 7 **Partners meet.** *Get together with your partner and compare the items you underlined. When you get to the end, be sure and discuss how each of you interpreted the ending.*

STEP 8 **Share.** Reconvene the class and invite pairs to point out the connections they noticed and ways different students interpreted the ending.

◀ *Variation*

Find an expert anytime: This strategy is useful whenever evoking and sharing relevant background knowledge enhances text comprehension. Which is pretty much always. Just start with the blank version of the "Find an Expert" form and fill in interesting items that relate to the piece of literature at hand. For *The Hunger Games*:

Watches reality shows on TV

Has lived in a rural area

Likes to dress up

Has been hunting

Knows how to use a bow and arrow

Has won a contest

Knows about mining

Has ridden a train

◀ *Shoptalk*

It helps students approach difficult text if they feel like they do know *something* about its setting, time period, writing style, specialized vocabulary, or author. However, many times kids get so overwhelmed with a complex text that they panic and completely forget to inventory their potentially relevant background knowledge. "Find an Expert" builds in the necessary step to bring students' schema into the open and begin working with it.

You may notice that we cast a pretty wide net in creating the horror story "Find an Expert" form, trying to find many possible entry points to the story. We figure that everybody has had some kind of scary experience or surprise. By doing this, we are emphasizing what's human and universal about this literature. "Find an Expert" can be especially valuable with a selection that kids initially see as alien—some obscure early American or British work—because it can help kids connect to timeless themes and emotions.

So, before you start your class on the next difficult text, make a list of background knowledge items that might come in handy to know and whip up a "Find an Expert" chart. Then, after the kids have finished the reading, pull out the chart and have them brainstorm the items that *really* should have been on it—and use their ideas with the next class.

FIND AN EXPERT WHO

Has read a novel by Stephen King	Remembers a really weird dream
Knows someone who's seen a ghost	Has gotten their fortune told
Seen a modern horror/slasher movie	Seen the movie *Jaws*
Seen a horror movie that took place mostly during the day	Played a "violent" videogame
Has something they worry about	Remembers a surprise

"Find an Expert" Steps

1. Move to the "dance floor" and wave your paper above your head to signal that you need a partner.

2. When you've found a new partner, make sure you can both help fill in a remaining box on each other's form. If so, then move off the dance floor. Remain standing and discuss.

3. Find a category that applies to your partner, interview them briefly, and write the information in the box.

4. Have your partner neatly sign under your notes. This is the *only* time your partner will write on your paper.

5. Now let your partner interview you on a topic. Be sure to sign the sheet after that interview is completed.

6. When you're both finished, thank each other and return to the "dance floor" for new partners. You must have a *different* partner for each topic box.

The Horror

Dave Eggers

Sandra never read horror novels, because everything scared her. Or rather, when she was young, just about everything scared her, so she never watched thrillers or slasher movies, much less read anything by King or Straub or Lovecraft. Her imagination was easily ignited, and the line between fiction and reality, for her, was much too malleable. Often, after a vivid dream, it took her days to come to terms with the fact that the dream was indeed a dream, and not something more—an alternative reality, a prophecy, a message from dead persons known or unknown. Nevertheless, when she was thirty years old, she had an idea for a horror novel or movie or perhaps both. The entire thing, she decided, would take place during the day. The only other scary movie she could think of that also took place during daylight hours was *Jaws*, and that didn't count, because the world underwater, as we all know, is much like night. Her movie would be light the entire time, and, even better, the night would be the time when everyone—all those oppressed by the terror—would rest. Everyone would get a good night's sleep each night. Having settled all that, Sandra was very satisfied. As a reward for having such a good brain, she walked to her fridge and made herself a sandwich with two types of bread, and speared it with a toothpick. All she needed now was to decide what exactly would be scary, and how people would die or be torn apart or maimed. She stood, eating her sandwich, and then had another revelation: What if no one died? Couldn't that be scary, in its own way? It certainly would be unexpected. Now, she felt, she was onto something. A horror movie that took place during the day in which no one was killed. But what would it be about? What would happen? The movie, she figured, could feature many surprises—people jumping out from closets and jabbing things quickly. That could be made suspenseful throughout, with the audience not knowing exactly when, for example, the jumping-out and jabbing-at would happen. But then again, wouldn't it be kind of scary—and better all around—if you (a) didn't know when or where jumping-out would occur, and also (b) didn't know whether or not such things would occur at all? Imagine watching the movie, fully expecting that something would happen, only to sit waiting, throughout, thus becoming ever more tense? She had now put down her sandwich, because her head was working too quickly and brilliantly; she dared not distract it with chewing. So an all-daylight horror movie with only the pretense of suspense, only the promise (to be broken) of chases, of danger and violence and untimely death. She would have her characters wander throughout, talking tensely—or laconically!—eyeing each other and every doorway warily. Or perhaps with great nonchalance. What if, she thought, her characters walked calmly through their lives, without threats, without suspense or shadows, expecting nothing and receiving nothing? Now, she thought, that is horror.

LESSON 7.2 Text on Text

Text on Text is a powerful combination of Text Annotation (Lesson 4.1, page 37) and Written Conversation (Lesson 5.1, page 66). It's silent but physically active, and it's less linear than passing literature letters clockwise around a circle. Look at this picture.

TEXT ▶ "I Am From," by Lorian Dahkai

TIME ▶ 20 Minutes

GROUPING SEQUENCE ▶ Whole class, groups of three, whole class

USED IN TEXT SET ▶ 6

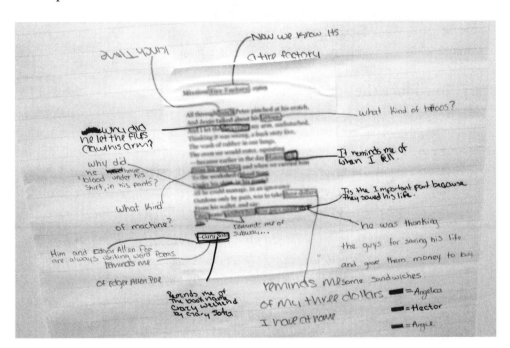

Here's what happened. Kids in this southern New Mexico classroom gathered in groups of three around a Gary Soto poem called "Mission Tire Factory." They read the poem and then marked it up with their comments, interpretations, and wonderings. As they worked, they were invited to read each other's postings and respond to them in the margins. So a written conversation broke out among the kids as they got deeper and deeper into the text. If you are looking carefully, you'll realize that this did not happen with kids hunched over one 8½ x 11-inch piece of paper. The preparations listed below are a little more complex than usual—but totally worth it.

For the upcoming lesson, we are using a classic pattern poem. "I Am From" is one of those helpful formulas we can use to jumpstart kids writing their own poetry. The template is simple: every line begins with "I Am From." Not only is this a great anxiety-reducing model for virgin poets, but every once in a while a student knocks it out of the park. Smokey's wife Elaine Daniels is also a teacher, and Lorian wrote this poem as a student in her class. Which reminds us that student writing, as well as the products of the pros, can make excellent text for our reading and thinking lessons.

This activity works for excerpts, very short stories, or shorter poems—rarely more than a hundred words on the page. So use Lorian's or another fascinating and artful short text and enlarge the font to the maximum size that will fit on one standard piece of paper. Now, stick the text onto a piece of chart paper (stolen from the local elementary school, perhaps), thus creating a big, wide margin. You'll need one set for every three students, because that is all the people who can fit around one text and work on it comfortably.

Better yet, let the kids finish the prep. Hand each group a glue stick, the poem, and a piece of chart paper and have them complete the final construction. Just make sure you have one prototype ready for display and emulation. Finally, you'll need different colored skinny markers so each group member writes in an immediately distinguishable color. Decide how kids will form into groups of three.

Steps & ▶ Teaching Language

COMMON CORE STANDARDS SUPPORTED

- Read closely to determine what the text says explicitly and to make logical inferences from it; cite specific textual evidence when writing or speaking to support conclusions drawn from the text. *(CCRA.R.1)*

- Analyze how specific word choices shape meaning or tone. *(CCRA.R.4)*

- Analyze the structure of texts. *(CCRA.R.5)*

- Assess how point of view shapes the content and style of a text. *(CCRA.R.6)*

- Participate effectively in a range of conversations and collaborations. *(CCRA.SL.1)*

STEP 1 **Introduce the activity.** *Today we are going to have yet another kind of literature discussion—a silent, written conversation about a poem, in groups of three. You can see that we have these large sheets of paper with a poem in the middle of each one.* (You can have these on the wall, flat on tables, or on the floor, depending on your room and how your kids are most likely to work well.) *When we are ready to start, you'll grab your own color marker and write your thoughts about the poem in the margins.*

After you have had a chance to jot a few of your own thoughts and reactions, start reading what your partners have been writing in the margins. Now you can engage in a silent discussion by writing notes to your friends about their ideas. You can comment, react, compare, or ask them questions. We want a lively conversation to break out right in the margins. Shall we try this?

So, get into your groups of three and position yourselves around the text—you'll have to form a U-shape so everyone can easily read the poem.

STEP 2 **Read the text aloud.** *OK, is everyone set? I am going to read this aloud first, and then you can go to work studying the poem and writing about it in the margins.* Read the poem aloud, with expression and drama.

STEP 3 **Give instructions for conversation.** *OK, now it's your turn. You'll take some time to reread the poem, annotate it, and join in a written conversation with your partners in the margins.* For crystal-clear accountability about who wrote what, have students first make a "map key" in the corner of the page that shows who's writing with which color pen.

What will you write about? First, since this is an "I Am From" poem, you obviously want to figure out who the author really is. How old? Where does she live? What has her life been like? Who are her friends and family? What are her beliefs and attitudes? And because this is a poem, you can pay attention to the poetic forms, tools, or techniques that the author uses. And finally, you can always refer to our chart, "Things to Think About While Reading" (page 38). So there's tons to think and write about. Enjoy.

STEP 4 **Monitor and assist as students reread, annotate, and jot notes.** You may need to remind kids to be silent, to use their most legible handwriting, or to keep on thinking and writing until you call time.

STEP 5 **Discuss.** Draw out the range of comments from different groups. If you wish, you can take this in the three steps mentioned above: talk about the poet's life and the poetic elements she uses, and share any of the thinking generated by the "Things to Think About" list.

◀ ***Variations***

- **Add a gallery walk:** At Step 5, instead of going directly into a whole-class discussion, you can have a gallery walk. The large posters are custom-made for sharing, so you can have kids hang them up at wide intervals around the room. Then groups travel around, visiting several other groups' posters, taking notes in their journals about how these other conversations were alike and different from their own. Or you can have visiting students leave Post-it notes with comments or questions beside other groups' charts. Then these ideas can plug into the whole-class meeting that comes up next.

- **Write our own:** Have kids (and you) write their own "I Am From" poems and then distribute them anonymously. Readers try to figure out which classmate is the author. In discussion, talk about the mysterious ways that arbitrary constraints, like the rules of an "I Am From" poem, can sometimes set us free creatively.

- **Watch it first.** There is a wonderful video of eighth graders doing this activity in one of our other resources, *The Best Practice Video Companion* (see Works Cited for details).

◀ ***Shoptalk***

If you are teaching a unit on poetic elements, select a poem that has the features you need to be teaching. Lorian's piece is obviously good for highlighting repetition, juxtaposition, and word choice. Other poems might be better suited to teaching metaphor, rhyme scheme, or personification. Your anthology should have plenty of poems to choose from—and then there is always the Poetry 180 website, with a great poem for each day of the school year.

I Am From

Lorian Dahkai

I am from red man and white man and brown man

I am from farmer and miner

I am from the bottom of a bottle

I am from hardship and surviving

I am from love at first sight

I am from attraction and youth

I am from salvation

I am from Sunday school and Baptist hymns

I am from higher education

I am from a teacher, a minister and nurse

I am from dirt roads and cattle guards

I am from giant cotton wood trees

I am from 2.5 kids a dog and picket fence

I am from Norman Rockwell

I am from the desert and the mountains

I am from camping and Disney

I am from Nintendo and rabbit ear antennas

I am from rebellion

I am from ripping and tearing

I am from heartache and death

I am from confusion.

I am from sex, drugs and rock and roll

I am from new birth

I am from adventure across the seven seas

I am from discipline, endurance and challenge

I am from One Nation Under God

I am from second and third chances

I am from Christian love

I am from a first kiss

I am from promises to love honor and cherish

I am from new life

I am from a hour ago

I am from a minute ago

I am from a second ago

I am now

LESSON 7.3 Frozen Scenes

How do you feel when you attend a meeting, conference, or workshop where you're expected to remain seated for hours? You can't sit all day. You need to periodically stretch, walk around, loosen up, right? So when you get sick of sitting, you take a break (whether everyone else is breaking or not). You refill your water bottle, make a quick trip to the washroom, survey the snack table to see if anything good is left. When you're ready, you sit back down. That's human.

But if your school/classroom is like the ones we work in, the traditional structure doesn't offer students many chances to move, so we've got to create some options that do. Yeah, we know how kids sometimes complain when you tell them to stand, but they really do want to get up out of those desks they've been sitting at for hours on end.

Frozen scenes (AKA tableaux) give students practice in noticing the text details that help readers visualize a scene. Basically, kids create statues of the characters frozen in midaction. Put several tableaux together and you have a series that can tell the whole story (if the piece is really short) or a section of a full-length text or chapter book. This activity is also very helpful for students who struggle with language proficiency. Sometimes they are the ones who are most creative physically. Plus, the physical interpretation allows them (and everyone) to return to the text and reread with greater confidence. If you need help showing kids what a frozen scene looks like, project a photograph of the Iwo Jima Memorial statue; that picture is worth a thousand explanations.

TEXT ▶ "This Is How I Remember It," by Betsy Kemper

TIME ▶ 30 Minutes

GROUPING SEQUENCE ▶ Whole class, groups of five, pairs, whole class

USED IN TEXT SET ▶ 4

> ### PREPARATION
>
> Each student will need a copy of the story and the script. Run them back to back. Determine how to form groups. The example script will work best if you have one group of three with the rest of the groups containing four to six students. Prepare a projection that highlights the elements of a good tableau.

STEP 1 **First reading of story.** We rate this story as "mature" just for the fleeting "God dammit." If this is a problem at your school, redact the curse and use it anyway. *Here's a really short story that we can have some fun with today. Go ahead and give it a read.* Invite a few comments when kids finish. That last line is a killer, and people will probably want to vent some critical comments about the mother.

STEP 2 **Second reading.** *Today we're going to create some three-dimensional pictures based on this story. Right now, let's reread it, and try to picture the different events and actions. How are the characters posed? What kinds of relationships do the kids have with their mothers? What are the different action scenes of the story?*

◀ **Steps** & **Teaching Language**

STEP 3 **Explain tableaux.** *Tableaux are frozen scenes that tell a story. Today you are going to work in groups to use your imaginations to create one scene from the story you just read. Turn the story over and look at the tableaux scripts. Each group is going to create a frozen scene that depicts a different caption.*

A good tableau reflects the following elements:

- Tight composition—characters should be close together
- Physical proximity indicates relationships—loving versus adversarial—which characters would be closer?
- Exaggerated gestures and facial expressions
- Variety of height levels—it's visually boring when everyone is standing, sitting, etc.
- Characters face the audience

STEP 4 **Assign groups and captions; monitor.** While the first caption needs only three players, the other captions can accommodate groups of four to six members. Once captions are assigned, tell groups they have about five minutes to get up and figure out how to stage their scene. As you monitor, don't be afraid to offer a blocking tip or two and definitely keep reminding the kids to figure out how to face the audience; otherwise, groups often create a tableau with several members turning their backs to the audience. (Once in a while, a face can be averted for artistic reasons—looking away in horror, e.g.).

STEP 5 **Perform tableaux.** Have groups perform their scenes in numerical order so that together they retell the story. Once a group gets in position, you can read the caption yourself, or draft different students to do the reading as you move through them. If you can, take a photograph of each tableau. You can use the photographs to review the next time you use this strategy. Also, if you can project the tableaux from several classes, it's interesting to discuss how different groups created very different scenes even though they worked with the exact same words.

STEP 6 **Third reading.** *Now, let's read the story one more time and look a little deeper.* Beforehand, pose these questions:

What do you make of the title?

Is the protagonist a girl or a boy? How old?

Why is this story all one paragraph?

Where is the period? How does the punctuation play a role in the story?

What are the three italic statements, exactly?

How might this story change if it were told from the mother's point of view?

What does the phrase "me for once not resisting" suggest to you?

STEP 7 **Discuss.** Start with a quick pair share and have partners report out. Then weave kids' observations into some talk about the way authors make deliberate craft decisions. In this case, every single element of the story contributes to its meaning and impact. The lack of paragraphs and periods creates a breathless whirlwind of activity. Many of the above questions might lead kids to a more nuanced understanding of the story. Given the title, it's a reasonable interpretation that the seemingly innocent kid might have been a hellion, in and out of the emergency room three times a week. Maybe innocent this time, but usually the guilty ringleader of untold mischief—with an exhausted and skeptical mother.

- **Have students pick lines:** You notice that we selected and prepared the frozen scene captions in this lesson. That's because certain lines lend themselves to creating scenes, while others fall flat. But once kids get the drift, they can and should be choosing and honing their own captions. One way to do this: assign each group a portion of the text and tell them how many scenes they need to find, hone, and depict. The captions should originate from the text, but it's OK to adjust the wording slightly or make edits to achieve brevity.

- **Bend the rules:** Tableau characters do not always have to remain silent or frozen. You can tell each group that one scene should include a decisive movement that enhances a scene or shifts the focus. Also, tableau characters can unfreeze one at a time to explain their roles and feelings. Feel free to experiment and find what works best for your students and your goals.

- **Audience preparation:** For more drama, have the viewers close their eyes briefly as groups assemble their frozen scene. Then they open their eyes as the caption is read, providing a more powerful, discrete performance to enjoy.

◀ *Variations*

As we have been saying throughout this chapter, these "up and thinking" activities help to bring literature alive, whether the readings come from our textbooks, or the district curriculum guides, or the CCSS exemplar texts. We English teachers are not alone in this view. In every school subject, educators seek out constructivist approaches—experiences that allow learners to reinvent each field of knowledge for themselves, from the inside. Teachers favor concrete manipulatives in math, hands-on experiments in science, and historical simulations in social studies. In the language arts, we take every opportunity to plunge kids into an interpretive community, gathered around the eternal campfire of *story*.

◀ *Shoptalk*

"THIS IS HOW I REMEMBER IT" FROZEN SCENES

1. Watching Joey pop the red berries into his mouth like Ju-Ju Bees and Mags only licking them at first, then chewing . . . and I laugh though I don't eat even one

2. Suddenly our moms are all around us

3. Mine doesn't panic till she looks at the others, then screams along with them . . . and shakes me

4. And then we're being yanked toward the house

5. Inside the moms shove medicine, thick and purple, down our throats in the bathroom

6. Joey in the toilet, Mags in the sink, me staring at the hair in the tub drain as my mom pushes my head down, and there is red vomit everywhere . . . except the tub where mine is coming out yellow, the color of corn muffins from lunch, not a speck of red

7. *I told you,* I want to scream and then it is over and I turn to my mother for a touch or a stroke on the head like the other moms (but she has moved to the doorway and lights a cigarette, pushes hair out of her eyes) and there is only her smeared lips saying, *This will teach you anyway*

This Is How I Remember It

Betsy Kemper

Watching Joey pop the red berries into his mouth like Ju-Ju Bees and Mags only licking them at first, then chewing, so both of their smiles look bloody and I laugh though I don't eat even one...then suddenly our moms are all around us (although mine doesn't panic till she looks at the others, then screams along with them things like *God dammit did you eat these?* and shakes me so my "No" sounds like "oh-oh-oh") and then we're being yanked toward the house, me for once not resisting as my mother scoops me into her arms, and inside the moms shove medicine, thick and purple, down our throats in the bathroom; Joey in the toilet, Mags in the sink, and me staring at the hair in the tub drain as my mom pushes my head down, and there is red vomit everywhere, splashing on the mirror and the powder-blue rugs, everywhere except the tub where mine is coming out yellow, the color of corn muffins from lunch, not a speck of red, *I told you,* I want to scream, and then it is over and I turn to my mother for a touch or a stroke on the head like the other moms (but she has moved to the doorway and lights a cigarette, pushes hair out of her eyes) and there is only her smeared lips saying, *This will teach you anyway.*

The Human Continuum

TEXT ▶ "Little Things Are Big," by Jesus Colon

TIME ▶ 50 Minutes

GROUPING SEQUENCE ▶ Whole class, lineup, pairs, lineup, whole class

USED IN TEXT SET ▶ 8

To keep kids on their toes (literally), we use lots of brief "up and thinking" activities, where students must stretch their bodies and their minds at once. Here's an upright "mingling" interaction that really challenges kids' thinking and requires them to defend their interpretation or position. But mingling needs a tight, purposeful structure, and the human continuum is entirely orderly. A big thank-out to Sara Ahmed of Burley School in Chicago, who developed this lesson from her training with the phenomenal organization, Facing History and Ourselves.

> **PREPARATION**
>
> Make copies of "Little Things Are Big" for all, on two separate pages as indicated. You'll hand these out at two different moments in the lesson. Practice reading the story aloud.

Steps & Teaching Language ▶

STEP 1 **Read aloud.** Hand out copies of page 1 only, and ask kids to follow along as you read the first section aloud. Read the story with your ever-increasing dramatic skills.

STEP 2 **Invite predictions.** *So what do you think is going to happen in this story? What will he decide to do? Help the woman or walk away? How will it end?* Take just two or three volunteers to prime the pump. Try to get competing answers by asking, *Who thinks it will end another way?*

STEP 3 **Explain the human continuum.** *In a minute, I'm going to ask you guys to stand up and put yourselves on a continuum. If you feel absolutely sure that Jesus will reach out to the woman and help her, stand over here at one end of the line. If you are just fairly sure he will help, then stand here closer to the middle. If you are unsure or on the fence, if you don't feel it's possible to predict the ending based on what we have read so far, stand right here in the center. If you are fairly sure he will not help her, stand here. And if you are totally convinced that Jesus is going to walk away and not get involved, then stand here at the far other end of the continuum.*

If your classroom is small, you can let the line meander around the room wherever space is available. You will have to be especially clear where the ends are. Some teachers put Post-its marking where each of the five positions might be standing, on the wall or even on the floor. Or better yet, take the whole activity out into the hall (if that's legal where you teach), where the continuum idea will be more visible—and linear.

Now before you stand up, a couple of instructions. Bring your copy of the first half of the story with you so you can refer to it in your discussions. What you're going to do is stand in the line where you think you belong and talk with a few of the kids standing nearby about why they also think the story is going to end the way you are predicting. Point out specific evidence in the story so far that makes you think this way. Ready? Line up and talk.

Allow for two or three minutes of conversation; encourage kids to turn both ways so they get different ideas from their continuum neighbors.

STEP 4 **The line speaks.** Now, have one or two kids from each continuum section explain why they are standing where they are, stating their prediction and the textual evidence that led them to their conclusion.

STEP 5 **Change places.** Give kids a chance to revise their thinking. *If your mind has been changed by what we have just discussed and heard, go ahead and move now to the appropriate spot.* Wait a minute while kids rearrange, keeping track of a few who have moved, especially long moves from one end to the other.

Now call on a couple of those kids, along the lines of: _____, *why did you change your position? What about our discussion changed your mind? Or did you discover something in the text that made you change your prediction?*

STEP 6 **Kids read the conclusion.** Hand out Part 2 of the story and let kids read it where they stand. And get ready to witness one of the most urgent readings you've ever seen your kids do. Savor their oohs and ahhs, the groans and the high fives, even some I-told-you-sos, as the end is revealed.

STEP 7 **Discuss**. With kids still standing, invite them to talk about why Colon's story ended as it did, and how helpful the clues in the text really were. Discuss what the powerful ending says to us all about stereotyping, ignorance, dignity, and humanity.

- **Stir more pointed debate:** After the initial lineup, "fold" the line in half, so people with extreme views are now facing each other. Mix up the kids in the middle just enough that they are facing new partners. Instruct each partner to attempt to persuade the other to change his or her initial conclusion. Give another two or three minutes for discussion and prediction. This would replace Step 4 in the preceding directions.

◀ *Variations*

- **Get the audio:** On the Facing History website there is an excellent dramatic reading of the memoir at http://www.choosingtoparticipate .org/explore/exhibit/stories/littlethings/hear-read. Instead of your own read-aloud, you could use this in the lesson—just be ready to pause the recording at the crucial line: "I hesitated."

- **Upstander or bystander?** The Facing History and Ourselves program is primarily about preventing genocide, and one of its recurring questions is, Who are the bystanders and who are the upstanders? On the day of the story, what was Jesus Colon, an upstander or a bystander? How does he feel about his choice now, looking back? Can we each remember a time when we took one of those roles and how it felt to us? Is this a valid metaphor for preventing crimes against humanity?

Shoptalk ▶ This lesson works very well for any story or poem that has a dramatic, unpredictable ending. Also, as the example illustrates, the human continuum is a great way to physically examine a character's moral dilemma. Think about how many of the texts you use have a character who arrives at a "fork in the road" where a personal choice must be made, neither of which will be easy or comfortable. Should Hester Prynne have revealed that Reverend Dimmesdale was the father of her "love child" Pearl? Should Lily have helped Rosaleen break out of police custody in *The Secret Life of Bees*?

Little Things Are Big

Jesus Colon

Part 1

"I've been thinking; you know, sometimes one thing happens to change your life, how you look at things, how you look at yourself. I remember one particular event. It was when? 1955 or '56 . . . a long time ago. Anyway, I had been working at night. I wrote for the newspaper and, you know, we had deadlines. It was late after midnight on the night before Memorial Day. I had to catch the train back to Brooklyn; the West side IRT. This lady got on to the subway at 34th and Penn Station, a nice looking white lady in her early twenties. Somehow she managed to push herself in with a baby on her right arm and a big suitcase in her left hand. Two children, a boy and a girl about three and five years old trailed after her.

Anyway, at Nevins Street I saw her preparing to get off at the next station, Atlantic Avenue. That's where I was getting off too. It was going to be a problem for her to get off; two small children, a baby in her arm, and a suitcase in her hand. And there I was also preparing to get off at Atlantic Avenue. I couldn't help but imagine the steep, long concrete stairs going down to the Long Island Railroad and up to the street. Should I offer my help? Should I take care of the girl and the boy, take them by their hands until they reach the end of that steep long concrete stairs?

Courtesy is important to us Puerto Ricans. And here I was, hours past midnight, and the white lady with the baby in her arm, a suitcase and two white children badly needing someone to help her.

I remember thinking; I'm a Negro and a Puerto Rican. Suppose I approach this white lady in this deserted subway station late at night? What would she say? What would be the first reaction of this white American woman? Would she say: "Yes, of course you may help me," or would she think I was trying to get too familiar or would she think worse? What do I do if she screamed when I went to offer my help? I hesitated.

Little Things Are Big

Jesus Colon

Part 2

And then I pushed by her like I saw nothing as if I were insensitive to her needs. I was like a rude animal walking on two legs just moving on, half running along the long subway platform, leaving the children and the suitcase and the woman with the baby in her arms. I ran up the steps of that long concrete stairs in twos and when I reached the street, the cold air slapped my warm face.

Perhaps the lady was not prejudiced after all. If you were not that prejudiced, I failed you, dear lady. If you were not that prejudiced I failed you; I failed you too, children. I failed myself. I buried my courtesy early on Memorial Day morning.

So, here is the promise I made to myself back then: if I am ever faced with an occasion like that again, I am going to offer my help regardless of how the offer is going to be received. Then I will have my courtesy with me again.

Character Interview Cards

If you read newspaper stories of disaster or crime, you'll notice that they all contain one key ingredient: the testimony of witnesses. These might be eyewitnesses; they might be expert witnesses; they might be character witnesses who haven't seen the perpetrator in twenty years. What's really cool about newspaper stories is that they inject all sorts of characters who aren't even in the original story. Think about it. If a wife kills her husband in cold blood, you've got a story with two characters. But once the newspaper grabs it, there will be two dozen: the parents of the wife and husband, the husband's ex-girlfriend, the wife's lawyer, her sorority sisters who hadn't seen her since she married that guy none of them liked. What if we read a story this way? The following activity incorporates elements from two related lessons, Literary Networking (pages 187–195) and Follow-Up Questions (pages 77–82). Best to try them individually first, before attempting this more complex activity.

TEXT ▸ "The Container," by Deb Olan Unferth

TIME ▸ 50 Minutes

GROUPING SEQUENCE ▸ Individuals, whole class, individuals, pairs

PREPARATION

Each student will need a copy of "The Container" and one index card. Determine how you will visually record and modify the character list. Be ready to project your own story copy so that you can model note taking. Later, be ready to project your own filled-out index card, or do it virtually on the computer.

Organize a "dance floor" area where students can go to find new partners. Plan how students will move about the room as they interview each other in pairs. Determine how pairs will form for quick sharing at the end of the activity.

On the Web

STEP 1 **Pass out the story and give directions.** *Today we're going to take a look at a story that you'll probably find a little odd. Before we do anything with it, I just want you to read it. Pay attention to the characters and what happens. You'll probably have some questions as you read. As I said, this story is puzzling, so just flow with it. If you see anything important that you want to mark, go ahead.*

STEP 2 **Give students time to read the story.**

STEP 3 **Brainstorm interview characters.** *Let's start by talking about the characters in this story. Who do we have?* Students should list:

Main character—woman

Neighbors

Two gas men

The container (you may need to nudge on this if kids don't already know that objects or settings can be characters also)

◂ **Steps & Teaching Language**

COMMON CORE STANDARDS SUPPORTED

- Read closely to determine what the text says explicitly and to make logical inferences from it; cite specific textual evidence when writing or speaking to support conclusions drawn from the text. *(CCRA.R.1)*

- Determine central ideas or themes of a text and analyze their development; summarize the key supporting details and ideas. *(CCRA.R.2)*

- Interpret words and phrases as they are used in a text, including figurative meanings. *(CCRA.R.4)*

- Assess how point of view shapes the content and style of a text. *(CCRA.R.6)*

- Participate effectively in a range of conversations and collaborations. *(CCRA.SL.1)*

Who else knows this woman, but isn't in the story? Students might brainstorm ex-husband, mother, Facebook friend, best friend from high school, coworker, doctor. Add these to the list.

Main character—woman

Neighbors

Two gas men

The container

Ex-husband

Mother

Facebook friend

Coworker

Doctor

Take a look at this list. Which characters would be most important to interview about the story events and their meaning? The main character, the neighbors, and the container must be interviewed. Now there's six left. Which two would provide the most insightful information? Imagine that you are a reporter and this is your assignment. You don't have time to interview everyone on the list before you have to write your story. Which two should you choose? Get consensus and cross out or erase the characters you won't be interviewing. *Did you notice that the main character doesn't have a name? Without a name it's going to be hard for the reporter to refer to her in the interview questions. What would be a good name for her?* Let the kids pick a name.

STEP 4 **Number off.** *Now we're going to count off by five. When you get your number, write it down in the top right-hand corner of the story.* Walk around the room, making sure the kids write down their numbers as they count off.

STEP 5 **Give directions.** *Everybody got their number written down? Good. Now I want you to write down the character that corresponds to your number.* Number the characters listed on the board 1 through 5. *When you read this story a second time, you will be taking on the role of a reporter who is going to interview that character about the story events. Jot some interview questions in the margin of the story, right near the spot where you thought of them. By the time you're finished reading, you should have five or six questions. Before you try this, I'm going to model the note taking.*

Project the story and use a character that was discarded. Begin to read the story aloud, stopping to jot down interview questions.

OK, I'm a reporter and I'm going to be interviewing this woman's coworker. Show the kids how, by reading two or three paragraphs of the story as you jot interview questions. Here are a few examples:

- What kinds of health problems did Ms. Every complain about at work?

- How was she to work with?

- What did Ms. Every say to you about her problem with the gas company?

Before we get started, what do you need clarified?

STEP 6 **Students reread and write interview questions.** Cruise the room, peer over shoulders, make sure that the kids are following directions. Answer questions as needed. As reading concludes, move to the next step.

STEP 7 **Pass out index cards and refine questions.** *When you get the index card, write your name on the top line. On the second line write your number and the name of your interview character. Now look back at your questions and find the best one, the one that will really help you write this article about the woman and her mysterious container. Neatly write that question on the card. Since you are a reporter, you are a masterful interviewer. What are two follow-up questions you could ask that would keep the character talking about the topic? Write those down underneath the first question. Let me show you what my card looks like.*

Project your own index card using one of the questions you modeled earlier. Add the two follow-ups.

STEP 8 **Give directions for interviewing.** *This is your chance to interview and be interviewed. Each time you find a partner, you'll be playing two roles: reporter and character. Let me show you.* Draft a student or take a volunteer to be your partner. *OK, who are you interviewing? So I'm* [the container—or whatever character the student has]—*right? Read the question. Now I'm going to answer in character by using the story details and my imagination. Watch.* Answer the question, and then have the reporter ask you the follow-up questions. You answer them. *Notice that when I answered the questions I tried to use story details and my imagination. I tried to make my answers logical, like they could fit into the story. My partner and I aren't done yet. Now it's my turn to be the reporter and his turn to be a character.* Continue modeling until the interview is complete. *Give _____ a big round of applause.*

STEP 9 **Interviewing begins.** *Grab your card and stand up. Whenever you need a new partner, go to the "dance floor" and wave your card. Try to meet and interview as many people as possible before I call time, but be sure to conduct full interviews just like I modeled. When it's your turn to* *answer in character, try your best to make your answers fit with the story; don't start making up crazy stuff. Make sure you work with a new partner each time; no repeats! People can only work in pairs.* If you have an uneven number of students, join the interviewing so that the "pairs only" rule will stick. *Any questions? Go.*

STEP 10 **Wrap up.** *You are now in your role of reporter. On the back of the index card, write down the most important information you uncovered in your interviews.* Give students a minute to write. *Turn to your partner, state your interview character and question, and tell them what you found out.*

STEP 11 **Share out.** Hear about interview details from a few volunteers. Then pose this question: *What is the significance of the container? What might it symbolize? Turn to your partner and come up with some ideas.*

Give pairs a couple of minutes and then call for their ideas. *This story is pretty wide open. Does the container symbolize her own paranoia, her isolation? Or does the container symbolize something bigger—like solving the problem of climate change? Lots of talk, but the solutions seem remote and no one takes action.* Use these questions/comments to invite some further speculation and a possible conclusion to this inconclusive story.

Variations ▶

- **Discussion questions:** Rather than being characters, students can just be themselves and write down a good discussion question on a piece of literature. Then kids get up and work in pairs, interviewing each other about the story and their ideas/opinions related to the question.

- **Card trade:** Once students understand the steps of this activity and how to be interviewed as different characters, have them trade cards at the end of each interview. When they return to the "dance floor," they will be waving someone else's questions rather than their own. This livens up being the reporter, because now with each new pairing you get to use different questions (and possibly interview a different character).

Shoptalk ▶

Talk about bringing literature alive. This lesson really does the job, and it's especially useful for those patches in long, hard books that send kids to Snoozeville. There's no place to hide when you are mingling with the whole class, switching partners every couple of minutes, on your feet and face to face. Compare that to the usual seated and sedate English class "lecture discussion." Want engagement? Stand the kids up and have it.

The Container

Deb Olan Unferth

She began to get headaches in the winter. Dull throbs and chills and a fever just above normal. She sat in bed and checked her temperature every two hours. This is too long, she thought, it's been weeks of headaches and low-grade fevers and this can't be normal—in fact, it's not normal, it's just above. She ventured into the hallway to ask the neighbors who passed by flipping through the mail whether they knew about such conditions as headaches and they paused to listen and discuss possible maladies. They agreed that it was possible, not too likely, but possible that she had a gas leak in her apartment, which could cause headaches and death and so on and shouldn't go unchecked. Anyway it's free to check—those gas people are so nutso about leaks and she should call the gas people, and she did.

Much faster than she expected, twenty minutes after the call, two gas men knocked on the door. They had on gas-man suits and carried liquid-filled containers and instruments with long antennas that they pointed at objects. The instruments beeped and ticked and the men walked through her apartment beeping and ticking and tapping and lifting oven lids and frowning into heat ducts, and she was brave and stood to one side and watched and answered their questions about headaches and fevers.

Then the gas men said there was no gas leak in any room, everything was tip-top and the headaches would go away, perhaps, if she didn't stay cooped up so much, if she went for more walks, for example, and that was an unpleasant comment, she thought, but she thanked them and showed them out. She stood in the hallway and rocked on her heels. She went back inside and into the kitchen.

There on the kitchen table sat a container. It had a long stick coming out of the top, much like a plunger, and two shadowy warning labels taped to the side: Danger. Hazardous. And: Not Responsible for Spillage or Leakage, Dispose of Properly, in smaller print below.

She ran out the door to the street, but the gas men were gone, and then she ran up the stairs to her apartment and into the kitchen. And the container was still there. It had a blue fluid in it which had to be thick because when she tipped the container the fluid moved slowly. She called the number she had called to get the gas men the first time.

Your gas men left their container in my apartment, she said to the man who answered the phone. The man asked her to describe it and she did. She told about the plunger sticking out and the blue fluid and the man on the phone put her on hold and then came back and asked her to describe it again and she read the warning labels firmly and twice and told him about the plunger coming out again and about the slow-moving blue fluid again and the man put her on hold again and then he came back and said, That's not ours.

Who else's would it be? she wanted to know.

Are you sure it wasn't there before they arrived? he asked.

No, it wasn't here, she said. She knew that for a fact and he put her on hold again. She sat on hold and looked at the container until he came back. He gave her a 1-800 number she could call for a dump site. There was one in Wyoming and one in Arizona. But I'm in Chicago, she said, and this is yours, not mine. The man hung up and she was alone with the container.

She went out into the hallway and asked the neighbors who passed by flipping through mail what they thought. Everyone came over to look at it, stopped in the doorway of the kitchen and peered in, made jokes about driving to Wyoming, but finally decided they were concerned and said, Are you going to leave that in the building, that nuclear waste? And she was concerned herself, called the 1-800 number and listened to the recorded message of directions off the interstate to the dump site. She called several times, sat in bed with the phone and a box of crackers, which she ate slowly, one small bite at a time, sucking on each biteful. Now the fever was gone. Now she was nauseated and nothing helped except to lie perfectly still and suck on small cracker bits and have one hand on the phone and not think about the container.

The neighbors slid notes under the door, messages scribbled on the backs of envelopes, Have you resolved the situation? She crept to the door and watched out the peephole at the neighbors gathering and whispering. They didn't flip through mail anymore but waited in clumps in the hallway, smoked cigarettes, and examined what looked like blueprints. They kept an eye on her door. Sometimes she could hear snatches of their conversation. She'll never part with it, they hissed from behind raised collars. She thought that was unfair. No one had asked her for it. She would have handed it over earlier and gladly had someone asked but no one did and she began to feel indignant and protective. After all none of this was her fault and, in fact, if it was anyone's fault it was the neighbors' whose idea it was to call the gas people in the first place and no one had asked her for the container and no one had asked her about her fever and headaches either, how she happened to be feeling these days, and this was the state of things.

She peered out the window and saw blue sky, a single square of it between buildings. One long surveillance helicopter circled. She went into the kitchen and picked up the container. Set it on the floor. She took hold of it by the long stick. Pushed down.

The Common Core Standards want kids not just to persuade, but to argue. *Interesting choice of words. When you think about it, "persuasive" sounds pretty genteel, while "argue" has a more aggressive connotation. The technical difference is that when we are persuading, we only need to make our own case. But to argue, you also have to acknowledge the other side's position—and then crush it. These lessons reflect our belief that to get good at this process, kids need lots of practice drawing on textual evidence to develop an interpretation, and then testing it against others' thinking.*

LESSON 8.1 Take a Position

Remember the last episode of *The Sopranos*? You don't? Then you might want to take some time off and devote eighty-three hours to watching the complete DVD collection. On the other hand, you can just keep reading and take our word for what follows . . .

. . . at this point, Tony is pretty much the last man standing, since an earlier mob war has wiped out his crew. To top it off, the feds have him cornered. Tony waits in a diner, sitting in a booth while a suspicious-looking guy at the counter is eyeing him. Who is this guy? Hit man? Mob celebrity stalker? Job applicant who heard there were openings? We don't know, but he's sure making us nervous! The camera keeps switching between the front door, Tony, guy at the counter. Anxiety mounts for the viewer, not so much for Tony. He seems pretty happy; maybe his new meds are kicking in? Someone's at the door. Oh no! Whew, it's only his wife, Carmella. The anxiety builds again, but then it's just A.J., his son. Finally Meadow walks in. Tony looks up. Screen goes blank and stays that way for about ten seconds, and then the credits roll silently.

What the !*@#? That was it. Every viewer had to make up his/her own ending based on the evidence they had gathered in the previous eighty-two episodes. At the time the final installment aired, it created quite a buzz and many viewers were angry. How could David Chase (writer, director, executive producer) do this to them after they had invested half a lifetime watching that show? The nerve of that guy! The next day, Chase stated, "I have no interest in explaining, defending, reinterpreting, or adding to what is there."

Yet months later Chase reneged on his "vow of silence" and claimed that Tony didn't die (reviving the chances of a future movie or Sopranos reunion episode), telling the *New York Daily News*, "Why would we entertain people for eight years only to give them the finger?" The ending was only an "artistic" decision. Personally we wish he had refused to give "the right answer," but probably

TEXT ▶ "We? #5" by Helen Phillips

TIME ▶ 20 Minutes

GROUPING SEQUENCE ▶ Whole class, pairs, whole class

USED IN TEXT SET ▶ 8

he was tired of being pilloried in YouTube comments as obsessed viewers watched and rewatched Tony's last five minutes. Luckily, few authors face the same degree of scrutiny about their endings.

How many times have you had students read a story or novel, get to the end, and say, "That's it? What happened?" But what we really want them to say is "Cool. I'm glad the author thought I was smart enough to use the clues to make my own meaning." Here's a chance to help your students make that transition.

PREPARATION

Make a copy of "We? #5" for each student. Practice reading the story aloud.

Steps & ▶ Teaching Language

STEP 1 **Define symbolism.** *A symbol is usually an object or graphic that represents more than its literal meaning; it also represents an idea or quality. Take U.S. currency, paper money. The literal value of a twenty-dollar bill is about the same as a single—same amount of ink, same paper, same cost of printing—yet they symbolize different values. And then there are all the different graphics on money that are more than just decoration: the eagle, the unfinished pyramid with the eye floating above it. We could probably spend the whole period just examining and deciphering the currency in our wallets, but we're not. Instead we're going to read a story.*

STEP 2 **Distribute the story and read aloud.** *To start off, I'm going to read this story aloud and I want you follow along. As the story unfolds, I want you to watch for something that seems to be working as a symbol. Any questions on what I mean by symbol? Also, I want you to notice something else. In the last paragraph, the point of view jumps from third to first person. What do you think that's all about?*

Read aloud. (If you think the title may be confusing to kids, you can tell them that Phillips' book has sets of stories that are numbered under the same title. Hence "We? #5" is the fifth story about "We," and the number has no significance within the story.)

STEP 3 **Highlight the story symbol.** *What object do you think is the symbol?* Students should readily recognize the blank die. *What led you to believe that's a symbol?* Students should mention the repetition.

STEP 4 **Reread the story.** *Before we talk about what the symbol might mean, I want you to reread the story once or twice (it's short!), and decide for yourself: What does that blank die represent? Once you think you know, write down your idea and make sure that you've found lines in the story to support your viewpoint.*

STEP 5 **Monitor and coach.** Let kids work for five minutes or so, checking in and coaching the ones who haven't marked up their sheet and jotted some symbolism notes.

STEP 6   **Pair share.** *Get together with your partner and discuss the blank die. What might it symbolize? How do you know? Where's the evidence? Listen carefully to your partner. If you have different ideas, that's OK. The important thing is that you can logically defend your answer with text evidence.*

STEP 7   **Share out.** *OK, let's hear some ideas. Anybody work with a partner who had a completely different idea than you?* Call on those students first and have them explain their divergent opinions. Remember to *always* require students to defend their opinions with text evidence. *Interesting. Anybody else have some other interpretations to share? I bet you're wondering what the right answer is, huh. I don't know. It's kind of like that last episode of* The Sopranos . . .

This activity lends itself to an extension into argumentative writing. Have students use their notes to develop a strong essay defending their interpretation of the central symbol of the story. Does the mysterious cube represent:

◀ *Shoptalk*

   conquering depression

   growing up

   taking control of your life

   breaking a bad habit

   leaving your "baggage" behind

   reaching out to other people

There are so many ways to look at this story and symbol. The kids will probably surprise you with things that neither we, nor *The Sopranos* writing staff, would ever think of.

We? #5

Helen Phillips

Once there was a person whose sadness was so enormous she knew it would kill her if she didn't squeeze it into a cube one centimeter by one centimeter by one centimeter. Diligently, she set about this task. Alone in her room, she grappled with her sadness. It was quite a beast, alternately foggy and slippery; by the time she managed to grip it, her skin was sleek with sweat, soaked with tears. (The sounds coming from her apartment worried the neighbors. What was that shy little woman up to?) She twisted her sadness like a dishrag. It strained against her, tugged, pulled. She sat on it to shrink it down the way old-fashioned ladies sat on their snakeskin suitcases.

Then, finally, there it was: a small white cube.

She slipped it into her pocket, went outside, noticed orange lichen growing on tenements, ordered lemonade in a café. The checkered floor nearly blinded her—it looked exactly like joy, and she almost covered her eyes. But instead, she fingered the thing in her pocket. Her eyes became bright prisms; they made her irresistible, and soon she had a friend. One day, passing some kids in the street who had just lost a die down the sewer, she discovered a die in her pocket. "Wow, lady," they said. "Where'dya get a blank one?"

"Gosh," she said, "I really can't remember." And she couldn't.

You know that book where they went all over the world and took pictures of families in front of their homes along with everything they owned? A hut in Kenya, a suburban house in Texas, a Tokyo apartment? I always loved to see the precious and unprecious items, the woven blankets and the TVs, the families standing nervously alongside. Sometimes I look around our home and imagine everything out on the street. But I hope that someday, when they come to take our picture with everything we own, it will just be us, standing before a building, your arm around me, a blank die in my palm.

LESSON 8.2 Finish the Story

Go to any art museum and you will see students sitting in front of the classics sketching away. Why? Are they practicing to be art counterfeiters? What's a convincing copy of the Mona Lisa going for these days? No, their studious practice is making them better artists because a great way to learn technique is through imitation. And once you've mastered that technique, you can reshape it and make it your own.

Students need to do the same thing with their own writing: imitate other writers' style and technique. Unfortunately, when we want kids to emulate a piece, we typically give them longish essays and then expect them to do everything: come up with their own topic, find the argument, research the details, and put it all together in a series of paragraphs that make sense. By the time they've finished all of that they're exhausted, we're exhausted, and any attention to craft details has long been kicked to the curb.

A more manageable way for kids to practice developing an eye for craft is to finish stories. Yes, we've all tried this at one time or another, but once again, we'll wager that the mentor text was long, like full-length novel long, and the assignment was to write an alternative ending chapter. Instead, let's shorten this up. Write the end of a story, but use a story short enough to emulate. And don't rewrite the ending. Just withhold the original ending and don't even read it until you've heard all the other alternatives. Who knows? It might turn out that one of your students writes a more satisfying ending than the original.

TEXT ▶ "Little Brother™"
by Bruce Holland Rogers

TIME ▶ 50 Minutes

GROUPING SEQUENCE ▶ Whole class, pairs, groups of four, groups of eight, whole class

USED IN TEXT SET ▶ 7

PREPARATION

Each student needs a copy of just the first part of "Little Brother™." We didn't label it Part 1 because we want the kids to think that's the whole story. Part 2, which begins with "Later, when Mommy came in to the living room . . . ," will be read aloud at the end of the lesson.

Determine how pairs will form to work together to write the ending. Determine how those pairs will combine to form groups of four, and how they will later combine to form groups of eight.

STEP 1 **Pass out and introduce the story.** *As I read the first few paragraphs of this story aloud, I want you to pay attention to what's going on, as well as details on character and setting.* Read the first three paragraphs aloud and then stop. *What did you notice in these first few paragraphs?* Take answers. Be sure to redirect the kids back to the details about Peter's little brother that make him different from a typical baby.

◀ **Steps & Teaching Language**

- Read closely to determine what the text says explicitly and to make logical inferences from it; cite specific textual evidence when writing or speaking to support conclusions drawn from the text. *(CCRA.R.1)*

- Analyze how and why individuals, events, or ideas develop and interact over the course of a text. *(CCRA.R.3)*

- Assess how point of view shapes the content and style of a text. *(CCRA.R.6)*

- Write narratives to develop imagined experiences or events. *(CCRA.W.3)*

- Apply knowledge of language to understand how language functions in different contexts, to make effective choices for meaning or style, and to comprehend more fully when reading or listening. *(CCRA.L.3)*

- Participate effectively in a range of conversations and collaborations. *(CCRA.SL.1)*

STEP 2   **Give students time to read the story.** *You've got the details right and you are following the story fine, so I'm confident you can read the rest on your own. Go ahead and do that now. Be sure to pay close attention to the dynamics between Peter, his mother, and his new little brother.*

STEP 3   **Examine craft.** *That story ended kind of suddenly, didn't it? Actually, there's a little bit more to go, but before we finish it up I want you to pause and take a look at the author's style. How does the author put this story together? Turn to your partner and take a look at the last section you read. Mark what you notice right on the text. Try to label what you see.*

Give pairs a few minutes to reread, discuss, and mark. Call them back and get suggestions. Students will probably notice these items.

- Third person-limited. We only know what Peter is thinking.

- Section starts and ends with narration: setting, plot.

- Most of the story told in dialogue.

- Lots of tension. Explanation points after what characters say.

- Arguing.

- Mom's explanations are longer than Peter's.

- Peter's little brother's name is Little Brother™.

Good. You've noticed that there is a specific style and rhythm to this story and that the author has made some specific choices about characterization and advancing the story.

STEP 4   **Give directions.** *Remember when I said that this wasn't the end of the story? Now we're going to get to that. Everyone stay with your partner, but get out a sheet of loose-leaf paper. How do you think the story is going to end? That's for you and your partner to figure out. Together you're going to write the ending in the style we just investigated. Now, don't panic. This is a short story. The original ending has 226 words, so it's not going to be any longer than about one to one and a half pages, depending on whether you type or handwrite it. What questions do you have?* Answer questions.

Oh, and even though you are working together, I want both of you to write down the ending you come up with so that you each have your own copy. Though you'll be tempted, don't share your ideas with any other pairs. We want the endings to be a surprise, and they won't be if you tell others what you're writing about. And remember, what you write has to be G-rated—we're still at school. Go ahead and get started.

STEP 5   **Monitor pairs.** Keep pairs focused on each other and on avoiding conversations with other groups that will slow down the writing. If a pair is struggling, direct them to reread the previous story section with this question in mind: How is Peter going to resolve this conflict with Little Brother™? The writing should take about ten minutes.

STEP 6 **Pairs combine to form groups of four.** *It's time to hear what you wrote. I want each pair to get with another pair to form a group of four. Partners, decide who will be your reader. The job in your group of four is to listen to both endings and decide which one does the best job matching the author's style and the clues in the first part of the story. Each group of four will choose of their two pieces to read aloud in the next round. Decide which pair is going first and get started.*

STEP 7 **Groups of four pair up to form groups of eight.** *OK, every group should know which piece you chose. Be sure to take that piece with you for the next step. Everyone stand up. Groups of four, point to another nearby group and move together so that you are a group of eight. Pay attention because I'm going to assign you to a different part of the room for your "on your feet" meeting.*

Direct groups to various corners and standable spaces. *It's your new group's job to listen to both of the endings brought to the meeting and decide which one most resembles the author's style and completes the story. That is the piece your group of eight will present to the class. Decide who's going first and get started.*

STEP 8 **Monitor groups of eight.** This shouldn't take long. Ascertain that each group has picked one piece to present to the whole class and make sure they know who is going to read it aloud. At this point, students can return to their seats or remain standing and listening respectfully. It will be easier to manage which groups have presented if the groups remain standing.

STEP 9 **Chosen pieces are read to the class.** Choose groups at random to send their reader up to the front. Encourage readers to make it interesting and dramatic. Keep it brisk. After each piece is read, call for a big round of applause. This shouldn't take long since you will be listening to only one piece from each group of eight students. Collect the pieces afterwards if you want, or have students file them in their binders for later retrieval.

STEP 10 **Read the original ending aloud.** Then ask: *Out of all the endings you heard, which one worked best? What was it about the writing that influenced your decision?*

◀ ***Variation***

To tell the truth: That was once the name of a game show where three people claimed to have a certain accomplishment or career, and the panelists had to decide which one was real and which two were the imposters. This variation works the same way. After the groups of eight have met and made their choices, collect those stories. Assuming that kids have created their endings on computers, grab those files. If handwritten, type them up, along with the last part of the original story, so that they look almost identical. Just identify the different endings with letters or numbers. Make copies of this "endings collection" for every student. Pass them out, have students read silently, and then vote on which one they think is the original. Tell the groups that they will recognize one piece as their own but the others should be unfamiliar. After the votes are in, reveal the winner and the original story ending.

Shoptalk ▶ There's a lot of talk these days—which we applaud—about "mentor texts." "Little Brother™" is a pretty good example. In the wide world of literature, there are certain pieces that particularly exemplify one or more literary elements: voice, tone, characterization, structure, dialogue, surprise endings, whatever. These special readings invite kids into an apprenticeship with them as readers—and, as we have shown in this lesson, as writers. But our friend Ted DeMille makes an important distinction about how we use these precious teaching tools: we want kids to riff on mentor texts, to write "impersonations," not simple imitations. Nice.

Little Brother™

Bruce Holland Rogers

Peter had wanted a Little Brother™ for three Christmases in a row. His favorite TV commercials were the ones that showed just how much fun he would have teaching Little Brother™ to do all the things that he could already do himself. But every year, Mommy had said that Peter wasn't ready for a Little Brother™. Until this year.

This year when Peter ran into the living room, there sat Little Brother™ among all the wrapped presents, babbling baby talk, smiling his happy smile, and patting one of the packages with his fat little hand. Peter was so excited that he ran up and gave Little Brother™ a big hug around the neck. That was how he found out about the button. Peter's hand pushed against something cold on Little Brother™'s neck, and suddenly Little Brother™ wasn't babbling any more, or even sitting up. Suddenly, Little Brother™ was limp on the floor, as lifeless as any ordinary doll.

"Peter!" Mommy said.

"I didn't mean to!"

Mommy picked up Little Brother™, sat him in her lap, and pressed the black button at the back of his neck. Little Brother™'s face came alive, and it wrinkled up as if he were about to cry, but Mommy bounced him on her knee and told him what a good boy he was. He didn't cry after all.

"Little Brother™ isn't like your other toys, Peter," Mommy said. "You have to be extra careful with him, as if he were a real baby." She put Little Brother™ down on the floor, and he took tottering baby steps toward Peter. "Why don't you let him help open your other presents?"

So that's what Peter did. He showed Little Brother™ how to tear the paper and open the boxes. The other toys were a fire engine, some talking books, a wagon, and lots and lots of wooden blocks. The fire engine was the second-best present. It had lights, a siren, and hoses that blew green gas just like the real thing. There weren't as many presents as last year, Mommy explained, because Little Brother™ was expensive. That was OK. Little Brother™ was the best present ever!

Well, that's what Peter thought at first. At first, everything that Little Brother™ did was funny and wonderful. Peter put all the torn wrapping paper in the wagon, and Little Brother™ took it out again and threw it on the floor. Peter started to read a talking book, and Little Brother™ came and turned the pages too fast for the book to keep up.

But then, while Mommy went to the kitchen to cook breakfast, Peter tried to show Little Brother™ how to build a very tall tower out of blocks. Little Brother™ wasn't interested in seeing a really tall tower. Every time Peter had a few blocks stacked up, Little Brother™ swatted the tower with his hand and laughed. Peter laughed, too, for the first time, and the second. But then he said, "Now watch this time. I'm going to make it really big."

But Little Brother™ didn't watch. The tower was only a few blocks tall when he knocked it down.

"No!" Peter said. He grabbed hold of Little Brother™'s arm. "Don't!"

Little Brother™'s face wrinkled. He was getting ready to cry.

Peter looked toward the kitchen and let go. "Don't cry," he said. "Look, I'm building another one! Watch me build it!"

Little Brother™ watched. Then he knocked the tower down.

Peter had an idea.

When Mommy came into the living room again, Peter had built a tower that was taller than he was, the best tower he had ever made. "Look!" he said.

But Mommy didn't even look at the tower. "Peter!" She picked up Little Brother™, put him on her lap, and pressed the button to turn him back on. As soon as he was on, Little Brother™ started to scream. His face turned red.

"I didn't mean to!"

"Peter, I told you! He's not like your other toys. When you turn him off, he can't move but he can still see and hear. He can still feel. And it scares him."

"He was knocking down my blocks."

"Babies do things like that," Mommy said. "That's what it's like to have a baby brother."

Little Brother™ howled.

"He's mine," Peter said too quietly for Mommy to hear. But when Little Brother™ had calmed down, Mommy put him back on the floor and Peter let him toddle over and knock down the tower.

Mommy told Peter to clean up the wrapping paper, and she went back into the kitchen. Peter had already picked up the wrapping paper once, and she hadn't said thank you. She hadn't even noticed.

Peter wadded the paper into angry balls and threw them one at a time into the wagon until it was almost full. That's when Little Brother™ broke the fire engine. Peter turned just in time to see him lift the engine up over his head and let it drop.

"No!" Peter shouted. The windshield cracked and popped out as the fire engine hit the floor. Broken. Peter hadn't even played with it once, and his best Christmas present was broken.

Little Brother™

Bruce Holland Rogers

Part 2

Later, when Mommy came into the living room, she didn't thank Peter for picking up all the wrapping paper. Instead, she scooped up Little Brother™ and turned him on again. He trembled and screeched louder than ever.

"My God! How long has he been off?" Mommy demanded.

"I don't like him!"

"Peter, it scares him! Listen to him!"

"I hate him! Take him back!"

"You are not to turn him off again. Ever!"

"He's mine!" Peter shouted. "He's mine and I can do what I want with him! He broke my fire engine!"

"He's a baby!"

"He's stupid! I hate him! Take him back!"

"You are going to learn to be nice with him."

"I'll turn him off if you don't take him back. I'll turn him off and hide him someplace where you can't find him!"

"Peter!" Mommy said, and she was angry. She was angrier than he'd ever seen her before. She put Little Brother™ down and took a step toward Peter. She would punish him. Peter didn't care. He was angry, too.

"I'll do it!" he yelled. "I'll turn him off and hide him someplace dark!"

"You'll do no such thing!" Mommy said. She grabbed his arm and spun him around. The spanking would come next.

But it didn't. Instead he felt her fingers searching for something at the back of his neck.

LESSON 8.3

Arguing Both Sides

TEXT ▶ "The Wallet,"
by Andrew McCuaig

TIME ▶ 50 Minutes

GROUPING SEQUENCE ▶ Individuals, pairs, groups of four, pairs

USED IN TEXT SETS ▶ 7, 8

The thing that makes literature so compelling is the human condition, the moral dilemma. Should George have shot Lenny in *Of Mice and Men*? In *One Flew Over the Cuckoo's Nest,* did Randle McMurphy ultimately help his fellow patients or harm them? In Walter Dean Myers' book *Monster,* is sixteen-year old Steve Harmon truly a monster, as the prosecutor declares at his trial?

If you start looking at the literature you teach, you'll find compelling argument possibilities in most of your pieces, even poetry. And you know what? That's good because the Common Core wants kids arguing, big-time. As a matter of fact, if you examine the Core Standards closely, you'll find argumentation built into the nonfiction reading, writing, and speaking and listening standards. And, even though argument doesn't play as prevalent a role in the literature standards, we shouldn't ignore it: making a case is making a case. When literature is the body of evidence, students must find text details and draw inferences as they develop their supports. Then they must present their conclusions articulately, while also paying close attention to the opposing viewpoint in order to refute it. And to complete the cycle of reasoning, students then switch sides to argue the opposing viewpoint as confidently as they did their own.

PREPARATION

Each student will need a copy of the story. Students will be working in two sets of pairs: they will have a "shoulder partner" (a student sitting beside them) and a "face partner" (one across a table or possibly behind them). With shoulder partners, students will be *planning* their arguments. With the face partners, they will be doing the actual *arguing*. Kids need to be able to turn quickly between two different partners, so think about how best to work this in your room.

Grab the projectable list of argument steps from the website (it also appears on page 183).

Steps & ▶ Teaching Language

STEP 1 **Read and annotate the story.** *As you read this story, pay attention to details of plot, setting, and character. Underline words or passages that seem important and jot down questions that will help you discuss the characters. If you finish the story before I call time, reread it and see what else you notice.*

STEP 2 **Preparation partners discuss the story.** *Turn to your shoulder partner and share what you've underlined. When you pose a question, be sure to let your partner answer first before you share your thoughts.* Allow three minutes. Students might discuss:

How does Elaine feel about Troy?

Why does Elaine keep the job if it's boring and she dislikes her coworkers?

What do you think went through Elaine's mind when the woman in the yellow Chevette said, "No, I mean I need money"?

What conclusions does Elaine draw when she sees the kids in the backseat?

Why did Elaine give the woman Troy's money instead of her own?

STEP 3 **Share out.** *What were some of the ideas that you discussed in your pairs? What do you think Elaine might like about her job as a tollbooth worker? Who was that woman with the kids who drove up at the end of the story? Why did Elaine give that woman money that wasn't hers? Was that the right decision?*

STEP 4 **Introduce argument.** *You seem divided on the last question I posed. Let's talk about that one a little bit more. But first, I want everyone to get out a sheet of loose-leaf paper. Ready? Shoulder partners, we're going to count off by twos (1, 2—1, 2—1, 2—and so on). As we count off, you and your partner should write down your number on your sheet of paper; you will end up being a one or a two.*

As this lesson progresses, students will be working with two different partners. Their shoulder partner will be their preparation partner and will support the same position, while their face partner will be their argument partner. *Number one shoulder partners raise your hands. Good. At the top of your papers write: Elaine did the right thing with Troy's money. Number two shoulder partners raise your hands. Excellent. At the top of your papers write: Elaine should not have given Troy's money away.*

STEP 5 **Give preparation instructions.** *With your preparation partner— your shoulder partner—I want you to come up with a list of reasons that support your side of the argument. Go back through the story and comb it for details that support your side. Remember that all of the support will not be stated in the story in black and white; you'll need to make some inferences using the text details as clues. Questions? Work with your partner on making as complete a list as possible for your side. If you get stuck, silently reread the story and look for other details you can use.*

Go to the end of this lesson for examples of what the preparation partners' notes should look like for each side.

STEP 6 **Give students time to work.** They'll probably need five to ten minutes. Monitor progress and cut off discussion as talk and note taking wind down.

STEP 7 **Partner one argues.** *It's almost time to begin arguing, but first thank your preparation partner for all the help in getting ready. Now turn to your face partner. If I planned this correctly, you should be facing someone who has the opposing viewpoint. Everybody good? Number ones—Elaine did the right thing—you're going to argue your position first. I'm going to give you one minute to convince your partner that Elaine did the right*

COMMON CORE STANDARDS SUPPORTED

- Read closely to determine what the text says explicitly and to make logical inferences from it; cite specific textual evidence when writing or speaking to support conclusions drawn from the text. *(CCRA.R.1)*

- Analyze how and why individuals develop and interact over the course of a text. *(CCRA.R.3)*

- Prepare for and participate effectively in a range of conversations and collaborations with diverse partners, building on others' ideas and expressing their own clearly and persuasively. *(CCRA.SL.1)*

- Demonstrate understanding of nuances in word meanings. *(L.CCR.5)*

thing giving Tony's money to that woman. Number twos, you need to just listen carefully. You can't talk, but you can take notes. As a matter of fact, I recommend you do take notes because they are going to come in handy later. Any questions? All right—go!

STEP 8 **Partner two argues.** *Stop! The minute is up. Now it's partner number two's turn to argue why Elaine should not have given away Tony's money. Same rules apply. Number ones, you can only listen, and you should take notes on your opponent's arguments. Go!*

STEP 9 **Refutation preparation.** *Stop! Turn back to your shoulder partner. What was the weakest argument your opponent gave you? Why was it weak? Talk this over with your preparation partner and decide how you will prove this with further points from your side.*

STEP 10 **Give pairs time to work.** This will only take about three minutes.

STEP 11 **Refutation.** *Get back with your argument partner. Each side is going to get one minute to point out the flaws in their opponent's arguments,* but *this time the opponents can talk back. Number ones, you are up. Go!* Call time after one minute. *Stop! Number twos, now it's your turn. Same rules apply. Go!* If time grows short, you can jump to Step 14, have students drop positions, and work in their groups of four to come up with the best solution.

STEP 12 **Reverse positions.** *Stop! Remember when I told you to take notes on your opponent's arguments? Now they are going to come in handy because you and your argument partner are going to switch positions. If you were originally a number one arguing that Elaine did the right thing, now you are a number two arguing that she made a mistake. Number twos, you are now number ones. Everybody understand what their new position is?*

At this point, you can move directly into the final argument round or you can add a brief meeting with the preparation partners first so they can organize their new positions.

STEP 13 **Argue new positions.** *Same rules apply as before. One minute for each side. New number ones go first. Number twos will go second. Listening only. No interrupting.* Begin the arguments and start timing.

STEP 14 **Groups of four brainstorm solutions.** *Stop! Now I want argument partners and preparation partners to form a group of four. You are no longer arguing whether or not Elaine did the right thing. Your job now is to come up with the best solution to Elaine's dilemma. Your group is free to use ideas from both sides or use new ideas that were not previously mentioned.* Give groups a few minutes to discuss and then quickly have each group state their solution.

STEP 15 **Bring solutions back to the story.** *How would your group's solution have changed the story?* Have students discuss briefly back in pairs and then conclude with some brief sharing as a few groups report out.

Argument Steps

1. Prepare positions
2. Argue positions
3. Prepare refutation
4. Refute arguments
5. Reverse positions and argue
6. Synthesize solution

POSITION 1: Elaine did the right thing giving Troy's money to that woman	TEXT DETAILS
Troy's a jerk and Elaine doesn't owe him any favors.	• Leaves his trash for Elaine to pick up (sweating cup of Coke); "left his food regularly . . . " • Purposely "rubs" up against her. He sexually harasses her.
Elaine is bored and feels disconnected from others.	• She thinks José is a lecher as well. • She counts the cars to fight the boredom. • It seems like a lonely job. She's all alone in the booth, she doesn't like her coworkers, she doesn't really talk to anyone.
The woman in the yellow Chevette looks like someone is chasing her, going to kill her.	• Brakes screech like she was speeding away, maybe not even going to stop. • Suitcase looks like it was thrown together in seconds—"overflowing with clothes."
She looks like she needs to see a doctor.	• She is physically injured—gash below one eye, face swollen and purple, dried blood at corner of mouth.
The woman had two young children who look traumatized.	• "Their eyes were wide and afraid." • Older kid is sucking thumb.
Woman in Chevette has no money, no one to turn to.	• Elaine sees the kids and puts herself in the woman's place. What would she hope Elaine did?

POSITION 2: Elaine should not have given Troy's money to that woman	TEXT DETAILS
Troy trusts her. If she steals money, she could lose her job, since her job is working with cash.	• He's left his wallet before and it's always been intact. What's he going to think when he finds out? Elaine might lose her job if he files a complaint!
$92 isn't going to get that woman very far.	• That money might just be encouraging the woman in the Chevette to jeopardize her children's safety. Where are they going? Where will they stay after that money runs out? Temporary solution.
Elaine's inferences might be completely incorrect.	• She assumes that the woman has been beaten by someone and is being chased. But maybe she just murdered someone!
Elaine knows she shouldn't have given Troy's money away. She's stealing.	• She "surreptitiously reached for Troy's wallet." If she thought she was doing the right thing, she wouldn't have been so sneaky.
If that woman was really in trouble, Elaine should have called the state police.	• State police would have investigated, helped her find a shelter, maybe get a restraining order against who hurt her (gash, swollen bruised face, blood on lip).

Shoptalk ▶ Though this lesson seems a little complicated at first, the more you practice it, the better the kids will get at moving quickly through the steps. Soon, this will be a strategy that you can plug into a lesson on an almost impromptu basis. Let's say you're studying *The Crucible*, and someone asks, "Why did Reverend Parris ever trust his niece Abigail?" Time for a quick argument! Pair the kids and number them off. Ones argue "trust her" and twos argue "don't trust her." Pairs work up their side of the argument by reviewing their notes and scanning the text for a few minutes—and then argue.

Revisit your textbook, hunting for potential controversies that can enliven almost any selection. Slogging through Emerson's "Self Reliance"? Time to argue whether "self-reliance" is an achievable reality for all Americans. When logical, academic argument becomes routine, transferring that thinking into writing— or Common Core assessments—will be much easier.

THE WALLET

Andrew McCuaig

When Elaine arrived at work the first thing she noticed was that Troy had left his wallet on the small shelf next to a half-finished cup of Coke. Troy left his food regularly, as if she were his maid, but he left his wallet less often—about once a month. The first time it happened was just her second night on the job, and she thought maybe he was testing her honesty, or, worse, that he had created some excuse to come back and see her. He had, in fact, returned half an hour later and deliberately rubbed his body up against hers as he retrieved his wallet instead of just standing at the door and asking her to hand it to him. They had made awkward small talk in the cramped booth before he finally raised his wallet in a salute, said good-bye and good luck and rubbed past her again.

Now, as she settled onto the stool for her shift, she could smell his lingering presence. She picked up the cup of Coke and placed it in the garbage can at her feet, careful to keep it upright. The cup had sweated out a puddle in the summer heat and she shook her head despairingly. She lined up her piles of quarters and dimes on the shelf in order to have something to do. Two booths down, Jose waved at her and gave her two thumbs up, a gesture he thought was cute. He was another lecherous type, always spending his breaks standing at her door looking her up and down and blowing smoke into her booth. She waved at him so he'd turn around.

In front of her now the highway was black. Every few minutes headlights would appear in the distance like slow trains but most of the time the drivers would pick the automatic lanes. Then three or four cars might come in a row and she'd be grateful to move into a rhythm—reach, grab, turn, gather, turn, reach, good night. It was annoying when people didn't bring their cars close enough, but at least it allowed her to stretch more. By midnight she had made change for twenty-six people. Several weeks ago she had started to keep track out of boredom. Her midnight record was seventy-two, her fewest, twelve.

At about three o'clock a car came toward her too fast, weaving like a firefly, before picking her booth. The brakes screeched, the muffler roared: it was a little yellow Chevette, an eighties car pocked with rust. Elaine leaned forward with her hand ready, but the driver, a young woman, made no move to pay her toll. She looked straight ahead, her face hidden by strings of brown hair, both hands locked tight to the wheel. Beside her in the front seat was a small beat-up suitcase overflowing with clothes.

Elaine said, "Good morning," and the woman said, "I need money."

Elaine hesitated. "You mean you don't have the toll?"

"No, I mean I need money." She turned now and Elaine saw her bleary eyes and splotched face. There was an ugly gash below one eye and the skin around it had swollen up and turned purple. There seemed to be an older scar on her nose, and dried blood in the corner of her mouth. Her stare was bitter and bold and it made Elaine look away.

She was about to raise the bar and tell her to go on ahead when she saw movement in the backseat. Looking closer, she saw there were two children, one about five, the other barely two, neither in car seats or seatbelts. Their eyes were wide and afraid and Elaine realized it was this that had drawn her attention to them in the dark. The little one held on to a gray stuffed animal, the older one was sucking her thumb.

José was watching her; he raised his palms and scowled. She had been trained to signal in a certain way if she was being held up, and José seemed to be waiting for this gesture. Instead, she gave him a thumbs up and surreptitiously reached for Troy's wallet. She opened the wallet to find ninety-two dollars inside. She pulled these bills out, wadded them in her fist and reached out to the woman, who took the money, gripped the wheel harder and sped away. The older girl's face, framed by the back window, receded into the darkness, her eyes like glowing stones.

9 COPING WITH COMPLEX AND CLASSIC TEXTS

Probably the word appearing most frequently in the Common Core Standards is complex. *There's a major emphasis on having students read tough, "grade-level" materials, often of the classic, time-tested variety. These lessons show how we can support kids to reach higher, while still reading engaging text and joining in sociable interaction.*

LESSON 9.1 Literary Networking

We hear about social networking all the time. What *do* people do on Facebook? They connect with others, update people on what's going on in their lives, and gossip about the friended and *unfriended.*

What do people do in real-time networking? Pretty much the same thing. Maybe the best example of real-time networking is when you hear the kids in your third-hour class questioning those who already took the geometry test first hour. *Was it hard? What was on it? Did it ask about . . . ? Was there anything on it from that one worksheet we got the day we had the sub?*

So what does all this networking have in common? Either electronic or real-time, groups of people are piecing together information and forming connections. And this is exactly what we want kids to do whenever they read: talk and share ideas related to the text. In addition, when text is complicated, "classic," or confusing, kids need to start talking about the text *before* they "officially" start reading it. And ideally, the way they talk about it introduces actual text bits and pieces; then, when the real reading begins, it won't be an ice-cold reading. The kids will recognize characters and lines they've already encountered.

One way to accomplish this is through literary networking, also known as *quotation mingle* or *tea party* (cocktail party not recommended until graduate school).

TEXT ▶ "The Storyteller," by Saki

TIME ▶ 40 Minutes

GROUPING SEQUENCE ▶ Series of partners, groups of four, whole class, groups of four, whole class

USED IN TEXT SET ▶ 4

PREPARATION

Make two or three copies of "The Storyteller" quotation card chart and cut the quotes apart. You'll need one card, or quote, for each student. Also, make copies of "The Storyteller" for all.

Figure out what area of the room will be your "dance floor." This is the part of the room students move to when they are looking for new partners. When students must return to the "dance floor," they cannot just hang with their friends in a corner or wait for new partners to come to them. Have the kids move some desks out of the way if you need more space. Solving the management issue of "nonminglers" is totally worth it. Plus, if everyone has to move to the "dance

On the Web

floor" for new partners, it's much easier for the shyer kids to pair up, and it's much easier for you to orchestrate the pairings when necessary.

Plan on actually modeling each lesson step with a volunteer student rather than just explaining them.

Steps & ▶ Teaching Language

STEP 1 **Give directions.** *Today we are going to read a story that has some subtle humor, but noticing that humor will be easier if you've already done a little thinking about the characters and what might be going on in the story. When I pass out these cards, just hang on to them while I explain how this is going work. Each person should have one card.* Pass out the cards.

STEP 2 **Think about the quotation.** *As you read your card, I want you to think about what this story quote might reveal about the characters and the unfolding events.*

STEP 3 **Mingling instructions.** *Those around you have different cards. Your job today is to network with the other people in this room to try to figure out who these characters are and what's going on. As you meet with each partner, start off by greeting them. Then read your quotes out loud and try to figure out how they fit together, like a jigsaw puzzle. The more people you talk to, the more quotes you'll see. Also, you just might run across someone who has the same quote as you. That's OK. Be sure to share what each of you has found out about how your quote fits with others you've run across.*

When you need a new partner, return to the "dance floor" and wave your card in the air, like this. And as soon as you find a new partner, get off the "dance floor." With each of your partners, take turns reading your quotations aloud—then talk. There are sixteen different quotations out there, so the more people you visit, the easier it will be to figure out the story. Now everybody stand up and get away from your desks. Work with each partner for about two minutes and then switch. No sitting allowed. Find a partner and start networking!

STEP 4 **Monitor and coach.** Let kids network for about ten minutes. Urge kids to the "dance floor" when they need a new partner. Keep it brisk. Call time when you see conversations winding down.

Remind the kids that there are sixteen different quotes to check out and discuss. If you have an uneven number of students, step up and be the missing partner to even things out. That way, you can ensure everyone works with only one partner at a time. Uneven numbers (like twenty-nine instead of thirty) invite trios, which in turn lead to less on-task conversation, cliques grouping together, and nonclique kids being frozen out.

COMMON CORE STANDARDS SUPPORTED

- Read closely to determine what the text says explicitly and to make logical inferences from it; cite specific textual evidence when writing or speaking to support conclusions drawn from the text. *(CCRA.R.1)*

- Determine central ideas or themes of a text and analyze their development. *(CCRA.R.2)*

- Analyze how and why individuals interact over the course of a text. *(CCRA.R.3)*

- Interpret words and phrases as they are used in a text, including determining connotative and figurative meanings. *(CCRA.R.4)*

- Demonstrate understanding of nuances in word meanings. *(CCRA.L.5)*

- Participate effectively in a range of conversations and collaborations. *(CCRA.SL.1)*

STEP 5 **Call time and form groups.** Have everyone freeze in place. Ask each pair to join up with another pair to form a group of four. Attach any stragglers, one at a time, making a couple of groups of five if needed.

Now, in your groups of four, start by reading aloud each of your cards. First talk about how your cards fit together and what order you think they go in based on what each of you knows from looking at other people's cards and comparing notes with them. Second, who are the characters in the story and what are they like?

STEP 6 **Monitor and support.** Allow three to five minutes for the groups to confer. Remind them that they'll need to share their ideas about how the story proceeds as well as who the characters are and what they're like. Also, they'll need to defend their conclusions with the quotes they've seen.

STEP 7 **Share.** Reconvene the class and ask for predictions the groups have made with regard to story and character.

STEP 8 **Read.** Now (at last!) it's time to distribute the story and give these directions. *As you read, put checks by the events and characterizations that you predicted correctly and be on the lookout for new details that tell you more. Finally, pay particular attention to the story the bachelor tells and how the tale finally ends. Why is the bachelor's "fairy tale" so funny compared to the aunt's and how does the story end ironically?*

STEP 9 **Discuss.** Have students turn back to their groups of four and quickly discuss the questions posed previously. Remind students to back up their findings with story details. Finally, end with a quick large-group share.

◀ **Variations**

- **Card trade:** Once students are familiar with how literary networking works, it's time to mix it up a bit. Instead of students hanging on to the same card the entire time, have them trade with each other before they leave to find a new partner. However, they cannot work with the same partner twice. Otherwise, the kids will keep going back to their same friends claiming, "But Jennifer has a different card now, so why can't we work together again?" (and again and again). Gently point out that though we are working to understand a story, another purpose of networking is to become skillful at striking up conversations with a wide variety of people!

- **Building schema with literary networking:** A modified version of this activity is a powerful way to get kids thinking and talking about allusions/historical background for texts that require that sort of thing—basically every single selection in American lit and Brit lit classes. For example, if students are reading Julius Caesar, you can prime them for the "The fault, dear Brutus, is not in our stars, / But in ourselves . . ." scene (I.ii) by giving kids cards with snippets of information about items that would be alluded to in the speech:

- A brief retelling of the story of Aeneas saving Anchises at the Tiber River
- The Elizabethan view of ambition as evil
- Roman/Elizabethan superstitions regarding signs and portents in nature on Earth and in the stars
- Very short biographies (a few sentences) of Cassius, Brutus, and Caesar
- A very short description of the symptoms of epilepsy

These information bits gives kids built-in buy-in—each of them gets to be a mini-expert when it's time to read.

Shoptalk ▶ You've probably figured out that some lessons in this book could be assigned to other chapters. For example, this networking activity is a kissing cousin of the five lessons in Chapter 7, where the focus is on getting students "up and thinking," physically engaging in literary interaction. When your kids are facing a long, hard, mandated text, remember this family of lesson options.

STORYTELLER QUOTATION CARD CHART

The occupants of the [railway] carriage were a small girl, and a smaller girl, and a small boy. An aunt belonging to the children occupied one corner seat.	"You don't seem to be a success as a storyteller," said the bachelor suddenly from his corner.
The further corner seat on the opposite side was occupied by a bachelor who was a stranger to their party.	"Perhaps you would like to tell them a story," was the aunt's retort.
Most of the aunt's remarks seemed to begin with "Don't," and nearly all of the children's remarks began with "Why?"	"Once upon a time," began the bachelor, "there was a little girl called Bertha, who was extraordinarily good."
"Don't, Cyril, don't," exclaimed the aunt, as the small boy began smacking the cushions of the seat, producing a cloud of dust at each blow.	"Bertha was rather sorry to find that there were no flowers in the park. She had promised her aunts that she would not pick any of the kind Prince's flowers."
"Oh, look at those cows!" exclaimed the aunt. Nearly every field along the line had contained cows or bullocks, but she spoke as though she were drawing attention to a rarity.	"She was so good," continued the bachelor, "that she won several medals for goodness, which she always wore, pinned on to her dress. They were large metal medals and they clicked against one another as she walked."
The frown on the bachelor's face was deepening to a scowl.	"It is the most beautiful story that I ever heard," said the bigger of the small girls, with immense decision.
"Come over here and listen to a story," said the aunt.	"A most improper story to tell to young children! You have undermined the effect of years of careful teaching."
"It's the stupidest story I've ever heard," said the bigger of the small girls, with immense conviction.	"Unhappy woman!" he observed to himself as he walked down the platform of Templecombe station; "for the next six months or so those children will assail her in public with demands for an improper story!"

The Storyteller

Saki

It was a hot afternoon, and the railway carriage was correspondingly sultry, and the next stop was at Templecombe, nearly an hour ahead. The occupants of the carriage were a small girl, and a smaller girl, and a small boy. An aunt belonging to the children occupied one corner seat, and the further corner seat on the opposite side was occupied by a bachelor who was a stranger to their party, but the small girls and the small boy emphatically occupied the compartment. Both the aunt and the children were conversational in a limited, persistent way, reminding one of the attentions of a housefly that refuses to be discouraged. Most of the aunt's remarks seemed to begin with "Don't," and nearly all of the children's remarks began with "Why?" The bachelor said nothing out loud. "Don't, Cyril, don't," exclaimed the aunt, as the small boy began smacking the cushions of the seat, producing a cloud of dust at each blow.

"Come and look out of the window," she added.

The child moved reluctantly to the window. "Why are those sheep being driven out of that field?" he asked.

"I expect they are being driven to another field where there is more grass," said the aunt weakly.

"But there is lots of grass in that field," protested the boy; "there's nothing else but grass there. Aunt, there's lots of grass in that field."

"Perhaps the grass in the other field is better," suggested the aunt fatuously.

"Why is it better?" came the swift, inevitable question.

"Oh, look at those cows!" exclaimed the aunt. Nearly every field along the line had contained cows or bullocks, but she spoke as though she were drawing attention to a rarity.

"Why is the grass in the other field better?" persisted Cyril.

The frown on the bachelor's face was deepening to a scowl. He was a hard, unsympathetic man, the aunt decided in her mind. She was utterly unable to come to any satisfactory decision about the grass in the other field.

The smaller girl created a diversion by beginning to recite "On the Road to Mandalay." She only knew the first line, but she put her limited knowledge to the fullest possible use. She repeated the line over and over again in a dreamy but resolute and very audible voice; it seemed to the bachelor as though some one had had a bet with her that she could not repeat the line aloud two thousand times without stopping. Whoever it was who had made the wager was likely to lose his bet.

"Come over here and listen to a story," said the aunt, when the bachelor had looked twice at her and once at the communication cord.

The children moved listlessly towards the aunt's end of the carriage. Evidently her reputation as a storyteller did not rank high in their estimation.

In a low, confidential voice, interrupted at frequent intervals by loud, petulant questionings from her listeners, she began an unenterprising and deplorably uninteresting story about a little girl who was good, and made friends with every one on account of her goodness, and was finally saved from a mad bull by a number of rescuers who admired her moral character.

"Wouldn't they have saved her if she hadn't been good?" demanded the bigger of the small girls. It was exactly the question that the bachelor had wanted to ask.

"Well, yes," admitted the aunt lamely, "but I don't think they would have run quite so fast to her help if they had not liked her so much."

"It's the stupidest story I've ever heard," said the bigger of the small girls, with immense conviction.

"I didn't listen after the first bit, it was so stupid," said Cyril.

The smaller girl made no actual comment on the story, but she had long ago recommenced a murmured repetition of her favourite line.

"You don't seem to be a success as a storyteller," said the bachelor suddenly from his corner.

The aunt bristled in instant defence at this unexpected attack.

"It's a very difficult thing to tell stories that children can both understand and appreciate," she said stiffly.

"I don't agree with you," said the bachelor.

"Perhaps you would like to tell them a story," was the aunt's retort.

"Tell us a story," demanded the bigger of the small girls.

"Once upon a time," began the bachelor, "there was a little girl called Bertha, who was extra-ordinarily good."

The children's momentarily-aroused interest began at once to flicker; all stories seemed dreadfully alike, no matter who told them.

"She did all that she was told, she was always truthful, she kept her clothes clean, ate milk puddings as though they were jam tarts, learned her lessons perfectly, and was polite in her manners."

"Was she pretty?" asked the bigger of the small girls.

"Not as pretty as any of you," said the bachelor, "but she was horribly good."

There was a wave of reaction in favour of the story; the word horrible in connection with goodness was a novelty that commended itself. It seemed to introduce a ring of truth that was absent from the aunt's tales of infant life.

"She was so good," continued the bachelor, "that she won several medals for goodness, which she always wore, pinned on to her dress. There was a medal for obedience, another medal for punctuality, and a third for good behaviour. They were large metal medals and they clicked against one another as she walked. No other child in the town where she lived had as many as three medals, so everybody knew that she must be an extra good child."

"Horribly good," quoted Cyril.

"Everybody talked about her goodness, and the Prince of the country got to hear about it, and he said that as she was so very good she might be allowed once a week to walk in his park, which was just outside the town. It was a beautiful park, and no children were ever allowed in it, so it was a great honour for Bertha to be allowed to go there."

"Were there any sheep in the park?" demanded Cyril.

"No;" said the bachelor, "there were no sheep."

"Why weren't there any sheep?" came the inevitable question arising out of that answer.

The aunt permitted herself a smile, which might almost have been described as a grin.

"There were no sheep in the park," said the bachelor, "because the Prince's mother had once had a dream that her son would either be killed by a sheep or else by a clock falling on him. For that reason the Prince never kept a sheep in his park or a clock in his palace."

The aunt suppressed a gasp of admiration.

"Was the Prince killed by a sheep or by a clock?" asked Cyril.

"He is still alive, so we can't tell whether the dream will come true," said the bachelor unconcernedly; "anyway, there were no sheep in the park, but there were lots of little pigs running all over the place."

"What colour were they?"

"Black with white faces, white with black spots, black all over, grey with white patches, and some were white all over."

The storyteller paused to let a full idea of the park's treasures sink into the children's imaginations; then he resumed:

"Bertha was rather sorry to find that there were no flowers in the park. She had promised her aunts, with tears in her eyes, that she would not pick any of the kind Prince's flowers, and she had meant to keep her promise, so of course it made her feel silly to find that there were no flowers to pick."

"Why weren't there any flowers?"

"Because the pigs had eaten them all," said the bachelor promptly. "The gardeners had told the Prince that you couldn't have pigs and flowers, so he decided to have pigs and no flowers."

There was a murmur of approval at the excellence of the Prince's decision; so many people would have decided the other way.

"There were lots of other delightful things in the park. There were ponds with gold and blue and green fish in them, and trees with beautiful parrots that said clever things at a moment's notice, and humming birds that hummed all the popular tunes of the day. Bertha walked up and down and enjoyed herself immensely, and thought to herself: 'If I were not so extraordinarily good I should not have been allowed to come into this beautiful park and enjoy all that there is to be seen in it,' and her three medals clinked against one another as she walked and helped to remind her how very good she really was. Just then an enormous wolf came prowling into the park to see if it could catch a fat little pig for its supper."

"What colour was it?" asked the children, amid an immediate quickening of interest.

"Mud-colour all over, with a black tongue and pale grey eyes that gleamed with unspeakable ferocity. The first thing that it saw in the park was Bertha; her pinafore was so spotlessly white and clean that it could be seen from a great distance. Bertha saw the wolf and saw that it was stealing towards her, and she began to wish that she had never been allowed to come into the park. She ran as hard as she could, and the wolf came after her with huge leaps and bounds. She managed to reach a shrubbery of myrtle bushes and she hid herself in one of the thickest of the bushes. The wolf came sniffing among the branches, its black tongue lolling out of its mouth and its pale grey eyes glaring with rage. Bertha was terribly frightened, and thought to herself: 'If I had not been so extraordinarily good I should have been safe in the town at this moment.' However, the scent of the myrtle was so strong that the wolf could not sniff out where Bertha was hiding, and the bushes were so thick that he might have hunted about in them for a long time without catching sight of her, so he thought he might as well go off and catch a little pig instead. Bertha was trembling very much at having the wolf prowling and sniffing so near her, and as she trembled the medal for obedience clinked against the medals for good conduct and punctuality. The wolf was just moving away when he heard the sound of the medals clinking and stopped to listen; they clinked again in a bush quite near him. He dashed into the bush, his pale grey eyes gleaming with ferocity and triumph, and dragged Bertha out and devoured her to the last morsel. All that was left of her were her shoes, bits of clothing, and the three medals for goodness."

"Were any of the little pigs killed?"

"No, they all escaped."

"The story began badly," said the smaller of the small girls, "but it had a beautiful ending."

"It is the most beautiful story that I ever heard," said the bigger of the small girls, with immense decision.

"It is the only beautiful story I have ever heard," said Cyril.

A dissentient opinion came from the aunt.

"A most improper story to tell to young children! You have undermined the effect of years of careful teaching."

"At any rate," said the bachelor, collecting his belongings preparatory to leaving the carriage, "I kept them quiet for ten minutes, which was more than you were able to do."

"Unhappy woman!" he observed to himself as he walked down the platform of Templecombe station; "for the next six months or so those children will assail her in public with demands for an improper story!"

Characters Texting

TEXT ▶ "Persephone and Demeter," Thomas Bulfinch

TIME ▶ 50 Minutes

GROUPING SEQUENCE ▶ Whole class, pairs, whole class

USED IN TEXT SET ▶ 4

COMMON CORE STANDARDS SUPPORTED

- Read closely to determine what the text says explicitly and to make logical inferences from it; cite specific textual evidence when writing or speaking to support conclusions drawn from the text. *(CCRA.R.1)*

- Summarize the key supporting details and ideas. *(CCRA.R.2)*

- Analyze how and why individuals interact over the course of a text. *(CCRA.R.3)*

- Participate effectively in a range of conversations and collaborations. *(CCRA.SL.1)*

- Produce clear and coherent writing in which the development, organization, and style are appropriate to task, purpose, and audience. *(CCRA.W.4)*

- Draw evidence from literary texts to support analysis. *(CCRA.W.9)*

- Apply knowledge of language to understand how language functions in different contexts, to make effective choices for meaning or style, and to comprehend more fully when reading or listening. *(CCRA.L.3)*

Are you sick of your students texting when you're trying to teach? Sure, there's a school rule—like that matters. We've learned to tell the girls to keep their giant purses on the floor and the guys to keep their hands out of their pockets. But kids can text without even glancing at the keys. You've gotta wonder how those texts turn out. Is the message exactly what was intended, or does the recipient text back "WTFDYJS?"

Nancy remembers one texting incident that particularly fried her:

I had to run to some meeting and the sub walked in just as I was simultaneously stamping composition book writing and giving directions for the work the kids would be completing while the sub was tending them. Just as I'm finishing up and getting ready to go, the sub says, in this how-blind-and-stupid-are-you? tone of voice, "You know that kid over there was texting right in front of you."

And I replied all in his face, "Listen, since I get paid to teach, I make that my main focus rather than hunting down rogue texters." And then the kids looked at each other like OMG and watched the drama unfold. It was so quiet you could hear that proverbial pin drop. I don't think they were even breathing. Even the texting kid put his phone away; finally something interesting was happening in sophomore English!

Nah, I'm pulling your leg. Here's what I really said: "Point him out to me." And then I wrote the referral and went to my meeting.

OK, this whole texting thing is here to stay, so we might as well turn it to our advantage. If we see something the kids love doing, we should co-opt it immediately and drag it into the curriculum. This lesson gives kids a chance to show off their mad texting skills as they follow a story and "text" about it (in writing) from the point of view of different characters. The difference is that students will be writing their texts on paper within the context of the story rather than floating all of them out into the ether.

PREPARATION

Make a copy of "Persephone and Demeter" and the texting shorthand list for each student. Determine how to project the story when you are giving directions and later when students are sharing their texts. Also determine how pairs will form after reading sharing.

STEP 1 **Pass out the story and give directions.** Project the text as you introduce the lesson. *Today you're going to read a mythology story that you might be familiar with, the story of Persephone and Demeter. It is the story that the Greeks and the Romans used to explain the change of seasons. Take a look at the story. As you read, you are going to stop and write a text at the prompts that begin with "Text from." Write texts only for these prompts. Ignore the prompts that begin with "Reply." We'll use those later. Notice that you're not texting as yourself, but as one character to another. You want the texts to reflect the story details, but also give personality— and maybe some humor—to the characters. However, the texts must be G-rated. I know there's a lot of texting shorthand that stands for swear words, sexual acts—heaven forbid!!—and so forth. You will be turning this story in to me afterwards, so keep that in mind. Got it? Good. You can use texting shorthand, but stick with the abbreviations on this list. Anything I need to clarify before you get started?*

STEP 2 **Monitor reading.** Gently nudge students to follow the directions and write the texts as they go along so that they have a spontaneous versus rehearsed feel to them. Also, make sure they are writing texts *only* for the first prompt in each pair. As you see students finishing up, tell them to review their texts, making sure that they make sense and use details from that part of the story.

STEP 3 **Pairs trade stories and text back.** *Now that everyone's done, trade with your partner. Go ahead and read the text series. As you read the texts, stop and reply as the character indicated in each of the prompts.*

Borrow one student's copy that already has the first prompts completed. Project this copy and point out the secondary prompts as you give the directions. *Any questions? Get started replying to the texts.*

STEP 4 **Monitor reply texting.** At this point, pairs will probably be highly engaged reading the original texts and having some fun with their replies as they pretend to be different characters. Your main job is to monitor for time and remind students that for the time being, all their conversation is of the silent texting variety.

STEP 5 **Trade back and read replies.** After students have worked through the entire story, completing their text responses, they will trade back. *It looks like everyone is just about done. As you finish up, trade back your stories and read the replies. Find the one pair of texts between two characters that is the best, the one that captures the characters, has some humor, really makes use of the story details. Put a star by it.*

STEP 6 **Share out.** Call for volunteers to project their best text string, using a document camera or whiteboard. Have students read them aloud to the class, using the real words the text shorthand stands for.

Variation ▶

- **Modern analogies/allusions/theme:** To make your own text set of short myth readings, pair this story with "Mother #1" (page 241) and the Rita Mae Brown essay (page 242.) Or expand this idea by skimming through your textbook for myths and legends. These "old" tales endure because they offer the character/plot/conflict archetypes on which most stories are built. Once you find a classic tale you like, match it up to something more modern that employs the same archetype. Here are some common mythological archetypes:

  - Women of power
  - Heroes
  - Mentors
  - Creation
  - Destruction/rebirth
  - The quest
  - Search for paradise (either on earth or elsewhere)
  - Search for immortality
  - Obtaining what's forbidden
  - Temptation of evil

Shoptalk ▶

Some teachers think we should stop kids from using texting language in school, like ASAP! And just FYI, texting is lowering teenagers' IQs, 24-7! We don't have to be all PC and let this happen. If our common language doesn't get some TLC pretty soon, it is going to be RIP for the English language. OMG!

—Harvey (AKA Smokey) Daniels

Smky-NTA. AAMOF, CCSS wnts us 2 teach kds 2 match lang 2 contxt. Txtng is just 1 of many. NUFF

—N

Persephone and Demeter

adapted from Thomas Bulfinch

A sudden earthquake roused Hades from his underworld kingdom. Worried that his dark world might be laid open to the light of day, he mounted his chariot with the four black horses and came to the earth's surface to investigate.

In the midst of his travels, he was observed by Aphrodite, who immediately noticed his lack of a wife or lover, something she interpreted as a personal affront being that she was the goddess of love! Not wasting a second, Aphrodite called for her son, Eros (though most of us now refer to him on Valentine's Day as Cupid). She said: "My son, take your darts with which you conquer all, even Jove himself, and send one into the breast of yonder dark monarch, who rules the realm of the underworld. Why should he alone escape? Seize the opportunity to extend your empire and mine. Do you not see those who despise our power? Athena the wise, and Artemis the huntress, are still single; and there is that daughter of Demeter, who threatens to follow their example. I want you to join these two in one."

The boy unbound his quiver, and selected his sharpest and truest arrow; then, straining the bow against his knee, he attached the string, and, having made ready, shot the arrow with its barbed point right into the heart of Hades.

As Hades was shot, his chariot passed directly over Persephone, who was playing with her companions, gathering lilies and violets, and filling her basket and her apron with them. When Hades saw her from his chariot, it was love at first sight, and in the blink of an eye he carried her off to be his wife and queen. Of course, from Persephone's perspective, she was being kidnapped by a complete stranger. She screamed for help to her mother and her companions and begged Hades to let her go.

Text from Persephone to her mother, Demeter:

Reply text from Demeter to her daughter, Persephone:

Deaf to her pleas, Hades urged his steeds on. In fright, Persephone dropped the corners of her apron and let fall her gathered flowers, their loss an addition to her grief. Then Hades' chariot plunged towards earth and, though terrified, Persephone hoped death might release her from her kidnapper. But at the very last instant, before the chariot smashed into the ground, the earth opened up to Hades, clearing the way for him to return to his dark kingdom.

Demeter sought her daughter all the world over. Bright-haired Aurora aided the search when she came forth in the morning, and Hesperus looked as well when he led out the stars in the evening. Even though Persephone was with companions, no one told Demeter about Hades' brutal act of abduction or how the earth opened and then shut its greedy mouth upon them both. All of the bystanders were afraid of Hades' wrath were they to tell the truth. At length, weary and sad, Demeter sat down and wept, believing her daughter was gone forever.

Text from friend of Persephone's to other mutual friend:

Reply text from mutual friend to friend of Persephone's:

Donning the colors of mourning, Demeter's sorrow gave way to anger. She blamed everyone for the loss of her daughter. Always known for her nurturing since she was the goddess of the harvest, Demeter decided that mankind would suffer her loss with her. She broke the farmers' ploughs and bade the fields to betray their trust. Young crops died, destroyed by violent rain, unending drought, or freezing cold.

Just as it appeared mankind might perish from starvation, the waters of a stream took pity on the grieving mother and revealed Persephone's whereabouts. Describing its journey through fissures, crevices, and hidden channels, the stream revealed that Persephone was the prisoner of Hades, trapped in the darkness of the underworld.

Alarmed beyond belief, Demeter went straight to Zeus and demanded that he intervene. "The daughter I have sought so long is found. Her theft I'll bear if Hades will but bring her back; a thief, a kidnapper is no proper husband for my child."

Secretly, Zeus was deeply concerned over the fate of his worshippers. If mankind became extinct, the gods would be robbed of their sacrifices. But being the supreme god, Zeus was not about to reveal his fears and cede the upper hand to Demeter. Instead he countered, "The only crime I see from Hades is one of love and passion. Such a son-in-law should not disgrace you. To be Zeus's brother, what a splendid thing! But if your heart's so set to part them, Persephone shall reach the sky again on one condition, that her lips have touched no food."

Text from Zeus to his brother, Hades:

Reply text from Hades to his brother, Zeus:

Demeter readily agreed since she had warned Persephone never to partake of any food from strangers. Zeus immediately dispatched Hermes with a message demanding Persephone's immediate release.

A good six months had passed between Persephone's sudden abduction and her mother's negotiations with Zeus. Though frightened and despondent at first, Persephone slowly became accustomed to her new surroundings and her new husband. In fact, a love for Hades began to stir within her heart.

Text from Persephone to her BFF:

Reply text from BFF to Persephone:

For the longest time, Persephone refused any food Hades proffered, tempting though it was, hoping that she would soon be returned to her mother. Finally, her hunger became overwhelming, the likelihood of ever leaving the underworld became ever distant, and her distrust of Hades became a faded memory. When offered a pomegranate, her favorite fruit, she ate six seeds. Embracing his beloved queen, Hades now knew that their betrothal was eternal.

Text from Persephone to her mother, Demeter:

Reply text from Demeter to her daughter, Persephone:

Upon Hermes' arrival, Hades told him of the pomegranate seeds.

At first, it appeared that Persephone would never see her mother again, but Hades softened and a compromise was made, by which she was to pass half the time with her mother, and the rest with her husband. Demeter allowed herself to be pacified with this arrangement, and restored the earth to her favor.

Text from Persephone to her husband, Hades:

Reply text from Hades to his wife, Persephone:

404	I haven't a clue
AAMOF	As A Matter of Fact
AFAICS	As Far As I Can See
AITR	Adult In The Room
AWHFY	Are We Having Fun Yet?
BBIAF	Be Back In A Few
BIO	Bring It On
BTD	Bored To Death
BTDTGTS	Been There, Done That, Got The T-shirt
BWTM	But Wait, There's More
BYKT	But You Knew That
CSL	Can't Stop Laughing
CWOT	Complete Waste Of Time
DKDC	Don't Know Don't Care
DYJHIW	Don't You Just Hate It When . . .
G2G	Got to Go
HHOK	Ha Ha, Only Kidding
IGYHTBTI	Guess You Had To Be There
IJS	I'm Just Saying . . .
IYKWIM	If You Know What I Mean
JK	Just Kidding
LOL	Laughing Out Loud
LONH	Lights On, Nobody Home

MTF	More To Follow
NIMJD	Not In My Job Description
NTA	Not This Again
NUFF	Enough said
ONNA	Oh No, Not Again
POV	Point Of View
PTMM	Please Tell Me More
RU	Are You?
SUP	What's up?
THX	Thanks
TISL	This Is So Lame
TNTL	Trying Not To Laugh
WBS	Write Back Soon
WBU	What 'Bout You?
WDDD	Woopie Doo Da Dey
WE	Whatever
YGLT	You're Gonna Love This
YKW	You Know What?
YKWIM	You Know What I Mean
YSIC	Why Should I Care?
ZZZ	Sleeping, bored, tired

(From http://www.netlingo.com/acronyms.php)

LESSON 9.3 Opening Up a Poem

There's poetry that kids like. They like the poems they write and post on their blogs and Facebook pages. They like the poems their friends write and post on their blogs and Facebook pages. They like the poetry in the songs they listen to. They like poems that are easy to grasp and on topics they can relate to. They like poems that you don't have to read a million times.

And there's poetry kid say they "hate." They hate poems that sound old-timey. They hate poems that use words they don't understand. They hate poems where every line might mean something other than what it appears to mean. They hate poems with metaphors they can't figure out until the teacher tells them. You know what kind of poems kids think they hate? The kind of poems found in most of our literature anthologies. The kind of poem we have selected for this lesson.

Where do kids get this negative attitude? Well, maybe we should reread that Billy Collins poem called "Introduction to Poetry." You know, the one about how "they" tie a poem to a chair and beat a confession out of it? And the "they" in the poem are English teachers. Yeah, Collins is pretty harsh on us, probably because he loves poetry and takes it personally when we turn kids off with intense analysis. However, if we can turn kids into lifelong poetry lovers, we teachers of English will be happier in the long run, and so will Collins, because he will sell more books!

So let's begin at the beginning, with poetry's capacity to bring joy. Instead of jumping immediately to the Correct Interpretation, let's support kids to have some fun trying to crack a poetry nut and collaborate in seeking its meaning. In this lesson, the teacher only structures the discussion, never delivering an official reading. The goal is for the students, together, to make meaning.

TEXT ▶ "The Listeners," Walter de la Mare

TIME ▶ 50 Minutes

GROUPING SEQUENCE ▶ Whole class, groups of three, whole class

PREPARATION

Make a copy of "The Listeners" for each student. Determine how students will form trios for poem reading and discussion.

STEP 1 **Pass out poems and form trios.** *This poem was written in 1912. It's not exactly modern language, but it isn't Shakespeare either, so don't go into freak-out mode. The first thing to do in your group is read through it a few times. That's the nice thing about poems. Compared to a lot of stories and any novel, they're really short and easy to quickly reread. However, when you read the poem in your group, I want you to read it aloud. Poems are a genre of literature that is actually meant to be read aloud. Poets like to play with sound and rhythm as well as meaning. When you just read silently, you won't catch that stuff.*

◀ **Steps** & **Teaching Language**

- Read closely to determine what the text says explicitly and to make logical inferences from it; cite specific textual evidence when writing or speaking to support conclusions drawn from the text. *(CCRA.R.1)*

- Determine central ideas or themes of a text and analyze their development; summarize the key supporting details and ideas. *(CCRA.R.2)*

- Interpret words and phrases as they are used in a text, including determining connotative and figurative meanings. *(CCRA.R.4)*

- Participate effectively in a range of conversations and collaborations. *(CCRA.SL.1)*

- Demonstrate understanding of nuances in word meanings. *(CCRA.L.5)*

STEP 2 **Read the poem aloud.** *To get started, I want each member of the group to read the poem aloud once while the others follow along. Yes, that means that each group will read the poem aloud three times. As you read and reread the poem, I want you to think about what jumps out at you. What do you notice? Also think about who's speaking to whom. And when it's your turn to read, try to add a little interpretation; give it some energy. Any questions? Go!*

STEP 3 **Monitor reading.** Observe students and remind them to follow the read-aloud directions. As groups finish up their third reading, tell them to go ahead and talk about what they notice.

STEP 4 **Reread silently.** *You're going to stay in your groups for further discussion, but right now I want you to read through the poem silently. As you read, keep a mental inventory of the lines you think you understand. And by the parts that are confusing, jot down a question you can ask the others in your group to see what ideas/insights they have. If you are done before I call time, silently reread the poem again and see if you notice anything else.*

STEP 5 **Trios discuss.** *Go ahead and take a couple of minutes to talk about the lines and discuss the questions you've jotted down. Remember to hear from everyone; take turns leading the discussion and sharing ideas. See if you can build on what one another says in order to make meaning.*

STEP 6 **Monitor discussion.** Encourage students to take turns and read lines aloud as they discuss.

STEP 7 **Last discussion prompts.** *As I've been eavesdropping, I've heard some pretty interesting comments. For people who visibly drooped when I passed out this poem, you really perked up. I liked the way you were sharing ideas and going back to the lines to see if they made sense. There are just a couple last things I'd like you to talk about.*

- *What kind of emotion or feeling does this poem convey to you? Are there any lines or words in particular that reflect that feeling?*

- *What does the title have to do with the poem?*

- *Turn back to your group and take a couple minutes to discuss those questions.*

STEP 8 **Share out.** *Now it's time for us to hear what you talked about. What's one idea from your discussion that stood out?* Call at random or take some volunteers.

Craft and style: In this lesson, we did not address literary devices directly. It was enough for the kids to machete their way through to meaning. However, once students gain confidence in tackling more challenging works, by all means direct some of their conversation toward the metaphors, symbolism, and imagery. We just don't want to overwhelm them before they are ready.

◀ *Variation*

After you've practiced this strategy two or three times and students have gained some confidence in reading puzzling poems, look through your anthology and pick out three or four of equal length and equal difficulty. Then give a little sales pitch for each poem and have each group pick one. It's OK if more than one group picks the same one. The purpose is to give the kids some choice *and* cover some of the other poems on your curriculum "to do" list. After discussion, each group can come up to the front of the class and give a short talk on what's great about their poem and why others should read it. As you listen to the presentations, try to refrain from following up with the definitive interpretation. Applaud the kids' efforts and affirm some of the noticings that were on target. Remember that the goal of this activity is not 100 percent accurate interpretation. It's for the kids to investigate a poem and enjoy the process. In the end, wouldn't it be amazing if you saw a student sneaking a peek at the textbook without your intervention? It could happen.

◀ *Shoptalk*

The Listeners

Walter de la Mare

"Is there anybody there?" said the Traveller,
Knocking on the moonlit door;
And his horse in the silence champ'd the grasses
Of the forest's ferny floor:
And a bird flew up out of the turret,
Above the Traveller's head:
And he smote upon the door again a second time;
"Is there anybody there?" he said.
But no one descended to the Traveller;
No head from the leaf-fringed sill
Lean'd over and look'd into his grey eyes,
Where he stood perplex'd and still.
But only a host of phantom listeners
That dwelt in the lone house then
Stood listening in the quiet of the moonlight
To that voice from the world of men:
Stood thronging the faint moonbeams on the dark stair,
That goes down to the empty hall,
Hearkening in an air stirr'd and shaken
By the lonely Traveller's call.
And he felt in his heart their strangeness,
Their stillness answering his cry,
While his horse moved, cropping the dark turf,
'Neath the starr'd and leafy sky;
For he suddenly smote on the door, even
Louder, and lifted his head:—
"Tell them I came, and no one answer'd,
That I kept my word," he said.
Never the least stir made the listeners,
Though every word he spake
Fell echoing through the shadowiness of the still house
From the one man left awake:
Ay, they heard his foot upon the stirrup,
And the sound of iron on stone,
And how the silence surged softly backward,
When the plunging hoofs were gone.

LESSON 9.4 Stop, Think, and React

Our students owe Edgar Allan Poe so much! Without his nightmarish ideas of torture and revenge, movies like *Saw 1-7* might never have been made! No wonder almost every single basal anthology includes at least one Poe selection for young readers salivating at the chance to study at the long-buried feet of the master. We only wish Poe could return from the dead to receive his Deadtime Posthumous Achievement Award for his ultimate influence on horror/slasher films and their companion video games. Not to mention how much the *Law and Order* TV franchise owes Mister Poe for inventing the detective story.

But seriously, have you ever *really* had kids read Edgar Allan Poe word for word? It's tough. The sentences and syntax speak of 1840, the vocabulary is vast, the settings unfamiliar, the narrators wildly unreliable. Kids generally like the "idea" of reading Poe until they actually have to do it. However, Poe—and other equally difficult authors—is listed in the CCSS exemplar texts, as well as in the table of contents of your textbook. Now, we could teach these texts the "old fashioned way," and assign the story for homework. At least half the kids don't even bother doing the reading, while the other half give it their best shot but quickly move into reader space-out territory. The next day they report that they "read it but didn't get it" (thank you, Cris Tovani). In response, we go over the story line by line, paragraph by paragraph, explaining everything and having kids write notes about the ideas we thought of.

There's got to be a better way, right? Yes, there is. We need to give students the chance to work through challenging material collaboratively, while we take the role of coach and resource instead of Teller. There's a bit of work on the setup end, but once it's rolling, it's all kids, all the time.

TEXT ▶ "The Cask of Amontillado," by Edgar Allan Poe (Stop and Think edition)

TIME ▶ 50+ Minutes

GROUPING SEQUENCE ▶ Groups of three, whole class

USED IN TEXT SET ▶ 8

PREPARATION

Copy our special version of "The Cask of Amontillado" for each student. It may already be in your textbook, but you will want ours, which you can print from our website.

Reread the story and determine what background knowledge kids will need to picture the setting and understand the plot. Remember, the Common Core Standards say it's just fine to preteach and build background knowledge when a text is difficult, old, or alien from kids' experience:

When necessary, extra textual scaffolding prior to and during the first read should focus on words and concepts that are essential to a basic understanding and that students are not likely to know or be able to determine from context. (CCSS Publishers Guidelines, May 12, 2012, p. 8)

To enter this Poe story successfully, most kids would benefit from a quick slide show of the time, era, and culture. To create this, Google:

- Catacombs in Italy
- Catacombs in Rome
- Dusty wine cellars
- Carnival in Italy
- Court jester costumes

Reread the story for vocabulary and think about which words you'll definitely need to preteach, which ones can slide, and which ones you should be ready to explain if a group asks. We'd say the five words kids definitely need to know up front are: *impunity*, *avenge*, *redress*, *amontillado*, and *masons*. In the story, we put those words in italics. You may find others.

Be ready to project the reading directions described in Step 3 and summarized at the end of this lesson.

Determine how trios will form for their think-aloud.

Steps & ▶ Teaching Language

STEP 1 **Pass out the story and introduce the setting. Show slides.** *Today you're going to be working in trios reading an Edgar Allan Poe story. I know you are all familiar with Poe, but you might not have ever sat down and carefully read one of his stories. They can be kind of challenging, but that's why you're going to be reading together instead of alone. Also, I'll give your group a hand if you have a question. But first, I want to show you some photos that will help you picture the setting.* Show and explain slides of carnival, catacombs, and court jester.

STEP 2 **Read the title and first paragraph aloud and define vocabulary words.** Have students mark these words (*impunity*, *avenge*, *redress*, *amontillado*, and *mason*) and jot down the definitions in the margin.

STEP 3 **Organize trios and explain directions.** *As I mentioned earlier, Poe can offer some challenging but interesting reading. How many of you have seen one of those* Saw *movies? Show hands. Anybody ever play the video game? Show hands. Believe it or not,* Saw *and a lot of other movies are indebted to Mister Poe, so when you read this story today, I want you to think about that. See if you can find the connection between* Saw *and "The Cask of Amontillado."*

Now take a look at the story while I explain the directions. Today, rather than reading this story straight through, you are going to take turns in your trio reading aloud while the other group members follow along. Each time you get to a broken line, I want you to stop and talk about the following:

- *Where are they—what setting details connect with the slides?*
- *Who are the characters and what do the story details reveal about them? What's their motivation to act as they do?*

- *What's going on? How is the story progressing? How do the characters and the setting tie into the plot?*

As you talk about these questions, jot down your thoughts on the story by that part. When you've finished discussing a section, it's the next person's turn to read. Continue this process until you are done with the story or until I call time. If you run across a word or a passage you are having trouble with, put an X by it and continue working. I'll be ghosting around the room, checking in with the groups. When I stop by, I'll be happy to give you a hand. Any questions? OK then, let's get to work.

STEP 4 **Monitor while groups read and think aloud.** Observe the groups, give a hand, remind members to read aloud, talk, jot notes.

STEP 5 **Homework.** This process is somewhat laborious and time consuming, so it is likely that students may need to finish a page or two for homework. *It looks like we're running out of time, and you'll need to finish this for homework. Though now you'll be reading on your own, I think you have a good command of the setting, characters, and plot so that you'll have no problem working alone on the last part. However, I still want you to follow the same format we were using in class. At the end of each broken line, stop reading and jot down some notes about how the setting, characters, and plot are tying together. Be sure to finish the reading since you'll be getting back into your groups tomorrow for a wrap-up discussion.*

STEP 6 **Concluding discussion.** *With your trio, talk about these questions:*

What kind of person is Montresor? How do you know?

What ironies exist in the story? How is the ending ironic?

What's the connection between Saw *and "The Cask of Amontillado"?*

STEP 7 **Share out.** End with a brief whole-class share. Remember, this doesn't have to be long, just enough to ascertain that the kids understood this revenge story in detail. Also, be sure to ask how the collaboration and the reading aloud helped ensure better understanding of the story.

◀ *Variation*

Stop and think marks: Once students are familiar with the idea of stopping to think at specific points while reading, you can determine these points for any story you assign. If the reading is not consumable—like in the textbook—pass out sticky notes and tell students where to stop and leave tracks of their thinking, hanging the notes right off the book edge. Designating specific places to stop and think is particularly important with challenging pieces, when students need to heighten their internal monitoring. Otherwise, kids may not catch their space-outs quickly, and will continue running their eyes over paragraphs or even pages they are not comprehending.

COMMON CORE STANDARDS SUPPORTED

- Read closely to determine what the text says explicitly and to make logical inferences from it; cite specific textual evidence when writing or speaking to support conclusions drawn from the text. *(CCRA.R.1)*

- Determine central ideas or themes of a text and analyze their development; summarize the key supporting details and ideas. *(CCRA.R.2)*

- Analyze how and why individuals, events, and ideas develop and interact over the course of a text. *(CCRA.R.3)*

- Interpret words and phrases as they are used in a text, including determining connotative and figurative meanings. *(CCRA.R.4)*

- Participate effectively in a range of conversations and collaborations. *(CCRA.SL.1)*

- Determine or clarify the meaning of unknown and multiple-meaning words and phrases by using context clues. *(CCRA.L.4)*

We chose to include "The Cask of Amontillado" because it is a shorter Poe piece, it's found in many literature textbook anthologies, and it's about wine. We're both into wine, though neither of us is a big fan of sherry. (That was a "distracting connection," right out of Lesson 4.2, for those of you keeping score.) We also realize that it does not qualify as a "fresh mentor text," as promised on the book's cover.

Anyway, your students may have other challenging, classic pieces in your textbook or curriculum to cover. Pretty much everything published before 1923 is public domain and available on the web. If you've got some tough older pieces you end up teaching year after year, we recommend grabbing that text and creating your own personally abridged pieces. We're not talking about "dumbing down the text"; we're mainly about shortening it up, making verbose writing styles (like Poe's) a bit more concise. Yes, we know this is going to take some time, but if you've taught the piece a million times already, you *so* totally know how you'd edit it given the chance. And guess what? That chance is now. And don't feel guilty at all. The CCSS frequently recommend that students read excerpts versus whole works.

Another option: summarizing some of the text and then digging into a portion of it just as the author wrote it. This lets kids work with difficult language in manageable chunks, without feeling like they're going to drown in it because it just keeps going on forever.

The Cask of Amontillado

Edgar Allan Poe (adapted)

The thousand injuries of Fortunato I had borne as I best could, but when he ventured upon insult, I vowed revenge. You, who so well know the nature of my soul, will not suppose, however, that I gave utterance to a threat. At length I would be avenged; this was a point definitively settled—but the very definitiveness with which it was resolved precluded the idea of risk. I must not only punish, but punish with impunity. A wrong is unredressed when retribution overtakes its redresser. It is equally unredressed when the avenger fails to make himself felt as such to him who has done the wrong.

It must be understood that neither by word nor deed had I given Fortunato cause to doubt my good will. I continued as was my wont, to smile in his face, and he did not perceive that my smile now was at the thought of his immolation.

He had a weak point—this Fortunato—although in other regards he was a man to be respected and even feared. He prided himself on his connoisseurship in wine. Few Italians have the true virtuoso spirit. For the most part their enthusiasm is adopted to suit the time and opportunity to practice imposture upon the British and Austrian millionaires. In painting and gemmary, Fortunato, like his countrymen, was a quack, but in the matter of old wines he was sincere. In this respect I did not differ from him materially; I was skilful in the Italian vintages myself, and bought largely whenever I could.

It was about dusk, one evening during the supreme madness of the carnival season, that I encountered my friend. He accosted me with excessive warmth, for he had been drinking much. The man wore motley. He had on a tight-fitting parti-striped dress and his head was surmounted by the conical cap and bells. I was so pleased to see him that I thought I should never have done wringing his hand.

I said to him—"My dear Fortunato, you are luckily met. How remarkably well you are looking to-day! But I have received a pipe of what passes for Amontillado, and I have my doubts."

"How?" said he, "Amontillado? A *pipe*? Impossible! And in the middle of the carnival?"

"I have my doubts," I replied; "and I was silly enough to pay the full Amontillado price without consulting you in the matter. You were not to be found, and I was fearful of losing a bargain."

"Amontillado!"

"I have my doubts."

"Amontillado!"

"And I must satisfy them."

"Amontillado!"

"As you are engaged, I am on my way to Luchesi. If anyone has a critical turn, it is he. He will tell me—"

"Luchesi cannot tell Amontillado from Sherry."

"And yet some fools will have it that his taste is a match for your own."

"Come let us go."

"Whither?"

"To your vaults."

"My friend, no; I will not impose upon your good nature. I perceive you have an engagement. Luchesi—"

"I have no engagement; come."

"My friend, no. It is not the engagement, but the severe cold with which I perceive you are afflicted. The vaults are insufferably damp. They are encrusted with nitre."

"Let us go, nevertheless. The cold is merely nothing. Amontillado! You have been imposed upon; and as for Luchesi, he cannot distinguish Sherry from Amontillado."

Thus speaking, Fortunato possessed himself of my arm. Putting on a mask of black silk and drawing a roquelaire closely about my person, I suffered him to hurry me to my palazzo.

There were no attendants at home; they had absconded to make merry in honour of the time. I had told them that I should not return until the morning and had given them explicit orders not to stir from the house. These orders were sufficient, I well knew, to insure their immediate disappearance, one and all, as soon as my back was turned.

I took from their sconces two flambeaux, and giving one to Fortunato bowed him through several suites of rooms to the archway that led into the vaults. I passed down a long and winding staircase, requesting him to be cautious as he followed. We came at length to the foot of the descent, and stood together on the damp ground of the catacombs of the Montresors.

The *gait* of my friend was unsteady, and the bells upon his cap jingled as he strode.

"The pipe," said he.

"It is farther on," said I; "but observe the white webwork which gleams from these cavern walls."

He turned towards me and looked into my eyes with two filmy orbs that distilled the rheum of intoxication.

"Nitre?" he asked, at length.

"Nitre," I replied. "How long have you had that cough!"

"Ugh! ugh! ugh! — ugh! ugh! ugh! — ugh! ugh! ugh! — ugh! ugh! ugh! — ugh! ugh! ugh!"

My poor friend found it impossible to reply for many minutes.

"It is nothing," he said, at last.

"Come," I said, with decision, "we will go back; your health is precious. You are rich, respected, admired, beloved; you are happy as once I was. You are a man to be missed. For me it is no matter. We will go back; you will be ill and I cannot be responsible. Besides, there is Luchesi—"

"Enough," he said; "the cough is a mere nothing; it will not kill me. I shall not die of a cough."

"True—true," I replied; "and, indeed, I had no intention of alarming you unnecessarily—but you should use all proper caution. A draught of this Medoc will defend us from the damps."

Here I knocked off the neck of a bottle which I drew from a long row of its fellows that lay upon the mould.

"Drink," I said, presenting him the wine.

He raised it to his lips with a leer. He paused and nodded to me familiarly, while his bells jingled.

"I drink," he said, "to the buried that repose around us."

"And I to your long life."

He again took my arm and we proceeded.

"These vaults," he said, "are extensive."

"The Montresors," I replied, "were a great numerous family."

"I forget your arms."

"A huge human foot d'or, in a field azure; the foot crushes a serpent rampant whose fangs are imbedded in the heel."

"And the motto?"

"Nemo me impune lacessit." [no one attacks me with impunity]

"Good!" he said.

The wine sparkled in his eyes and the bells jingled. My own fancy grew warm with the Medoc. We had passed through walls of piled bones, with casks and puncheons intermingling, into the inmost recesses of the catacombs. I paused again, and this time I made bold to seize Fortunato by an arm above the elbow.

"The nitre!" I said: see it increases. It hangs like moss upon the vaults. We are below the river's bed. The drops of moisture trickle among the bones. Come, we will go back ere it is too late. Your cough—"

"It is nothing" he said; "let us go on. But first, another draught of the Medoc."

I broke and reached him a flagon of De Grave. He emptied it at a breath. His eyes flashed with a fierce light. He laughed and threw the bottle upwards with a gesticulation I did not understand.

I looked at him in surprise. He repeated the movement—a grotesque one.

"You do not comprehend?" he said.

"Not I," I replied.

"Then you are not of the brotherhood."

"How?"

"You are not of the masons."

"Yes, yes," I said; "yes! yes."

"You? Impossible! A mason?"

"A mason," I replied.

"A sign," he said.

"It is this," I answered, producing a trowel from beneath the folds of my roquelaire.

"You jest," he exclaimed, recoiling a few paces. "But let us proceed to the Amontillado."

"Be it so," I said, replacing the tool beneath the cloak, and again offering him my arm. He leaned upon it heavily. We continued our route in search of the Amontillado. We passed through a range of low arches, descended, passed on, and descending again, arrived at a deep crypt, in which the foulness of the air caused our flambeaux rather to glow than flame.

At the most remote end of the crypt there appeared another less spacious. Its walls had been lined with human remains piled to the vault overhead, in the fashion of the great catacombs of Paris. Three sides of this interior crypt were still ornamented in this manner. From the fourth the bones had been thrown down, and lay promiscuously upon the earth, forming at one point a mound of some size. Within the wall thus exposed by the displacing of the bones, we perceived a still interior recess, in depth about four feet, in width three, in height six or seven. It seemed to have been constructed for no especial use in itself, but formed merely the interval between two of the colossal supports of the roof of the catacombs, and was backed by one of their circumscribing walls of solid granite.

It was in vain that Fortunato, uplifting his dull torch, endeavored to pry into the depths of the recess. Its termination the feeble light did not enable us to see.

"Proceed," I said; "herein is the Amontillado. As for Luchesi—"

"He is an ignoramus," interrupted my friend, as he stepped unsteadily forward, while I followed immediately at his heels. In an instant he had reached the extremity of the niche, and finding his progress arrested by the rock, stood stupidly bewildered. A moment more and I had fettered him to the granite. In its surface were two iron staples, distant from each other about two feet, horizontally. From one of these depended a short chain, from the other a padlock. Throwing the links about his waist, it was but the work of a few seconds to secure it. He was too much astounded to resist. Withdrawing the key I stepped back from the recess.

"Pass your hand," I said, "over the wall; you cannot help feeling the nitre. Indeed it is very damp. Once more let me implore you to return. No? Then I must positively leave you. But I must first render you all the little attentions in my power."

"The Amontillado!" ejaculated my friend, not yet recovered from his astonishment.

"True," I replied; "the Amontillado."

As I said these words I busied myself among the pile of bones of which I have before spoken. Throwing them aside, I soon uncovered a quantity of building stone and mortar. With these materials and with the aid of my trowel, I began vigorously to wall up the entrance of the niche.

I had scarcely laid the first tier of my masonry when I discovered that the intoxication of Fortunato had in a great measure worn off. The earliest indication I had of this was a low moaning cry from the depth of the recess. It was NOT the cry of a drunken man. There was then a long and obstinate silence. I laid the second tier, and the third, and the fourth; and then I heard the furious vibrations of the chain. The noise lasted for several minutes, during which, that I might hearken to it with the more satisfaction, I ceased my labours and sat down upon the bones. When at last the clanking subsided, I resumed the trowel, and finished without interruption the fifth, the sixth, and the seventh tier. The wall was now nearly upon a level with my breast. I again paused, and holding the flambeaux over the mason-work, threw a few feeble rays upon the figure within.

A succession of loud and shrill screams, bursting suddenly from the throat of the chained form, seemed to thrust me violently back. For a brief moment I hesitated—I trembled. Unsheathing my rapier, I began to grope with it about the recess; but the thought of an instant reassured me. I placed my hand upon the solid fabric of the catacombs, and felt satisfied. I reapproached the wall. I replied to the yells of him who clamored. I reechoed—I aided—I surpassed them in volume and in strength. I did this, and the clamorer grew still.

It was now midnight, and my task was drawing to a close. I had completed the eighth, the ninth, and the tenth tier. I had finished a portion of the last and the eleventh; there remained but a single stone to be fitted and plastered in. I struggled with its weight; I placed it partially in its destined position. But now there came from out the niche a low laugh that erected the hairs upon my head. It was succeeded by a sad voice, which I had difficulty in recognizing as that of the noble Fortunato. The voice said—

"Ha! ha! ha!—he! he!—a very good joke indeed—an excellent jest. We will have many a rich laugh about it at the palazzo—he! he! he!—over our wine—he! he! he!"

"The Amontillado!" I said.

"He! he! he!—he! he! he!—yes, the Amontillado. But is it not getting late? Will not they be awaiting us at the palazzo, the Lady Fortunato and the rest? Let us be gone."

"Yes," I said, "let us be gone."

"FOR THE LOVE OF GOD, MONTRESOR!"

"Yes," I said, "for the love of God!"

But to these words I hearkened in vain for a reply. I grew impatient. I called aloud—

"Fortunato!"

No answer. I called again—

"Fortunato!"

No answer still. I thrust a torch through the remaining aperture and let it fall within. There came forth in return only a jingling of the bells. My heart grew sick—on account of the dampness of the catacombs. I hastened to make an end of my labor. I forced the last stone into its position; I plastered it up. Against the new masonry I re-erected the old rampart of bones. For the half of a century no mortal has disturbed them.

In pace requiescat! [rest in peace]

LESSON 9.5 Reading with Expression

As English teachers, we get plenty of time on stage. And when we are up there modeling our thinking, it's time well spent. But we also want kids performing, a lot. If we want them to get better at things like reading aloud with expression, *they* must be the ones doing the interpretive planning and testing out their readings before an attentive audience.

For this excursion into interpretation, we've chosen an abridged version of the "Witches Chant" from *Macbeth*. If you've been looking over the Common Core Standards (who hasn't?), Shakespeare comes up quite a bit. This excerpt is a playful way to introduce or reengage kids with the bard. Plus, if you save this lesson for Halloween (always one of the craziest days of the year in school), you'll have a standards-based way of channeling the sugar buzz in your room.

TEXT ▶ "Witches' Chant" from *Macbeth*, William Shakespeare

TIME ▶ 50 Minutes

GROUPING SEQUENCE ▶ Groups of three or four, whole class

USED IN TEXT SETS ▶ 2, 6, 7

PREPARATION

Make a copy of the "Witches' Chant" for each student. Place students in their groups of three or four before the lesson starts.

This lesson assumes that you'd have kids learn the witches' chant without first having read the play. If that's the deal, practice telling the story of Macbeth yourself so you can set the context. We've included a heavily edited synopsis; if you memorize the main details and then tell it as a story, it will be most effective. Just a little more legwork: Google some images—cauldron, harpy, hedgehog, adder—that will help you define key vocabulary in Step 3.

**◀ Steps &
Teaching
Language**

STEP 1 **Tell the story of Macbeth.** *Today we're going to look at an excerpt from the Shakespeare play* Macbeth. *However, in order for you to understand the context, I need to briefly tell you the plot of this play.* Then synopsize, drawing on the summary on page 221.

STEP 2 **Pass out the "Witches Chant."** *This is from the scene when the witches give Macbeth their prophecies regarding Birnam Wood and Macbeth's invincibility. As Macbeth approaches them, he overhears the witches talking about a recipe they are in the act of cooking up.*

STEP 3 **Groups do first reading.** *With your group, read this piece aloud a couple of times and figure out what the witches are talking about. Don't try to read the whole thing through at once. Stop every few lines and discuss. On the second reading, be sure to circle any words that you have not been able to define.* Allow a good five minutes as you circulate and provide support.

STEP 4 **Regather and discuss vocabulary.** *What words were you having trouble with?* Make a list of those words on the board toward the side and discuss. Keep your projection area clear to show some pictures you've retrieved from Google Images: cauldron, harpy, hedgehog, adder.

STEP 5 **Mark image words.** *Now that we've discussed the unfamiliar words, I want you to read the chant aloud again and mark the words your group thinks are the most powerful, the ones that really conjure up vivid sensory images.*

STEP 6 **Practice reading aloud.** *With your group, practice reading this piece aloud expressively. In a few minutes, your group is going to come up and read in front of the class. Think about how you are going to read the lines so that you seriously sound like witches. But instead of just changing your voice to sound like the Wicked Witch of the West from* The Wizard of Oz, *instead think about how to say those really important words you marked earlier so their power reaches the audience. What are good places to pause, so that a word or line can sink in? Also, discuss each line with your group and agree on the interpretation. Then mark down your notes on each copy.*

STEP 7 **Divide lines.** *Now that you've determined your interpretation, you need to figure out your solo parts. Read the lines marked "all" together, but the other parts I want you to evenly divide so that all of you have an equal number of solo lines. There are tons of different ways to split up those lines, so be creative.*

STEP 8 **Practice applause.** *All of you have seen a television show filmed before a live audience, like* Saturday Night Live, Conan O'Brien, Tosh.0, *or* The Big Bang Theory. *Though the audiences are definitely enjoying the shows, they have rehearsed their responses beforehand because their enthusiastic applause helps the actors. Today we want to help everyone in this room do a great job. When each performance is finished, I'm going to say, "Big round of applause!" and that's when you clap loudly. Let's give it a try.* Practice until they kids have got it right. *All right, that sounds great. Remember to make it sound just like this when I give you the cue.*

STEP 9 **Listen to performances.** Take volunteers or choose randomly. Remind students to listen attentively and save the applause for the cue. Listeners can offer feedback along the lines of "One thing you did really well" or "One thing that made your reading different was . . ."

Variations ▶

- **Characterization:** If you want to spend a little more time on this, have students fill out the Character Resume sheet where they'll create a name and character profile for their witch. This profile should inform how each student interprets the lines to reflect his/her witch's personality.

- **Fleshing out characters:** The Character Resume can be used to help kids get to know characters in just about any literary work, especially characters that are a little flat—the perfect women in Dickens' novels, the folktale-ish good people and bad people in early American literature, the distant and out-to-lunch adults in YA novels.

- **Branching out:** Once students understand the steps of developing an interpretive reading, expand to longer poems where each pair or group reads a different stanza. Putting all the performances together creates the entire poem; no group repeats a part. Poems that tell a story work best for this purpose. A couple of accessible classics are "Casey at the Bat" by Ernest Thayer or "The Highwayman" by Alfred Noyes. A more contemporary piece is Dean Koontz's children's book called *Santa's Twin*. It's a very adolescent-appealing story about Santa's evil twin kidnapping the *real* Santa and then really messing with the kids. Think Grinch on steroids.

◀ *Shoptalk*

Audio and video recordings of the "Witches' Chant" abound on the web. We'd love to recommend one or two, but the quality (at least as we go to press) ranges from poor to execrable. Maybe your students can make a breakthrough and post a performance that becomes the gold standard!

There's a whole "performance poetry" movement out here that is very attractive to many of today's teenagers. Sara Holbrook and Michael Salinger, who each have several poems in this book, are leaders in that world, and have written several books for teachers (see Chapter 12) on how to bring live poetry to school and integrate it with the curriculum.

"Witches Chant" from *Macbeth* (abridged)

William Shakespeare

A dark Cave. In the middle, a caldron boils. Thunder.

Thrice the brinded cat hath mewed.
Thrice and once, the hedge-pig whined.
Harpier cries:—'tis time! 'tis time!

Round about the caldron go;
In the poisoned entrails throw.—
Toad, that under cold stone,
Days and nights has thirty-one;
Sweltered venom sleeping got,
Boil thou first in the charmed pot!

[ALL.] Double, double toil and trouble;
     Fire burn, and caldron bubble.

Fillet of a fenny snake,
In the caldron boil and bake;
Eye of newt, and toe of frog,
Wool of bat, and tongue of dog,
Adder's fork, and blind-worm's sting,
Lizard's leg, and owlet's wing,—
For a charm of powerful trouble,
Like a hell-broth boil and bubble.

[ALL.] Double, double toil and trouble;
     Fire burn, and caldron bubble.

Cool it with a baboon's blood,
Now the charm is firm and good.

Macbeth Plot Overview

Following a battle defending Scotland, Macbeth encounters three witches who prophesy that Macbeth will eventually become king. Macbeth is skeptical.

However, when Macbeth talks to his wife, Lady Macbeth, she is all about making the prophecy a reality and encourages Macbeth to murder King Duncan and take the throne. The plan works, Macbeth assumes kingship, and Duncan's sons flee the country, fearing that whoever killed Duncan will want to kill them as well.

Insecure in his power, Macbeth returns to the witches for advice. First they warn him about Macduff, a Scottish nobleman who hates Macbeth's rule. But then the witches calm Macbeth's fears by telling him that no man born of woman can kill him and that he will be king until Birnam Wood, the forest outside of his castle, moves. Since all men are born of women and that forest has been in the same spot for hundreds of years, Macbeth leaves feeling pretty good. Yet just to be on the safe side, he attacks and murders Macduff's family; unfortunately, Macduff, the guy Macbeth *really* wants to kill, happens to be out of town.

Of course, when Macduff hears what happened to his family, he starts planning a war of revenge, enlisting Prince Malcolm, the son of King Duncan, whom Macbeth had murdered to get the throne in the first place. In the meantime, Lady Macbeth is finally starting to feel guilty about all the murders and develops obsessive-compulsive disorder, spending most of her days trying to wash the "blood" off her hands. When the soap doesn't work, she commits suicide. Though Macbeth is pretty depressed over his wife's sudden death, he's still confident that, based on the witches' prophecy, he will triumph over the impending army attack. But witches are tricky. As the army approaches Macbeth's castle, they camouflage themselves with branches from the forest, so technically Birnam Wood moves! This fulfills half of the witches' prophecy and the army invades Macbeth's castle.

Macbeth ends up in hand-to-hand combat against Macduff. When Macbeth tells Macduff that he is invincible thanks to the witches' prophecy, Macduff laughs bitterly and gives Macbeth the news: Macduff's mother died in childbirth and he was delivered by cesarean so therefore, technically, he was not born of woman. Macbeth is like, "What?" but continues fighting until Macduff gains the advantage and beheads him. Afterwards, Prince Malcolm, the rightful heir, takes the throne of Scotland. The End.

May be photocopied for classroom use. *Texts and Lessons for Teaching Literature* by Harvey "Smokey" Daniels and Nancy Steineke, © 2013 (Portsmouth, NH: Heinemann).

CHARACTER RESUME

Witch's Name _____

1. Favorite actor: _____

2. Favorite movie: _____

3. One thing I do very well: _____

4. Favorite Internet site: _____

5. If I had $100, I'd spend it on: _____

6. Favorite outfit: _____

7. I am known for: _____

8. Sometimes I worry about: _____

9. An important goal for me: _____

10. Favorite vacation spot: _____

11. Best gift ever given: _____

12. Best gift ever received: _____

13. Favorite food: _____

Now we offer you eight teaching units built around collections of two to five readings, each one addressing a powerful and important literary theme.

Readings. Unlike the strategy lesson pieces, these thirty are more diverse, ranging over many genres and occasionally venturing into nonfiction territory. Some are also more mature than earlier selections, and we have marked them as such. Most readings are right here in the book; a few need to be grabbed from the web, and we supply links on our website.

Instructions and directions. Every text set is built on a sequence of lessons from the first part of the book. (We indicate where each one comes up and give the page number for quick reference.) Because all the lessons have already been described, the instructions here can be quite concise. Any teaching language you might need is found back in the lessons, and in the few spots where any new "connective tissue" is needed, we provide it right here.

Standards correlations. Throughout the book, we have shown how each lesson meets certain Common Core Standards for 6–12 Reading, Writing, Speaking and Listening, and Language. The upcoming text set lessons do similar work, but on steroids. Each of these multitext lessons meets most—sometimes all—of the Reading anchor standards. And every one involves active and sustained speaking and listening activities centered on challenging texts.

Make it your own. These units can ignite all kinds of extensions, variations, explorations, and inquiries. The plans we offer are just jumping-off points, waiting for your unique adaptations, twists, and flourishes.

Memory

▶ *Texts Used*

TITLE	AUTHOR	GENRE	WHERE TO FIND IT
Kennedy in the Barrio	Judith Ortiz Cofer	story	page 226
Excerpt from the Warren Commission Report	Warren Commission	nonfiction	page 227
Announcement of President Kennedy's Death	Walter Cronkite	video	http://www.youtube.com/ /watch?v=2K8Q3cqGs7L or search "Cronkite" + "Kennedy Assassination" (make sure you have the six-minute version)

Why These Selections?

The Kennedy assassination. Everyone who was alive on that day—and many who weren't—have a personal story about it. Judith Ortiz Cofer gives us a child's eye view of this monumental event as it rippled through an immigrant community. Cofer's story is a classic and highly compressed demonstration of how authors use historical materials to create literary works. The Warren Commission excerpt occupies a nearly opposite genre—it is almost technical nonfiction focused on facts, not feelings. (Of course, there is still controversy over whether the Warren Commission actually did get to the truth of the assassination.) Finally, the archival black-and-white footage of Walter Cronkite's announcement is about as dramatic as primary source documents can get. His broadcast is literally what those people in the second half of Cofer's story are watching, huddled around their TV. We prefer the longer, six-minute version, because its early, wide shots reveal the near chaos in the newsroom, and allow you to see Cronkite exercising his editorial judgment as conflicting and unconfirmed reports pour in.

Lesson Suggestions

1. **View the Cronkite video.** Have kids use Two-Column Notes (Lesson 6.3, page 112) to capture their responses while viewing: *On the left side, jot down what you are seeing, hearing, and noticing. Pay special attention to the process of the newsroom and to Cronkite's exact words. On the right-hand side, jot down any questions, wonderings or uncertainties you have.*

2. **Prepare to read the Warren Commission excerpt.** Have kids review their questions in the right-hand column. They will probably have plenty since the Kennedy assassination happened at least thirty-five years before they were born. Build upon these to create a whole-class list of questions people have about the assassination.

3. **Read the Warren Commission excerpt.** Have students read with the class-made question list in mind (Lesson 4.4, page 51). Have them make check marks in the text margin as questions are answered. Invite discussion, and pay attention to questions that are *not* answered. (If there is significant energy for lingering questions, kids could spin off into inquiry circle groups for some quick online research. Quick, because this stuff can be addictive and we probably do not want to turn our kids into obsessed conspiracy theorists.)

4. **Read and synthesize the Cofer story.** Read the text using Drawing Text Details (Lesson 4.3, page 47). *Try to make a picture of Elenita, either at the Puerto Habana or back at the apartment. Share with a classmate.*

5. **Synthesize.** After rereading text, have students create a note that Elenita might have sent to a friend that night (today it might be an email), as she is sitting alone and trying to sort out her feelings from the day.

6. **Whole-class discussion.** *Consider how all three documents provide different parts of the picture of November 22, 1963. How do these different sources help you think about these questions?*

   Her family and friends' reaction to the assassination seemed overwhelming to Elenita. Do you think this Puerto Rican family and their friends were more upset than other Americans or immigrants?

   How do you think other groups and families reacted? Are there any stories about the Kennedy assassination from your own family?

   What does it say about Elenita that she has to escape?

   Why on this of all nights did her mother let her walk alone?

   How do people react to a national tragedy? How and why might people's reactions change over time?

   Even if we live through world-changing historical events, what we remember is always us, ourselves, our own reactions and feelings, and those of the people around us at that time. Has there been a public event that changed you? Or can you imagine one that *could* change you?

Kennedy in the Barrio

Judith Ortiz Cofer

My sixth-grade class had been assigned to watch the Kennedy inauguration on television and I did at the counter of Puerto Habana, the restaurant where my father worked. I heard the Cuban owner Larry Reyes say that an Irish Catholic being elected meant that someday an Hispano could be president of the United States too. I saw my father nod in automatic agreement with his boss, but his eyes were not on the grainy screen; he was mainly concerned with the food cooking in the back and with the listless waitress mopping the floor. Larry Reyes turned his attention to me then and raised his cup as if to make a toast: "Here's to a puertorriqueño or puertorriqueña president of the United States," he laughed, not kindly I thought.

"Right. Elenita?"

I shrugged my shoulders. Later my father would once again reprimand me for not showing Mr. Reyes the proper respect.

Two years and ten months later I would run to Puerto Habana on a cold Friday afternoon to find a crowd of people around the television set. Many of them, men and women both, were sobbing like children. "Dios mio, Dios mio," they kept wailing. A group of huddling women tried to embrace me as I made my way to my parents, who were holding each other tightly, apart from the others. I slipped in between them. I smelled her scent of castile soap, cafe con leche, and cinnamon; I inhaled his mixture of sweat and Old Spice cologne—a man-smell that I was afraid to like too much.

That night at Puerto Habana Larry Reyes and my father served free food. Both of them wore black armbands. My mother cooked and I bussed tables. An old woman started reciting the rosary aloud, and soon practically everyone was kneeling on that hard linoleum floor, praying and sobbing for our dead President. Exhausted from the outpouring of public grief and exasperated by the displays of uncontrolled emotion I had witnessed that day, the *ay benditos,* the kisses and embraces of strangers I had had to endure, I asked if I could go home early. For the first time in my life, my vigilant mother trusted me to walk alone at night without the usual lecture about the dangers of the streets. The dark, empty silence of our apartment gave me no solace, and in a turmoil of emotions I had never experienced before, I went to sleep the night of the day President Kennedy died. I rose the next day to a world that looked the same.

Excerpt from the Warren Commission Report (1964)

Narrative of Events

www.archives.gov/research/jfk/warren-commission-report/chapter-1.html

At 11:40 a.m., CST, on Friday, November 22, 1963, President John F. Kennedy, Mrs. Kennedy, and their party arrived at Love Field, Dallas, Texas. Planned for later that day were a motorcade through downtown Dallas, a luncheon speech at the Trade Mart, and a flight to Austin where the President would attend a reception and speak at a Democratic fundraising dinner. From Austin he would proceed to the Texas ranch of the Vice President. Evident on this trip were the varied roles which an American President performs—Head of State, Chief Executive, party leader, and, in this instance, prospective candidate for reelection.

By midmorning of November 22, clearing skies in Dallas dispelled the threat of rain and the President greeted the crowds from his open limousine without the "bubbletop," which was at that time a plastic shield furnishing protection only against inclement weather. To the left of the President in the rear seat was Mrs. Kennedy. In the jump seats were Governor Connally, who was in front of the President, and Mrs. Connally at the Governor's left. Agent William R. Greer of the Secret Service was driving, and Agent Roy H. Kellerman was sitting to his right.

Directly behind the Presidential limousine was an open "follow-up" car with eight Secret Service agents, two in the front seat, two in the rear, and two on each running board. These agents, in accordance with normal Secret Service procedures, were instructed to scan the crowds, the roofs, and windows of buildings, overpasses, and crossings for signs of trouble. Behind the "follow-up" car was the Vice-Presidential car carrying the Vice President and Mrs. Johnson and Senator Ralph W. Yarborough. Next were a Vice-Presidential "follow-up" car and several cars and buses for additional dignitaries, press representatives, and others.

The President's car which had been going north made a sharp turn toward the southwest onto Elm Street. At a speed of about 11 miles per hour, it started down the gradual descent toward a railroad overpass under which the motorcade would proceed before reaching the Stemmons Freeway. The front of the Texas School

Book Depository was now on the President's right, and he waved to the crowd assembled there as he passed the building. Dealey Plaza—an open, landscaped area marking the western end of downtown Dallas stretched out to the President's left. A Secret Service agent riding in the motorcade radioed the Trade Mart that the President would arrive in 5 minutes

Seconds later shots resounded in rapid succession. The President's hands moved to his neck. He appeared to stiffen momentarily and lurch slightly forward in his seat. A bullet had entered the base of the back of his neck slightly to the right of the spine. It traveled downward and exited from the front of the neck, causing a nick in the left lower portion of the knot in the President's necktie. Before the shooting started, Governor Connally had been facing toward the crowd on the right. He started to turn toward the left and suddenly felt a blow on his back. The Governor had been hit by a bullet which entered at the extreme right side of his back at a point below his right armpit. The bullet traveled through his chest in a downward and forward direction, exited below his right nipple, passed through his right wrist which had been in his lap, and then caused a wound to his left thigh. The force of the bullet's impact appeared to spin the Governor to his right, and Mrs. Connally pulled him down into her lap. Another bullet then struck President Kennedy in the rear portion of his head, causing a massive and fatal wound. The President fell to the left into Mrs. Kennedy's lap.

TEXT SET 2 # Citizenship

TITLE	AUTHOR	GENRE	WHERE TO FIND IT
"Canvassing for the School Levy"	Sara Holbrook	poem	page 231
"Canvassing for the School Levy"	Sara Holbrook reading	audio recording	http://www.heinemann.com /textsandlessonsliterature

Why These Selections?

We feel Holbrook's piece is one of those special, knock-your-socks-off poems. We savor the irony that as a citizen participating in her local democracy, Sara is reminded how undemocratically assets are distributed in our country. We also know that her voice could add a whole other level of meaning to the print poem. She's been to the finals of the national Poetry Slam. The girl can bring it.

Lesson Suggestions

1. **Read the poem aloud.** (See Teacher Read-Aloud, Lesson 3.2, page 22.) Stop at the title and make sure that kids understand what *levy* and *canvassing* mean. In many states these school funding elections are called "millage" or some other name. And *canvassing* means knocking on voters' doors to get out the vote—for your side, usually. Then continue reading aloud. Invite a few brief reactions or comments.

2. **Study the printed version.** Now, have kids reread the poem on their own, using Rereading Poetry (Lesson 6.8, page 137) and its accompanying note sheet. That means students will be stopping to jot down what they notice about the poem, its effect on them, and the poet's craft.

3. **Pairs meet.** For one minute, have partners share some insights into the poem. Then, add this direction: *How do you think this poem should be read aloud? How would the poet sound? How could you best communicate the feel and meaning of this poem?* Partners get ten minutes to work up their ideal reading of the poem, using steps from Reading with Expression (Lesson 9.5, page 217). Both kids must be ready to perform.

4. **Share readings.** Have partners sit with another pair and take turns performing their interpretations. Have them discuss how the readings relate back to the poetic elements they identified in Step 2.

COMMON CORE STANDARDS SUPPORTED

- Read closely to determine what the text says explicitly and to make logical inferences from it; cite specific textual evidence when writing or speaking to support conclusions drawn from the text. (CCRA.R.1)

- Determine central ideas or themes of a text and analyze their development; summarize the key supporting details and ideas. (CCRA.R.2)

- Interpret words and phrases as they are used in a text, including determining connotative and figurative meanings, and analyze how specific word choices shape meaning or tone. (CCRA.R.4)

- Analyze the structure of texts, including how specific sentences, paragraphs, and larger portions of the text (e.g., a section, chapter, scene, or stanza) relate to each other and the whole. (CCRA.R.5)

- Integrate and evaluate content presented in diverse media and formats, including visually and quantitatively, as well as in words. (CCRA.R.7)

- Read and comprehend complex literary and informational texts independently and proficiently. (CCRA.R.10)

- Engage effectively in a range of collaborative discussions. (CCRA.SL.1)

5. **Listen to the author's reading.** Before listening to the recorded version, have students jot down expectations of what they think the poet will sound like—her tone, attitude, pacing, emphasis.

6. **Discuss reading.** After they listen to the recording, have the groups of four discuss: *How did Holbrook's reading enhance or change your understanding of the poem? How was her reading alike or different from what you expected? Which version seemed most powerful or effective, and why?*

7. **Optional: kids' choice.** Kids choose their own poems and prepare readings that enhance or extend the impact of the printed versions, using instructions from Reading with Expression (Lesson 9.5, page 217).

Variation ▶

The web abounds with countless recordings of poems, legal and illegal, performed by the author, by a professional actor, or by amateurs around the globe. Many prominent poets have committed at least a few of their works to audio or video, and we can happily use them in our teaching. Interestingly, it's not hard to find a recording that makes you say, "Ugh, that's a terrible reading! What is that guy thinking? We could do better!" And then you put the kids to work.

The go-to resource for inspiration on teaching poetry is the Poetry Foundation, which hosts a wonderful website at http://www.poetryfoundation.org.

Canvassing for the School Levy

Sara Holbrook

These are the front doors
made of steel
that open into throbbing bass apartments
of coffee table filing systems
for wrappers from burgers bought
       four for five bucks,
of wide-eyed kids
leg-clinging scared of
kids who knock on front doors.
Doors opened by parents whose
crossed brows and weak smiles
take the literature hesitantly.
Nothing good never come from
door knocks before.

These are not the front doors
made of steel
that open into foyers of marble tile
and direct eye contact that demands explanations
accompanied by a smoke screen of
lavender, violins, and steak.
Not the doors anointed by well oiled brass knockers.
Not the focal point of brick walks and twin shrubs.
Not the doors that open on down payment gifts
from parents who are downsizing,
of diplomas hanging on walls warmly
illuminated by glowing fires held safely behind glass
reflecting on family rooms floors floored in hard wood.

These are the front doors
opened between shifts of minimum wage.
Doors accustomed to hard knocks
and routine downsizing
that open off of hallways
scented by a stewing of onions,
urine and beer,
littered by broken toys.
These are the front doors
made of steel
opened when the world wants more.

May I have your vote?

Life Stories

Texts Used ▶

TITLE	AUTHOR	GENRE	WHERE TO FIND IT
"Nikki-Rosa"	Nikki Giovanni	poem	page 235
Nikki Giovanni bio	Wikipedia	biography	http://en.wikipedia.org/wiki/Nikki_Giovanni
Giovanni Timeline	Nikki Giovanni	website	http://nikki-giovanni.com/timeline.shtml

Why These Selections?

Nikki Giovanni is one of America's strongest poets, but we think her work has been slightly overlooked in the school world. So we are always happy to have the chance to bring her poetry forward. There's also a stinging accusation in this poem suggesting that white people, especially scholars, critics, and biographers, are inclined to focus too much on the saddest and hardest parts of black people's lives. They seem not to notice or accept the fact that, even amid poverty and struggle, most black families are suffused with joy and love, and their children grow up with plenty of happy memories.

In this set we have Giovanni's poem, a short biography, and a website with a timeline of her life. These materials allow for a close study of the poem itself, an opportunity for some high-level teacher modeling, and the chance for students to further explore this author's life and her work in the context of the African-American literary tradition.

Lesson Suggestions

1. **Introduce and read the poem.** Preview for students that you will be reading aloud a poem, and they will respond to it in writing. Distribute and then read aloud "Nikki Rosa" as students follow along (Lesson 3.2, page 22).

2. **Students write a response.** Immediately invite kids to do a One-Minute Write (Lesson 3.3, page 26) in response to the poem. If they need prompting, you can project these suggestions (these are possibilities to choose from, not a list of required responses):

   What were you seeing as I read this piece?

   What do you think the poem is mostly about?

   Does this remind you of your own childhood in some ways?

   What are some poetic elements at work here, and how do they add meaning to the text?

   Are there words or passages you do not understand?

COMMON CORE STANDARDS SUPPORTED

- Read closely to determine what the text says explicitly and to make logical inferences from it; cite specific textual evidence when writing or speaking to support conclusions drawn from the text. *(CCRA.R.1)*

- Determine central ideas or themes of a text and analyze their development; summarize the key supporting details and ideas. *(CCRA.R.2)*

- Interpret words and phrases as they are used in a text, including determining connotative and figurative meanings, and analyze how specific word choices shape meaning or tone. *(CCRA.R.4)*

- Analyze the structure of texts, including how specific sentences, paragraphs, and larger portions of the text (e.g., a section, chapter, scene, or stanza) relate to each other and the whole. *(CCRA.R.5)*

continues

3. **Partners discuss their writings.** Using Pair Share (Lesson 3.1, page 18), have students join with a classmate and talk about their reactions to the poem for about one minute each. Then invite volunteer pairs to share with the whole group.

4. **Show students how you grapple with an unknown reference.** If it hasn't come up already, point out the puzzling mentions of "meetings" and "stock" related to "Hollydale." Explain that sometimes we can just read along, hoping that later lines will fill in a blank like this. But here, that strategy doesn't fully work. Though you can still grasp the poem, this "meaning gap" may nag at you. So now, model how you'd stop and look up a reference, in real time, to ensure your full understanding. Do a quick Teacher Think-Aloud (Lesson 3.4, page 29) of lines 12–19 (from "and somehow" to "and another dream goes"). Project Google and search "Giovanni + Hollydale." You'll find information about the failed black housing development that was undermined by racially discriminatory banks, and cost the Giovanni family its dream home.

5. **Discuss.** *What do we do when writers use references we have no way of understanding? Is it OK for them to do that, making us a little curious or puzzled? So maybe we want to learn more? Or is it inconsiderate? What about really old text, where the author's references aren't widely known anymore, by anyone? How do we cope with that? Let's list the strategies we can use in coping with these kinds of roadblocks to comprehension:*

   Reread the sentence

   Read on

   Look it up/search the web

   Ask someone for help

6. **Read the biography and timeline.** Invite students to read the other two documents in the set, using as their lens Giovanni's fear that her biographers will make her life look sad even though "all the while I was happy." Allow reading time.

7. **Discuss in pairs.** *What do you think Giovanni might say about the Wikipedia biography? Does it seem to misrepresent her childhood, as far as we can tell?* Offer students one or more of these focusing questions: *Do you agree with the idea that "outsiders" can never quite understand the lives of others? Does a person always get the last say about the truth of his life? Is it possible that another person might know someone better than he knows himself?*

8. **Optional:** Giovanni was a professor at Virginia Tech University when the classroom shootings happened there in 2007. In fact, she was one of the shooter's teachers, and had reported him to school authorities as being hostile and threatening. There are many news accounts online that detail the shooting, its aftermath, and Giovanni's role throughout the crisis. Later that same year, at the university's grief-inflected graduation

ceremony, Giovanni delivered a poetic speech alluding to that tragedy. Students may read or hear the speech at:

www.remembrance.vt.edu/2007/archive/giovanni_transcript.html

9. **Optional: Learn more about Giovannni.** If your kids want to take up the poem's challenge and find out more about who the real Nikki Giovanni is and was, there are many resources on the web for doing so. Giovanni's own website has lots of good material, including links to other valuable sites, which include video interviews and poetry readings.

http://nikki-giovanni.com/wwwresources.shtml

http://nikki-giovanni.com/nikkirosa.shtml

Nikki Rosa

Nikki Giovanni

childhood remembrances are always a drag
if you're Black
you always remember things like living in Woodlawn
with no inside toilet
and if you become famous or something
they never talk about how happy you were to have
your mother
all to yourself and
how good the water felt when you got your bath
from one of those
big tubs that folk in chicago barbecue in
and somehow when you talk about home
it never gets across how much you
understood their feelings
as the whole family attended meetings about Hollydale
and even though you remember
your biographers never understand
your father's pain as he sells his stock
and another dream goes
And though you're poor it isn't poverty that
concerns you
and though they fought a lot
it isn't your father's drinking that makes any difference
but only that everybody is together and you
and your sister have happy birthdays and very good
Christmases
and I really hope no white person ever has cause
to write about me
because they never understand
Black love is Black wealth and they'll
probably talk about my hard childhood
and never understand that
all the while I was quite happy

Biography Highlights

(from Wikipedia)

Nikki Giovanni (born **Yolande Cornelia Giovanni**; June 7, 1943) is an American poet, writer, commentator, activist, and educator. Her primary focus is on the individual and the power one has to make a difference in oneself and in the lives of others. Giovanni's poetry expresses strong racial pride, respect for family, and her own experiences as a daughter, a civil rights activist, and a mother. She is currently a distinguished professor of English at Virginia Tech.

Nikki Giovanni was born in Knoxville, Tennessee, and grew up in an all-black suburb of Cincinnati, Ohio. In 1960 she began her studies at Fisk University in Nashville, Tennessee, and graduated with honors in 1967, receiving a B.A. in history. Afterward she went on to attend the University of Pennsylvania and Columbia University.

Giovanni gave birth to her only child, Thomas Watson Giovanni, on August 31, 1969, while visiting Cincinnati, Ohio, for Labor Day Weekend. She later stated that she had a child out of wedlock at twenty-five because she "wanted to have a baby and she could afford to have a baby," and because of her conviction that marriage as an institution was inhospitable to women and would never play a role in her life.

The civil rights and black power movements inspired her early poetry. She has since written more than two dozen books, including volumes of poetry, illustrated children's books, and three collections of essays.

Some of her more recent work tones down the militant, edgy conscience that Giovanni has become famous for and portrays her softer, more nostalgic side. The work is a celebration of love and recollection directed at friends and loved ones and recalls memories of nature, theater, and the glories of children. However, her fiery persona still remains a constant undercurrent, as her own life struggles (being a black woman, a cancer survivor, and a professor at Virginia Tech) place her to the wider frame of African-American history and the continual fight for equality.

TEXT SET 4 Mothers and Daughters

◀ *Texts Used*

TITLE	AUTHOR	GENRE	WHERE TO FIND IT
"Persephone and Demeter"	Thomas Bulfinch	myth	page 199
"Mother #1"	Helen Phillips	story	page 241
"Mother Disapproved of Him" (mature)	Rita Mae Brown	speech	page 242

Why These Selections?

Almost any story about mothers and daughters has its roots in the story of Persephone and Demeter. It is a classic archetype: daughter falls for "bad boy" even after mother's repeated warnings about men. Finally, mother accepts son-in-law/boyfriend because she knows she will lose her daughter forever if she doesn't. This text set lesson explores mother and daughter relationships while also asking students to analyze how contemporary authors use a classic story archetype, another Common Core Standard.

You'll notice that we marked (mature) next to "Mother Disapproved." That's because the mother in this story warns, "Honey, let me give you a piece of motherly advice. If it's got testicles or tires, it's gonna be trouble." *Testicles* is a word that is repeated twice more before this speech concludes. Read the piece. The word is totally in context, but you are the best expert on your students' maturity. However, if you choose to forgo this second follow-up text to Persephone, your students will still have done sufficient work studying how a modern story draws from a classic one.

Lesson Suggestions

If students have already read "Persephone" (used in our Lesson 9.2 on page 196), skip Steps 1 and 2. Instead, give students a few minutes to individually skim through the story and their previously written "texts." Then have students form partners and discuss the attitudes of the characters as they engage in these relationships:

> Hades and Persephone
>
> Persephone and Demeter
>
> Hades and Demeter (remember Hades is now Demeter's son-in-law!)

Afterwards, share out and move directly to Step 3, instructions for reading "Mother #1."

1. **Introduce the story with a mingle.** Begin with Literary Networking (Lesson 9.1, page 187). Networking cards for Persephone and Demeter are included on page 240 (and are available on the website). Let students network for about ten minutes. Urge kids to the "dance floor" when they need a new partner. Keep it brisk. Remind the kids that there are fourteen different quotes to check out and discuss and the more people they get to the easier it will be to put the story together.

2. **Read "Persephone and Demeter."** Now, have kids read the full story, using the Characters Texting notation lesson (Lesson 9.2, page 196). The version we've provided prompts students at various points in the story to text as one character to another. For example, when Persephone is kidnapped by Hades, she immediately texts her mother, Demeter. Once students have completed the reading and initial texting, they trade with a partner and respond to each of the texts, taking on the roles of the text recipients. (Our version of the story offers many texting opportunities. Feel free to select just a few of these stop-and-text spots.)

3. **Read "Mother #1."** The following day, prepare students for two readings of Mother #1. For the first reading, use Reading with Questions in Mind (Lesson 4.4, page 51). Suggest this question: *Why do mothers disapprove of boyfriends and why are daughters drawn to guys their mothers won't like?* While keeping this question in mind, students should read with the goal of jotting down additional discussion questions. When finished, students meet briefly with their partners and discuss the initial question as well as the others they've created.

   For the second reading, focus on tone, using Text Annotation (Lesson 4.1, page 37). Have students underline the words and phrases that best portray the tension and that contrast how the mother and daughter feel about the boyfriend. When finished, partners meet and compare the words they've underlined and discuss how those choices create the tension present in the story. Then ask partners to decide which three words best depict the tension between mother and daughter. End with a whole-class discussion of tone, allowing pairs to share and compare their word choices.

4. **Compare the texts.** To conclude the study of the myth and its modern-day counterpart, pose these questions: *How does the author of "Mother #1" use the classic myth of Persephone and Demeter in her own story? What new meaning does the contemporary story bring to the myth? How are both stories inspired by human nature?* Begin the discussion with the pairs used in Step 3 and then have those pairs share their ideas with the whole class.

5. **Read "Mother Disapproved."** If you would like to continue this theme and text comparison study for one more day, this is a valuable story to include. However, please read it first since it is geared toward an older audience.

Form groups of three or four and pass out the first two-thirds of the story. Students should read only as far as the mother's advice "Honey, let me give you . . . it's gonna be trouble." As students read, they should underline the lines that they could imagine working as a caption for a photograph. Prompt students to notice key details describing the narrator's boyfriend and the mother's attitude toward him.

After reading, groups meet and briefly discuss what they underlined. Then assign a portion of the text—a half to a whole paragraph—to each group and review the steps for creating tableaux (Lesson 7.3, Frozen Scenes, page 153). Give groups about ten minutes to create two frozen scenes based on the underlined lines found in their assigned portion. Perform the tableaux in sequence and then have each group speculate how the story will end. Pass out the conclusion and read. Most students will be surprised that the narrator's boyfriend is a cat!

6. **Reread "Mother Disapproved."** Now have students work individually to reread the story, specifically looking for how the author intentionally fooled the reader into thinking the narrator's boyfriend was a human. When students are finished, have them return to the groups used in Step 5 and review the evidence of the author's intentional misdirection. Then have groups compare the mothers of all three stories and discuss these questions:

How are the mothers alike?

How are the mothers different?

What do the boyfriends always seem to have in common?

Why do the mothers oppose their daughters' wishes?

Is this a sign of love for their daughters—that they are willing to have their daughters dislike them if they feel they can keep them safe—or are the mothers trying to control their daughters' lives and prevent them from making their own decisions?

End with a whole-class discussion, inviting groups to share their ideas.

COMMON CORE STANDARDS SUPPORTED

- Read closely to determine what the text says explicitly and to make logical inferences from it; cite specific textual evidence when writing or speaking to support conclusions drawn from the text. (CCRA.R.1)

- Determine central ideas or themes of a text and analyze their development; summarize the key supporting details and ideas. (CCRA.R.2)

- Analyze how and why individuals, events, and ideas develop and interact over the course of a text. *(CCRA.R.3)*

- Interpret words and phrases as they are used in a text, including determining connotative and figurative meanings, and analyze how specific word choices shape meaning or tone. *(CCRA.R.4)*

- Analyze the structure of texts, including how specific sentences, paragraphs, and larger portions of the text (e.g., a section, chapter, scene, or stanza) relate to each other and the whole. *(CCRA.R.5)*

- Assess how point of view or purpose shapes the content and style of a text. *(CCRA.R.6)*

- Analyze how two or more texts address similar themes or topics in order to build knowledge or to compare the approaches the authors take. *(CCRA.R.9)*

- Read and comprehend complex literary and informational texts independently and proficiently. *(CCRA.R.10)*

- Engage effectively in a range of collaborative discussions. *(CCRA.SL.1)*

A sudden earthquake roused Hades from his underworld kingdom.	Zeus was not about reveal his fears and cede the upper hand to Demeter.
Demeter decided that mankind would suffer her loss with her.	Persephone hoped death might release her from her kidnapper.
Hades was observed by Aphrodite, who immediately noticed his lack of a wife or lover.	"Persephone shall reach the sky again on one condition, that her lips have touched no food."
Young crops died, destroyed by violent rain, unending drought, or freezing cold.	Demeter sought her daughter all the world over.
Aphrodite called for her son, Eros (though most of us now refer to him on Valentine's Day as Cupid).	For the longest time, Persephone refused any food Hades proffered.
Secretly, Zeus was deeply concerned over the fate of his worshippers.	All of the bystanders were afraid of Hades' wrath were they to tell the truth.
As Hades was shot, his chariot passed directly over Persephone.	When offered a pomegranate, her favorite fruit, she ate six seeds.

Mother #1

Helen Phillips

We the daughters of the twenty-first century are not mystified by Persephone's behavior. In school, we learn that Persephone is frolicking in a field when Hades kidnaps her and takes her underground. Persephone's mother Demeter, the goddess of the harvest, freaks out. Every plant in the world dies. Eventually Persephone is found, sitting beside Hades on an obsidian throne. He's drinking something from a wooden goblet. She looks anorexic. Hades says she can leave if she must but first why doesn't she eat this.

It's not til she emerges into the weird sunlight—it's not till she's in her mother's kitchen sipping pumpkin soup—it's not till Demeter sighs with relief to know her daughter didn't eat anything down there—that Persephone makes her confession about the six pomegranate seeds. Her mother smashes plates, slams doors. Meanwhile, Persephone sits, quitely disliking the freshness of the day, the soft winds carrying the smells of plants growing.

What Persephone will never mention is the rich unending night, the earthy smell of scotch on his breath, the way he mocked the universe and everyone in it but was so tender with the dead, with her, with beasts and ghosts. How low his voice got when he told her attempts would be made to separate them.

Now we the daughters of the twenty-first century are going to marry men our mothers don't quite love. These men seem dark to them, dangerous, lacking in good posture. We sit at our mothers' tables, trying to explain why we have chosen to settle in distant, inhospitable cities where the gray days outnumber the sunny. We try to explain that our future husbands are at once cynical and compassionate. We fight bitterly over wedding invitations and veils, as though these are matters of life and death, which they are. We suggest to our mothers that they read a certain Greek myth; they raise their eyebrows at us as they always do nowadays; the grass begins to shrivel in the ground, and in the orchard the apples sicken on the branch.

Mother Disapproved of Him

Rita Mae Brown

Mother disapproved of him. Said he was lazy and "no 'count." When she'd really get mad at him she said if he was a mule she wouldn't feed him hay. But I watched him beguile her even as he beguiled me. Not even Mother, the only five-two linebacker I have ever met, could resist Mick's green eyes or his deep, throaty voice when he chose to talk. He wasn't talky though, which was a good thing because Mother liked being the center of attention. When my homework or chores dragged me down like fathoms of chain, I could hear her on the front porch taking a break from her relentless work ethic. Mickey visited with her while waiting for me to finish. People would pass by and Mother would bestow upon my boyfriend her assessment of their characters. Mrs. Mundes cruised by in a brand-new Cadillac and Mother whispered into his eager ear, "She's so good, poor thing." Then she'd laugh at her own opinion. Mrs. Mundes was holier than thou. But I suspected as I doodled on my school tablet that Mother was jealous because of the new Cadillac. If Mickey thought that he never said a word.

Mrs. Mundes dug a pool that summer to which all of Coffee Hollow was invited at the opening party. Mickey and I left in disgrace because when all the adults were yakking away I threw Baby Ruths in the pool. Actually we didn't leave in disgrace. We ran like scalded dogs. Because Mother was hot on our tails and she was fast. To make matters worse Mrs. Mundes appeared at our porch the next day and Mother hauled me out for an apology. Mick of course was nowhere to be found. So I listened to how my generation was contributing to the moral and spiritual decline of America. Mrs. Mundes's generation knitted socks for the doughboys in World War I, thereby proving for all time to come that they sacrificed for the war effort, whereas I threw Baby Ruths in the swimming pool. Swathed in purple as she delivered this tirade, I could hardly wait for her to leave. Mickey peeped around the porch and then disappeared. I could've killed him. As Mrs. Mundes waddled off Mother whispered, "Looks like an eggplant, the old windbag." And then, as if I'd grasped the full import, she commented on Mrs. Mundes's marriage, a union for which her husband lacked enthusiasm.

"Mislaid his love like he mislaid his keys."

"I'll always love Mickey," I eagerly piped up.

"Hah!"

"I will!"

"You're too young to know about love."

"I am not!"

She drew deeply on her Chesterfield, which was stapled to her lip. "Honey, let me give you a piece of motherly advice. If it's got testicles or tires it's gonna be trouble."

I pondered this, and then replied, "Mickey doesn't have testicles!" She laughed, and Mickey jumped back on the porch. He'd been underneath all along waiting for the Gorgon to leave. "Come here, you lazy good-for-nothing cat!" He traipsed over to her and she scratched his ears. Then he leapt onto my lap and purred like Mrs. Mundes's Cadillac on full accelerator. He did love me truly and totally. Later, Mickey as my sidekick, I rubbed poison ivy on Mrs. Mundes's steering wheel. People didn't lock their houses or cars then and I didn't get caught for that one.

Many years have passed since that summer day. But Mother was wrong to say I didn't know about love. I did. And I still love Mickey and pay honor to his memory, for I'm never without a big tiger cat. After what Mother told me about testicles and tires I have had ample occasion to discover she was right about that!

Narcissism

Texts Used ▶

TITLE	AUTHOR	GENRE	WHERE TO FIND IT
Narcissus	Caravaggio	painting	Google Images
"Narcissus and Echo" (adaptation)	Ovid	myth	page 246
"Narcissism"	Wikipedia	nonfiction	page 248
"The Stag and His Reflection"	Aesop	fable	page 249

Why These Selections?

Mythology and fables, though truly ancient, influence modern culture. The story of Narcissus emerged in Greek mythology, was retold by Ovid from a Roman perspective, and now exists as a bona fide psychological disorder. Tracing a classical story through its various incarnations is a Common Core Standard, and it's also pretty interesting.

Lesson Suggestions

1. **View *Narcissus* by Caravaggio.** Though this work is not included in the book (we couldn't get the necessary permission from the museum in Rome where the painting resides), the image is plastered on the walls of the Internet. Search Google Images using the phrase "Narcissus Caravaggio" and dozens of usable images will appear as well as invitations to buy "Narcissus" T-shirts, aprons, coffee mugs, and key chains. Prepare the image so that it can be examined as a whole and in quadrants, using the directions from Setting the Scene (Lesson 6.2, page 108). As students jot down and discuss what they notice in the different parts of the painting, be sure to also draw their attention to what *isn't* there.

2. **Read "Narcissus and Echo."** Using Text Annotation (Lesson 4.1, page 37), have kids look for similarities and differences between painting and myth. Within the discussion of differences, point out that Ovid wrote his version of the Narcissus myth around AD 8, while Caravaggio completed his painting around 1599, a little less than 1,600 years later.

3. **Read the Wikipedia definition of narcissism.** Or watch psychiatrist Rhoda Hahn explaining the condition at www.videojug.com /interview/narcissistic-personality-disorder. How are the psychological disorder symptoms reflected in the myth and the painting?

4. **Read "The Stag and His Reflection."** Aesop lived between 620 and 560 BC, so this story was written well before Ovid's version (AD 8). Discuss how the story of the stag is initially informed by human nature and then reinvented by a succession of storytellers informed by their contemporary society.

5. **Make contemporary connections.** *Some psychologists have said that we Americans are now living in an "age of narcissism," where everything is geared to immediately meeting our own selfish needs. What examples of narcissism do you see in current society and culture? Some critics point to the behavior of sports and music stars as examples of contemporary narcissism. Using the historical versions you've studied, as well as the diagnostic symptoms list, defend or refute the idea that we are living in a narcissistic time.*

Narcissus and Echo

Adapted from Ovid's Metamorphoses

Tiresias' fame of prophecy was known through all the cities. A lovely nymph, named Liriope, came to him with her son Narcissus, who at fifteen was unequalled for his beauty. Liriope asked Tiresias if Narcissus might attain a ripe old age. The blind seer answered, "If he but fail to recognize himself, a long life he may have beneath the sun." The odd prophecy forgotten, Narcissus became a man and many a damsel sought to gain his love, but such was his mood and spirit and his pride, none gained his favor.

One day, Echo, a nymph, spied Narcissus deer hunting. Though once a keen conversationalist, Echo had lost her full power of speech as punishment for deceiving Juno, queen of the gods. One day Juno was seeking her husband, Jupiter, who she suspected was amusing himself among the nymphs. Echo stalled the goddess with talk until the nymphs made their escape. When Juno discovered it, she passed sentence upon Echo in these words: "I shall give you less power over that tongue by which I have been deluded, and the briefest ability to speak." After that, Echo could only repeat the last of what was spoken and return only the words she heard.

Echo observed Narcissus wandering in the pathless woods and she fell in love with him. The more she followed him the hotter did she burn. Oh, how she longed to make her passion known! To plead in soft entreaty! To implore his love!

By chance, Narcissus became separated from his fellow hunters and called out, "Is anyone here?" and "Here," Echo replied. He glanced everywhere, and shouted in a loud voice, "Come to me!" Echo called as he called. He turned to see who called him and, beholding naught, exclaimed, "Avoid me not!" *"Avoid me not!"* Narcissus called again and again, until finally calling out, "Oh let us come together!" Echo cried, *"Oh let us come together!"* No sound seemed sweeter to the Nymph, and from the woods she hastened to wind her arms around his neck, but Narcissus flew from her shouting, "Take off your hands! You shall not fold your arms around me. Better death than such a one should ever caress me!" Echo answered, *"Caress me!"* Thus rejected, she hid in the deep woods, yet her great love for Narcissus only increased with neglect. Over time Echo faded away until only her voice remained.

As Narcissus had scorned Echo, so had he scorned the other nymphs until one rejected lover cried to the skies, "So may he himself love, and so may he fail to command what he loves!" The goddess Nemesis heard this just request and acted upon it.

There was a fountain silver-clear and bright, which neither shepherds nor goats nor any cattle had touched; its waters were unsullied. Neither birds nor fallen boughs disturbed it. Here Narcissus, tired of hunting and the heated noon, lay down, attracted by the peaceful solitude and glassy spring. As he stooped to quench his thirst another thirst increased. While drinking, he saw himself reflected in the mirrored pool—and loved who he saw. He could not move, so transfixed he was by his image, and lay with countenance unchanged, as if he were indeed a statue carved of marble.

Unknowingly he desired himself, and though his image matched his passion, when he plunged his arms into the water, he could not catch himself within them!

When Echo saw Narcissus in his hapless plight, though angry at his scorn, she only grieved. As often as the lovesick man complained, "Alas!" "Alas!" her echoing voice returned. And as he gazed upon the mirrored pool he breathed a last sad *"farewell!"* "Farewell!" sighed Echo too. Narcissus laid his wearied head on the verdant grass and those bright eyes, which had so loved to gaze, entranced, on their own master's beauty, closed. And in his body's place a sweet flower grew, golden and white, the white around the gold. And now among the nether shades his sad sprite roams, Narcissus ever loves to gaze on his reflection in the Stygian wave.

Narcissism

Wikipedia, July 27, 2012
http://www.videojug.com/interview/narcissistic-personality-disorder

The word *narcissism* comes from the Greek myth of Narcissus. Narcissus was a handsome Greek youth who rejected the desperate advances of the nymph Echo. As punishment, he was doomed to fall in love with his own reflection in a pool of water. Unable to consummate his love, Narcissus "lay gazing enraptured into the pool, hour after hour," and finally changed into a flower that bears his name, the narcissus.

The concept of excessive selfishness has been recognized throughout history. In ancient Greece the concept was understood as hubris. It is only in recent times that it has been defined in psychological terms.

Traits and signs

Narcissists typically display most, and sometimes all, of the following traits:

- An obvious self-focus in interpersonal exchanges
- Problems in sustaining satisfying relationships
- A lack of psychological awareness
- Difficulty with empathy
- Problems distinguishing the self from others
- Hypersensitivity to any insults or imagined insults
- Vulnerability to shame rather than guilt
- Haughty body language
- Flattery toward people who admire and affirm them
- Detesting those who do not admire them
- Using other people without considering the cost of doing so
- Pretending to be more important than they really are
- Bragging (subtly but persistently) and exaggerating their achievements
- Claiming to be an "expert" at many things
- Inability to view the world from the perspective of other people
- Denial of remorse and gratitude

The Stag and His Reflection

Aesop

A Stag, drinking from a crystal spring, saw himself mirrored in the clear water. He greatly admired the graceful arch of his antlers, but he was very much ashamed of his spindling legs.

"How can it be," he sighed, "that I should be cursed with such legs when I have so magnificent a crown."

At that moment he scented a panther and in an instant was bounding away through the forest. But as he ran his wide-spreading antlers caught in the branches of the trees, and soon the Panther overtook him. Then the Stag perceived that the legs of which he was so ashamed would have saved him had it not been for the useless ornaments on his head.

We often make much of the ornamental and despise the useful.

Labels

Texts Used ▶

TITLE	AUTHOR	GENRE	WHERE TO FIND IT
"Labels"	Sara Holbrook	poem	page 252
"Sitting Bull Returns" at the Drive-In	Willard Midgette	painting	Google Images
"Sure You Can Ask Me A Personal Question"	Diane Burns	poem	page 254
"On Making Him a Good Man by Calling Him a Good Man"	Dave Eggers	story	page 256
Speech at the U.S. Capitol	Mandeep Chahal	speech	page 257

Why These Selections?

We each have an identity that is shaped by our family, our experiences, our personality, our uniqueness. And then someone else slaps on a label, reducing us from a multifaceted being to a one-dimensional stereotype. Instead of people getting to know us, labels encourage others to assume they already do. How can we think about this issue? How do labels influence behavior? How can we get to know others authentically versus superficially? These are the questions we hope students will think about, discuss, and explore as they unpack these pieces.

Lesson Suggestions

1. **Read and discuss "Labels."** Place copies of the poem on large sheets of chart paper. Then have groups of three or four gather around, read the poem, and have a written conversation via Text on Text (Lesson 7.2, page 149).

2. **View and analyze an image.** Invite students to view *"Sitting Bull Returns" at the Drive-In* using Thirty-Second Look (Lesson 5.2, page 73). (Search for "Sitting Bull Midgette" in Google Images.) After initial observation and notation, have students categorize their details on a Venn diagram (page 125) using these labels: left circle—reality; right circle—stereotype. Leave the intersecting section blank for now.

3. **Read and discuss annotations of Burns poem.** Students read the poem "Sure You Can Ask Me a Personal Question." During reading, they should mark lines that they think make connections with *"Sitting Bull Returns" at the Drive-In*. After reading, students discuss in small groups, using Save the Last Word for Me (Lesson 5.4, page 83).

COMMON CORE STANDARDS SUPPORTED

- Read closely to determine what the text says explicitly and to make logical inferences from it; cite specific textual evidence when writing or speaking to support conclusions drawn from the text. *(CCRA.R.1)*

- Determine central ideas or themes of a text and analyze their development; summarize the key supporting details and ideas. *(CCRA.R.2)*

- Analyze how and why individuals, events, and ideas develop and interact over the course of a text. *(CCRA.R.3)*

- Interpret words and phrases as they are used in a text, including determining technical, connotative, and figurative meanings, and analyze how specific word choices shape meaning or tone. *(CCRA.R.4)*

continues

4. **Small groups compare the poem and image.** After the discussion of the poem, groups decide what feelings or messages the art and the poem share. Students then jot notes in the middle section of the Venn.

5. **Read and annotate the speech.** Next, tell students that they will be reading the speech of a college student in fear of being deported. Have students read Mandeep Chahal's speech on being "a dreamer" twice. On the second reading, they should underline the words and phrases they would emphasize if they were giving the speech as well as the places they would pause when they really wanted to give the audience time for the message to sink in (Reading with Expression, Lesson 9.5, page 217). Have students share their interpretation with a partner and then watch Ms. Chahal's speech (http://weareamericastories.org/videos/mandeep-chahal-dreamer-calls-on-president-obama-and-congress-to-bring-relief-to-undocumented-youth/). Afterwards, ask volunteers to compare Chahal's interpretation to the notes they took during reading.

6. **Read and discuss the story.** Students read the story "On Making Him a Good Man by Calling Him a Good Man," using Reading with Questions in Mind (Lesson 4.4, page 51): Offer students this guiding question before they begin reading: *Can we influence those around us by the way we label them?*

7. **Written Conversation** (Lesson 5.1, page 66). Get students into groups of three or four for a culminating written discussion, using this prompt: *Pulling from all these texts, do you think a community can help its members become better people by viewing each other and speaking about each other more positively?*

Research: Let students investigate the situation of children and young adults caught up in the snare of possible deportation through no fault of their own. In reviewing the many sources available, take note of the ways that labels can heighten tension and misunderstanding around such issues. There's a big difference between "undocumented worker," "illegal alien," and "wetback."

We Are America: Stories of Today's Immigrants
http://weareamericastories.org/stories/

American Children, Now Struggling to Adjust to Life in Mexico
By Damien Cave, June 18, 2012, *The New York Times,*
http://www.nytimes.com/2012/06/19/world/americas/american
-born-children-struggle-to-adjust-in-mexico.html?ref=
immigrationandemigration

My Life as an Undocumented Immigrant
By Jose Antonio Vargas, June 22, 2011, *The New York Times,*
http://www.nytimes.com/2011/06/26/magazine/my-life-as-an
-undocumented-immigrant.html?pagewanted=all

COMMON CORE STANDARDS SUPPORTED *(CONT.)*

- Analyze the structure of texts, including how specific sentences, paragraphs, and larger portions of the text (e.g., a section, chapter, scene, or stanza) relate to each other and the whole. *(CCRA.R.5)*

- Assess how point of view or purpose shapes the content and style of a text. *(CCRA.R.6)*

- Integrate and evaluate content presented in diverse media and formats, including visually as well as in words. *(CCRA.R.7)*

- Analyze how two or more texts address similar themes or topics in order to build knowledge or to compare the approaches the authors take. *(CCRA.R.9)*

- Read and comprehend complex literary and informational texts independently and proficiently. *(CCRA.R.10)*

- Engage effectively in a range of collaborative discussions. *(CCRA.SL.1)*

◀ *Variations*

Labels

Sara Holbrook

People get tagged with these labels,
like African-American,
Native-American,
White,
Asian, Hispanic,
or Euro-Caucasian—
I just ask that you get my name right.
I'm part Willie,
part Ethel,
part Suzi and Scott.
Part assembly-line worker,
part barber, a lot of dancer
and salesman.
Part grocer and mailman.
Part rural, part city, part cook
and part caveman.
I'm a chunk-style vegetable soup
of cultural little bits,
my recipe's unique
and no one label fits.
Grouping folks together
is an individual waste.
You can't know me by just a look,
you have to take a taste.

Willard Midgette, *"Sitting Bull Returns" at the Drive-In*, 1976. Smithsonian American Art Museum, Washington, DC / Art Resource, NY.

Sure You Can Ask Me a Personal Question

Diane Burns

How do you do?
No, I am not Chinese.
No, not Spanish.
No, I am American Indian, Native American.

No, not from India.
No, not Apache
No, not Navajo.
No, not Sioux.
No, we are not extinct.
Yes, Indian.

Oh?
So that's where you got those high cheekbones.
Your great grandmother, huh?
An Indian Princess, huh?
Hair down to there?
Let me guess. Cherokee?

Oh, so you've had an Indian friend?
That close?

Oh, so you've had an Indian lover?
That tight?

Oh, so you've had an Indian servant?
That much?

Yeah, it was awful what you guys did to us.
It's real decent of you to apologize.
No, I don't know where you can get peyote.
No, I don't know where you can get Navajo rugs real cheap.
No, I didn't make this. I bought it at Bloomingdales.

Thank you. I like your hair too.
I don't know if anyone knows whether or not Cher
is really Indian.
No, I didn't make it rain tonight.

Yeah. Uh-huh. Spirituality.
Uh-huh. Yeah. Spirituality. Uh-huh. Mother
Earth. Yeah. Uh-huh. Uh-huh. Spirituality.

No, I didn't major in archery.
Yeah, a lot of us drink too much.
Some of us can't drink enough.

This ain't no stoic look.
This is my face.

On Making Him a Good Man by Calling Him a Good Man

Dave Eggers

Stuart has the face of a Scottish warrior. He has been told this, though he is unsure if this means that he has a historically accurate and fierce Highlands look, or that he simply looks like a particular actor from *Braveheart*. Stuart has been friends with Margaret since they were very small. Margaret, soft in every way, recently married Phillipe, who is an idiot. Stuart feels no jealousy toward Phillipe, for he and Margaret were never romantic, and he actually wanted to like Phillipe, from the start he tried to like Phillipe, but Phillipe has always made this difficult because Phillipe is a moron. Phillipe does not work, or does not work often, and feels no guilt at all about allowing Margaret to pay for food, for car repairs that he makes necessary, and for rent. When he has his own money, he goes on sportfishing vacations without Margaret. As we said, he is an idiot. Is he charming? He is not. Is he handsome? Passably. What, then, is his appeal? The narrator is not sure. Anyway, one day, Stuart and Phillipe were standing near each other at one of the many birthdays, bar mitzvahs, and christenings at which they find themselves. As they were talking about sport-fishing, which at least means Phillipe will not talk about the ineffectiveness of the U.N., Phillipe noticed, at the corner of the building, a young boy being taunted by three others. Before Stuart could react, Phillipe sprinted toward the scrum, and chased away the offenders, and was soon consoling the young boy, who after a few minutes was laughing at Phillipe's jokes. When Phillipe returned to the gathering, Stuart, who saw the entire scene unfold, patted Phillipe on the back and said, "Phillipe, you're a good man." Stuart said this very seriously, because he was greatly impressed by Philippe's heroics, and because the words *good man* are used with the utmost sincerity in his family. In fact, the primary aspiration of the men in his family is to be called, by their father or grandfather or great uncle Daniel, a "good man." So Stuart called Phillipe a good man, and although he felt initially that he might have jumped the gun, that one decent act doesn't necessarily define a man, Stuart was surprised to see that over the next weeks and months, Phillipe seemed to change. He stood straighter, he showed up on time. He was kind to, even chivalrous to, Margaret, and undertook a steady job. He sent her and two of her friends to a weekend spa, and fixed the broken door to her closet. Phillipe never said a word about being called a good man, and Stuart couldn't believe that the words had any effect on him. But the change in him was clear: he was becoming what Stuart had called him, a good man. Stuart wondered if we, all or any of us, are so easily improved. If all we need is this kind of semantic certainty. If to be named is to be realized. If once something like that is settled—I *am* a good man—we no longer need to struggle, to guess, to err.

Speech at the U.S. Capitol

Mandeep Chahal, 2011

*http://weareamericastories.org/videos/mandeep-chahal
-dreamer-calls-on-president-obama-and-congress-to-bring
-relief-to-undocumented-youth/*

My name is Mandeep Chahal, I am a college student, a sister, a daughter, a friend, and an activist, and for the first time in my life, I am standing before you as a proud dreamer.

I came to this country at age six knowing nothing but the alphabet and phrases like "thank you" and "please" that my mom had taught me. Today, I stand before you as an honors college student on her way to med school. It's been 14 years since I walked into my first grade classroom, and I've come a long way since then.

Like Jose Antonio Vargas, I grew up in the San Francisco Bay Area: headquarters of tech giants like Google and Facebook, and also home to the SF Giants, who I might mention are World Series champions. It's a place of opportunity and innovation, and a place that's full of immigrant families like my own.

As a kid in California, I was obsessed first with Arthur, then Harry Potter, and eventually human rights. In high school, I helped found One Dollar For Life, a 501-c3 that has since become a national poverty relief organization. I was also president of my high school's Amnesty International chapter and have continued to volunteer with Amnesty in college.

I went to Los Altos High School, which just so happens to be the rival school of Mountain View High School, where Jose went. Jose and I actually grew up in the same town—I just went to the school with the better football team.

It was during high school that my parents sat me down, and told me about my illegal status. The knowledge that I was undocumented rocked my teenage reality of soccer practice and Spanish homework. It scared me, and so I told almost no one. I focused on my grades and devoted my free time to human rights activism. I graduated high school with honors, and was voted "Most Likely to Save the World" by my class. I thought that, if I ignored my secret problem, it would go away. That is not what happened.

Last summer, the summer after my freshman year at UC Davis, Immigration and Customs Enforcement found me. They took me in and fitted my ankle with an electronic tracking device. They told me I was lucky I wasn't in prison instead. They treated me like a criminal, and to be honest there were moments when I felt like one.

This past school year, I tried to keep my life at school somewhat normal. I declared my major: Neurology, Physiology and Behavior. I expanded campus outreach for STAND, UC Davis's anti-genocide coalition and was elected co-president. I even managed to pass Chemistry 2C.

Three weeks ago, I finished all of my finals and came home excited to relax and enjoy summer vacation with my family and friends. Little did I know that my life was about to be turned upside down.

On June 16th, I was summoned to the ICE office. My case officer told me that within a week, my mom and I would be deported. He ordered me to purchase a one-way plane ticket to India. The nightmare that I had warded off for years was coming true, and fast.

I walked out of my meeting with ICE knowing I had to stop this. I could not be sent to a country I no longer know, ripped away from my family, my friends, and the beautiful place that I had called home for almost as long as I could remember.

I went to the few people I had trusted with the truth about my status. We sat down and decided that with deportation just five days away, the only way to stop this was to "go public."

To an undocumented immigrant, that's a scary, scary term. The fear of being discovered is one that's constantly on our minds. You learn to avoid bringing attention to yourself, to live below the radar of authority at all times, to stay hidden in the shadows.

Having kept my status a secret from even my closest friends for so long, going to my community for help was not easy. To expose my secret to everyone I've ever known, and put my future in their hands, was one of the hardest things I've ever had to do.

When the Facebook group went up, and the message was sent out to hundreds of my friends, classmates, and community members, I was scared. I didn't know what to expect. I had no idea how people would respond.

What happened next was bigger than anyone had expected.

The news spread across Facebook like wildfire. The overwhelming support I received knocked me off my feet. Once the news was out, my friends sent the petition to their friends, who sent it their friends, who in turn invited more and more people.

In the end, nearly 20,000 faxes were sent to senators, ICE and the Department of Homeland Security. Thousands of people signed a letter on my behalf, hundreds of people called senators.

And it worked.

My mom and I went to ICE last Tuesday, and as ordered we reported to be taken into custody. For a fleeting moment, I thought I might never see my friends again. But we were there less than two hours before ICE changed their minds and let us go.

And so I'm here. We've been granted a stay for one year. But that doesn't change the fact that last week I was just hours away from being deported from my home.

As a student, I work hard. I'm in the honors program at one of the country's top public universities, and I'm on track to go to medical school. I plan to spend my life working for the public good in the United States of America.

If it took this, for me, to stay in my country, then something is wrong. It shouldn't be this hard.

President Obama has made it clear that he fully supports the DREAM Act. He has even said that its failure to pass has been one his biggest disappointments as President.

And yet, he hasn't acted. He has the power to stop the deportations of people like me. He can bring relief so that no family has to go through what mine has. He can end our pain, but he is still deporting DREAMers.

I am standing here today, in my country's capital, because of you. Had it not been for the support of my community and the activism of DREAMers from all across America, I would be gone.

I cannot describe what it means to have all of you. After hiding for so long, to be completely embraced by other dreamers and allies has been incredible. It gives me hope for our future, and the future of our country.

My story is your story; yours is mine. We are a community held together by our common dream.

Such *hai vi meh kali nai. La verdad es que no soy la unica.*

Abuse

Why These Selections?

Anger, often manifested as domestic abuse, plays out in many arenas and ensnares more than those directly brutalized: friends, family, children. Victims of abuse sometimes seek escape—on their own or with help—but just as often remain in the relationship. Students need to understand the dynamics of these relationships in order to avoid them and to support others safely. We teach this unit in full knowledge that there will be kids in the class affected by this issue, and stand ready to help if they reach out.

"Dozens of Roses," written by acclaimed young adult author Virginia Euwer Wolff, is a play depicting the cyclical pattern of an abusive dating relationship. In "The Wallet," a stranger has to make a snap decision to help a victim of abuse she has never met before and will probably never see again. And Pat Conroy's memoir, "My Father," portrays the brutal reality some children face when living with an abusive parent.

Besides theme, each of these pieces makes strong use of symbolism or metaphor. In addition, "Dozens of Roses" employs a Greek chorus.

You'll notice that "My Father" is marked "mature." Please read this memoir carefully and determine its suitability for your students. Also, notice that you have two choices for analyzing this memoir. Even if you choose not to use "My Father," you will still be able to complete the culminating activity.

Lesson Suggestions

1. **Read "Dozens of Roses" aloud.** Have students work in groups of four, each group member taking one of the parts: Lucy, Chuck, Chorus, the Rememberer. If your class count does not divide by four evenly, it's OK to have some groups of five since the chorus is actually meant to have several voices reading in unison.

2. **Quick initial discussion.** After reading, groups have a quick Partner Think-Aloud (Lesson 3.5, page 33). Since students are now working in groups larger than pairs, have each member take a turn explaining his ideas using this prompt: *What do you notice or think?*

3. **Students prepare their interpretations.** Have the groups go back through the story, discussing and marking interpretation notes as outlined in Reading with Expression (Lesson 9.5, page 217). How should each member read his/her lines so that the character's personality and feelings come across in the words? After completing their interpretation discussion and note taking, the groups practice their interpretations, reading and rereading the play aloud until you call time.

4. **Collaborative performance.** Finally, call on a volunteer from each group to read the part they prepared. in front of the class; the whole-class performance will include members from all of the preparation groups. Since you will likely have more than four groups of four, groups that have not volunteered a "lead" character can volunteer their chorus member. If time permits, listen to a second collaborative performance with different leads and different chorus members.

5. **Analyze symbolism.** Using the lesson Drawing Text Details (Lesson 4.3, page 47), students respond in drawing to this question: How do the red roses symbolize something different for Lucy, Chuck, the Chorus, and the Rememberer? Rather than drawing about all four characters, students might choose one of the four.

6. **Read and annotate "The Wallet."** (See Lesson 8.3, page 180.) After students have discussed their underlined passages and accompanying questions, groups can discuss the symbolism of the tollbooth for the attendant and the driver. How can the same physical structure symbolize something very different for these two characters?

   Note: If students have already read "The Wallet" (used in Lesson 8.3), have them focus on the symbolism of the tollbooth as they quickly reread the story. After reading, the groups should move directly into the symbolism discussion.

7. **Finish the story.** Distribute only the first portion of "My Father," ending on the first time the sentence "I was eleven" is used. Have students read up to that point and then each write the ending (Lesson 8.2, page 173). Remind students to imitate the author's style.

8. **Write a Six-Word Memoir.** After reading all three pieces, have each student return to his or her favorite story and reread it. Then, choosing one of the characters from that piece (or an inanimate object that witnesses events, such as the roses, the tollbooth, the butcher's knife) have students write a six-word summary that captures the event from that character's perspective (Lesson 4.5, page 56). Students then share in their groups, nominating one memoir from their group to be read to the entire class.

COMMON CORE STANDARDS SUPPORTED

- Read closely to determine what the text says explicitly and to make logical inferences from it; cite specific textual evidence when writing or speaking to support conclusions drawn from the text. *(CCRA.R.1)*

- Determine central ideas or themes of a text and analyze their development; summarize the key supporting details and ideas. *(CCRA.R.2)*

- Analyze how and why individuals, events, and ideas develop and interact over the course of a text. *(CCRA.R.3)*

- Interpret words and phrases as they are used in a text, including determining connotative and figurative meanings, and analyze how specific word choices shape meaning or tone. *(CCRA.R.4)*

- Analyze the structure of texts, including how specific sentences, paragraphs, and larger portions of the text (e.g., a section, chapter, scene, or stanza) relate to each other and the whole. *(CCRA.R.5)*

- Analyze how two or more texts address similar themes or topics in order to build knowledge or to compare the approaches the authors take. *(CCRA.R.9)*

- Read and comprehend complex literary and informational texts independently and proficiently. *(CCRA.R.10)*

- Engage effectively in a range of collaborative discussions. *(CCRA.SL.1)*

Variations ▶ **Take an alternative point of view:** In the spirit of Point-of-View Note Taking (Lesson 6.4, page 117), have students write a letter of advice to Lucy ("Dozens of Roses") from one of the following characters:

> Woman driver—"The Wallet"
>
> The driver's five-year-old daughter—"The Wallet"
>
> Mother—"My Father"
>
> Nine-year-old daughter—"My Father"
>
> Eleven-year-old male narrator—"My Father"

Adding another story: "Fight #3" is the piece we used in Lesson 6.6, Metaphorically Speaking (page 126). But it also fits "hand in glove" into this text set and offers a nice contrast to the extreme dysfunction displayed in the other texts. As author Helen Phillips' email suggests, we all have anger, we all have a complex nature, and we sometimes engage in behavior we later regret. However, unlike characters in the earlier stories, the couple in "Fight #3" emerges from these lows relatively unscathed. What can we learn from them?

Connecting fiction with research: Send students online for further nonfiction research on this issue.

> **Domestic Violence and Abuse**
> Signs of abuse and abusive relationships:
> http://www.helpguide.org/mental/domestic_violence_abuse_types
> _signs_causes_effects.htm
>
> **National Domestic Violence Hotline**
> http://www.thehotline.org/
>
> **Medline Plus**
> A service of the U.S. National Library of Medicine and National
> Institutes of Health: http://www.nlm.nih.gov/medlineplus
> /domesticviolence.html
>
> **Domestic Violence**
> United States Department of Justice:
> http://www.ovw.usdoj.gov/domviolence.htm

Dozens of Roses: A Story for Voices

Virginia Euwer Wolff

Voices:
Lucy
Chuck
Chorus
The Rememberer

Chorus: They are bloodred, floating on long stems, stiffened with invisible wire so they stand up straight among maidenhair ferns, and there are a dozen of them.

Lucy: I don't want them.

Chorus: But they came for you! A dozen red roses! Delivered by a florist's messenger! Right to the school office! An announcement came over the air, through the walls, into all the hallways, asking for you to come to the office!

Lucy: I don't want them. Please, don't make me take them.

The Rememberer: I used to know her when we were little. She was full of energy then. We had picnics and we played jump rope. She had pep.

Chorus: Who sent them to you?

Lucy: Please don't make me say.

Chorus: You can't ignore flowers. There they are, standing up straight in a vase full of water, right in front of the secretary's desk. It's really a sight to see: the dull old school office, with the tan walls and the tan filing cabinets and bad lighting—And those dozen romantic, red roses.

Chuck: She'll know how I feel about her when she sees the roses.

Lucy: I can't go get them.

Chorus: That's ridiculous. Of course you can go get them. Who would turn down such a gift?

Lucy: You don't understand.

Chorus: Oh—you mean your sprained ankle? They must be get-well roses.

Lucy: I don't care what kind of roses they are.

The Rememberer: Something has taken the fire out of her. She isn't the same.

Chorus: Take a friend with you. To help carry them while you limp along. Read the card and tell us who sent them.

Chuck: She'll love them. That's a lot of money I spent.

Chorus: Whoever he is, he must adore you.

Lucy: I won't look at them! I won't go to the office. I won't read the card.

Chuck: She'll forget she was mad.

Chorus: You're a lucky girl.

Lucy: My ankle hurts.

Chorus: People who feel sorry for themselves aren't any fun at all.

Chuck: She fell.

Lucy: I can't leave my math class.

Chuck: She fell right over the end of the chair.

Lucy: Please, somebody, take the roses home with you.

Chorus: You must be crazy.

Chuck: She had her weight distributed the wrong way. I barely touched her.

Chorus: She must be very stubborn.

Chuck: She looked at him. I saw her look at him. Making plans to meet him behind my back.

Lucy: I need to do my math.

The Rememberer: Maybe it was that cut on her forehead last fall. Maybe it did something to her brain. Maybe the emergency room was a shock to her system.

Chorus: She's so ungrateful.

Lucy: Please don't make me talk about it.

Chuck: She'll know when she gets the roses. How much I feel for her.

Lucy: I want to stay in class, where I can breathe.

Chuck: I need her. She'll know when she gets the roses.

The Rememberer: That was it. When she had to go to the hospital that time. With the cut on her forehead. She's been different ever since.

Lucy: Can math class please go on forever?

Chorus: There's a time to be moody and a time to snap out of it. She should snap out of it.

Chuck: I can't live without her. She'll know when she gets the roses.

The Rememberer: She got a dozen roses that other time, too.

My Father

Pat Conroy

My father, a Marine Corps fighter pilot, 220 pounds, six-two, a blunt instrument: a semiautomatic assault weapon. My father waged war against the Japanese, the North Koreans, the Vietnamese, and his family. My first memory: my mother trying to stab my father with a butcher knife while he was beating her. I knew this was going to be a long and involved life. My mother—from the hills of Alabama. Her relatives were named this (and I give you the exact names): There was Jasper Catlit, Plumma, Clyde. There was an uncle in the graveyard named Jerrymire Peak. And I said, "Where did he come from?" and she said, "He was named for the prophet, Jer-ry-mire."

These two improbable people got together, had a marriage that produced seven children, six miscarriages. My sister called the miscarriages the lucky ones. In the dance of this particular family, in this horrible dance—you know, when I read Eudora Welty's thing that her mother and father sang to each other from the stairways—not my mother and father. This was martial art. This was a terrible, terrible union, but it was the one that caused me to be a writer.

The worst thing that happened: Dad was stationed at the Pentagon and a fight broke out between my mother and father when my sister had her birthday party, her ninth birthday party. I was eleven.

My Father *(continued)*

A fight started. My role was to get the other six kids out of harm's way. So I rushed them out of the room. My second Job was to get Mom away from Dad. I went roaring in. I was eleven. Dad could eat Ollie North for breakfast. I got between them. I looked over my head and saw the butcher knife I'd seen when I was a child. My mother connected this time. Blood got on me, my sister. Mom took us to Hot Shoppes and said she was going to leave Dad. She did not. What she did instead was wash my shirt and my sister's dress that had the blood of my father on it.

Later, when I asked my sister if it happened, she said no, it didn't happen. I said, why not? She said we didn't write it down. If it's going to be real, you got to write it down. My sister's book of poetry is coming out next year, published by Norton. My father made one mistake. He was raising an American novelist and an American poet—and we wrote it down.

Soldiers and Heroes

TITLE	AUTHOR	GENRE	WHERE TO FIND IT
"Broadcaster Refuses to Label Dead Soldiers 'Heroes'"	Lee Terrell	news item	page 271
The Advance-Guard, or the Military Sacrifice (the Ambush)	Frederic Remington	painting	Google Images
"Three Soldiers"	Bruce Holland Rogers	story	page 273
"The News from Iraq"	Sara Holbrook	poem	page 274
"Heroes"	Tim O'Brien	speech	page 277

◀ *Texts Used*

Why These Selections?

Much of the literature we teach centers on war. From *The Iliad* to the Arthurian legend to Shakespeare's *Henry IV*, many of the characters our students encounter are soldiers. In celebrated literature, these soldiers are often high-ranking warriors—generals, commanders, and kings—who are portrayed as heroes. A neglected theme in war literature, we think, is the experience of the common soldier, the recruit, the conscript, the grunt.

Just as this book was going to press, a modest-sized media controversy blew up over whether it is mandatory to refer to *all* American soldiers as *heroes*. Pundits, talking heads, and even NPR linguist in residence Geoffrey Nunberg weighed in on this issue. So that's our guiding question for this multiday unit: Are all soldiers heroes?

This text set draws on five kinds of media to illuminate the real world of the soldier: a news clipping, a nineteenth-century painting, a poem, a story, and a speech by PEN/Faulkner Award winner Tim O'Brien. This is potentially the most extensive text set unit of the bunch; with the writing steps at the end, it could easily take a week or more. It is also a topic with plenty of edges, passions, and controversies. Your class will have kids with military connections, so approach this subject with foresight, respect, and openness. But don't back away from it because it's risky. Life is too short to teach literature that doesn't matter.

Lesson Suggestions

1. **Introduce guiding questions.** Hand out or project the news item and read it aloud. Have kids do a quick Pair Share (Lesson 3.1, page 18). Then evoke and list their thoughts about questions like these: What is the definition of a hero? Should all U.S. soldiers be called heroes? The soldiers of other countries? WWII Nazis? The drug armies of southeast Asia? What makes the difference? Create this list under the heading

- Read closely to determine what the text says explicitly and to make logical inferences from it; cite specific textual evidence when writing or speaking to support conclusions drawn from the text. *(CCRA.R.1)*

- Determine central ideas or themes of a text and analyze their development; summarize the key supporting details and ideas. *(CCRA.R.2)*

- Analyze how and why individuals, events, and ideas develop and interact over the course of a text. *(CCRA.R.3)*

- Interpret words and phrases as they are used in a text, including determining connotative and figurative meanings, and analyze how specific word choices shape meaning or tone. *(CCRA.R.4)*

- Analyze the structure of texts, including how specific sentences, paragraphs, and larger portions of the text (e.g., a section, chapter, scene, or stanza) relate to each other and the whole. *(CCRA.R.5)*

- Assess how point of view or purpose shapes the content and style of a text. *(CCRA.R.6)*

continues

"What makes a solider a hero?" Take some time and care in creating this list, and then update it regularly throughout the lesson that follows. The culminating activity will be to revisit the list and see how students' definitions of heroism may have changed or broadened.

2. **Pairs view painting and discuss.** Project the image of the cavalrymen on the American frontier, telling kids it was painted in 1890 by Frederic Remington, one of the most respected artists of the American West. (Search for "Advance Guard Remington" in Google Images.) Have them study the picture in pairs, looking patiently for details for at least one full minute, trying to figure out what has happened in the painting (a variant of Lesson 6.2, page 108). Then have kids make up and share their own titles for the picture, using details in the image to support their decisions. Remington actually gave this painting a triple title: *The Advance-Guard, or the Military Sacrifice (the Ambush).* According to the painter, the soldier has been fatally wounded in an Indian ambush, but because of this sacrifice, his comrades can live to fight another day. Reveal these titles one at a time, asking kids to talk about how each one confirms or changes their understanding of the painting. And finally discuss: Is this fallen (or falling) soldier a hero?

3. **Read and reread the Holbrook poem.** This is a form called a "cut-up," in which the author patches together lines from different sources, voices, and documents. As Holbrook explains in her acknowledgment, the poem was partly built on email correspondence that a military family shared with her. Use the appropriate steps from Stop, Think, and React (Lesson 9.4, page 207) to ensure that students understand this complex poem. They should stop at the three indicated points to make notes as they go, then gather to discuss their thinking. Revisit and revise the class list on what makes a soldier a hero.

4. **Read aloud the Rogers piece.** Here's a sergeant's-eye view of the troops he is directly responsible for. After you read it aloud (Lesson 3.2, page 22), ask kids to talk about what information or understanding this adds to the ongoing investigation of soldiering and heroism. Revise the chart as needed.

5. **Students read the Tim O'Brien speech.** To finish the set, kids read an untitled speech that O'Brien gave upon accepting the PEN/Faulkner Award in 1979 for his first novel, *Going After Cacciato.* He speaks as a combat veteran and writer, and also talks about himself as a young man in the Vietnam era, trying to decide whether to become a soldier or flee to Canada. In the last lines of the speech he directly addresses the topic of who is, and isn't, a hero. After reading, have students compare his definition of a hero to the whole-class list, making revisions to the chart as needed.

6. **Where do you stand?** Based on their study of all readings in the text set, have kids line up on a continuum that expresses their level of agreement with the proposition "All soldiers are heroes." Line up along five points: all are heroes, some are heroes, unsure, a few are heroes, none are heroes. Kids should be ready to talk about why they are standing where they are. Find instructions in Lesson 7.4, The Human Continuum (page 158), and be sure to include "folding the line," so kids must talk with classmates holding different positions.

7. **Optional: Debate.** Following the appropriate steps in Arguing Both Sides (Lesson 8.3, page 180), have students plan and argue for and against the proposition "All soldiers are heroes."

8. **Optional: Culminating writing experience.** Using steps from Lesson 8.1, Take a Position (page 169), have kids write an essay outlining their own view of this issue, based on all the evidence they have found and sifted from the whole five-piece text set—plus, if desired, any further research they conduct.

9. **Optional: Peer-led discussions.** The stepwise plan above is comprehensive and very structured. You might offer guided instruction for just one or two texts, and then let kids read and discuss tackle the remaining texts using the model of Literature Circles (Lesson 5.5, page 89).

- **First-hand testimony:** Your students will be a huge resource in this inquiry unit, because many of them have relatives who are now serving or have served in the military. We find this to be true everywhere we travel; kids burst out with passionate stories of their dad, or their older brother, or their sister in uniform somewhere in the world. Even in highly affluent neighborhoods, where the proportion in service is lower, military families are out there among the student body. Think about it: some of your own students may be planning on entering the service right after high school.

  In our previous book, *Texts and Lessons for Content-Area Reading* (2011), we created a soldiers text set with five nonfiction pieces focusing on post-traumatic stress disorder (PTSD). If you wanted to create a mega soldiers-at-war text set and inquiry lesson, you could combine the literary pieces here with those informational texts.

- **Add images to the text set:** One of the most powerful war "texts" we have ever encountered is a series of photographs of a U.S. marine being ambushed in Afghanistan, caught by combat photographer Goran Tomasevic. We could not obtain rights to print these photos, but at publication time you could view them at http://blogs.reuters

- Integrate and evaluate content presented in diverse media and formats, including visually and quantitatively, as well as in words. *(CCRA.R.7)*
- Delineate and evaluate the argument and specific claims in a text, including the validity of the reasoning as well as the relevance and sufficiency of the evidence. *(CCRA.R.8)*
- Analyze how two or more texts address similar themes or topics in order to build knowledge or to compare the approaches the authors take. *(CCRA.R.9)*
- Read and comprehend complex literary and informational texts independently and proficiently. *(CCRA.R.10)*
- Engage effectively in a range of collaborative discussions. *(CCRA.SL.1)*

◀ *Variations*

.com/photographers-blog/2008/05/19/close-enough/. Though the ambushed solider survived, the pictures explain, in a way that no text ever could, where PTSD can come from. It also correlates beautifully with the Remington painting and can be added to or substituted in the lesson.

- **More on Tim O'Brien:** In 1999, Tim O'Brien gave a now-legendary lecture at Brown University, in which he talked about soldiering and authoring, about literal truth and "heart-truth," and closed with a story—maybe true, maybe not—that chills the bones even as it demonstrates his artistic mastery. Luckily, this document still lives on the web at http://www.stg.brown.edu/projects/WritingVietnam/ obrien.html. Interestingly, in this talk O'Brien repeats the Rainy River story told in his PEN/Faulkner acceptance speech (Step 5), and then reveals it to be a fiction, a way of representing how he really felt, even though he just played golf all summer waiting for the draft to take him. Thus, the story is "heart-true."

Broadcaster Refuses to Label Dead Soldiers "Heroes"

Today's World News Bulletins, May 28, 2012
by Lee Terrell

AN MSNBC HOST HAS APOLOGIZED after saying on the air that he was "uncomfortable" calling fallen soldiers "heroes." Chris Hayes made the remark on his MSNBC program over the weekend.

Hayes's verbatim statement was: "I feel uncomfortable about the word 'hero' because it seems to me that it is so rhetorically proximate to justifications for more war."

The newsman added, "There are individual circumstances in which there is genuine, tremendous heroism, you know, hail of gunfire, rescuing fellow soldiers," but "it seems to me that we marshal this word in a way that is problematic."

Frederic Remington, *The Advance-Guard, or The Military Sacrifice (The Ambush),* 1890. The Art Institute of Chicago.

Three Soldiers

Bruce Holland Rogers

1. The Hardest Question

My marines bring me questions. "When do we get to shower?" "Sergeant, how do you say 'Good afternoon' again?" "Sarge, where can I get more gun oil?"

I have answers. "Tomorrow, maybe." "Maysuh alheer." "Use mine."

Answering their questions is my job. But when Anaya was shot and bleeding out, he grabbed my arm and said, "Sergeant? Sergeant?" I understood the question, but damn. I didn't have an answer.

2. Foreign War

No U.S. soldier who could see that kid would have shot him. But that's long-range ordnance for you. Calder stood next to me in the street, looking at the pieces. "We've come so far from home," he said, "that we'll never get back."

"You dumbass," I said. But a year later, I stood on the tarmac hugging my child, thinking of that kid in pieces, and I wasn't home.

3. Decisions, Decisions

In morning twilight far away, my men are making up their minds:

What's that guy carrying?

Friend or foe?

I should be there, helping them decide. My wife and my parents do their best to make Christmas dinner conversation around my silence. An hour ago, I was yelling at Angie for turning on the damn news. My father, carving, won't meet my eyes. He says, "White meat, or dark?"

The News from Iraq

Sara Holbrook

The helicopter burst into flames immediately on impact.
Secondary explosions from all the rockets, missiles, and 30mm rounds.
All four radios going off all at once,
F16s over head, 1 BCT Commander, our team internal frequencies,
and flight flowing.
I could only tell them what I saw.

> **ABC News:** *The AH-64 Apache went down north of Baghdad, killing its two crew members and becoming the third US helicopter to be shot down in 10 days.*

There were 250 ft power lines in the vicinity of the crash site
so we couldn't get very low,
but we did see.
It was a bad situation
We had to come off of what we were doing
to provide security for the downed aircraft.
I knew the two pilots of the aircraft,
but not very well
Really bad situation.

>**Email Subject: Notification**
>ALL CAPS THIS IS A NEGATIVE NOTIFICATION
>AFTER NOTIFICATION HAS BEEN MADE
>Our Combat Aviation Brigade, 4ID lost an aircraft
>two pilots
>Monday 16 January. The immediate family members have been
>notified. This is an official negative notification
>the death did not occur in your unit.

>> **<Reply:** Once again, I personally thank you
>> <on behalf of all of the 4th Infantry Division families.
>> <your personal touch
>> <the phone call to our home in Cleveland
>> <Apache lost
>> <more than words can express.
>> <Once again, terribly relieved
>> <Our son not lost.
>> <Relief. Heartache. Sorrow for the other families.
>> <Continue to pray for the safe return . . .

Dear Dad,

If you saw the news, you saw two Apaches flying over the crash site,
one of them was me.
We provided overwatch
as a bunch of Iraqi civilians were trying to get to the crash site,
you don't know if they are curious or trying to steal pieces of the
helicopter for propaganda.
Ground guys coming to secure the site,
F16s trying to relay what they saw.
All this leads to a bad situation
Tense. Very tense.
In the air.
Turned into sadness when we finally got back
When we landed.

●

   MSNBC: *Apache down, north of Baghdad*

We are still flying, I generally fly 3 days a week.
Everything is good.
We couldn't get very low, but we did see.
flames immediately on impact
secondary explosions.
I could only tell them what I saw.
It was a bad situation.

>THIS IS A NEGATIVE NOTIFICATION

Dad, I would like some bedding.
Sheets for my single bed.
I have been sleeping on a mattress and a sleeping bag.

   CNN: *A Russian-made surface-to-air missile launched by anti-American
   insurgents brought down a US military helicopter that crashed in Iraq on
   Monday . . .*

If mom could please send me some sheets for the bed that would be great.
I already got her other package of socks and boxers. Thank you.

   CBS: *The shootdown represented "a troubling new development," there are
   hundreds and possibly thousands of SA-7 missiles that remain unaccounted
   for in Iraq.*

Troubling new development.
30mm rounds.
　　Flames upon impact.
　　A very bad situation.
We pray for the safe return

　　>ANOTHER NEGATIVE NOTIFICATION
Please.
　　Thank you.

Acknowledgement: Thanks to Captain Thad Weist and his father, Sargeant Dan Weist (retired) for letting me read their mail.

Heroes

Tim O'Brien

This is a dazzling array of talent and I feel as if I'm on an all-star team, a literary all-star team, and I'm honored to be in the lineup even if I'm batting way down the order. I'm glad too that the event will raise money; I'm glad the money won't go for hair spray for sheiks in Kuwait, I'm glad the money will go in one form or another to writers. Writers can use it. I'm a writer, by the way. The reason we're all here, aside from hearing about heroes, is that America sometimes gets absentminded about paying writers. For instance, the guy who bats in my slot tonight for the Boston Red Sox makes twelve times what I do. He's not even an all-star. He doesn't get to give speeches. Now and then he gets to explain on television why he can't stop striking out. "No can see the ball too hot," he says. Anyway, I'll bet you can guess that the hero I want to tell you about tonight does not play baseball for the Boston Red Sox. The Boston Red Sox, I might add, often do not play baseball for the Boston Red Sox; they play for Baltimore a lot.

The hero I want to tell you about does not play baseball for Baltimore either. He's a dead old man—at least I think he's dead. Elroy Birdall was eighty-some years old when I last saw him and that was two decades ago. I was twenty-one then. There was a war on which I despised and thought was immoral. Certain blood, I thought, was being shed for uncertain reasons. I didn't want to die in that war. I didn't want to die. The war was named after a country called Viet Nam or Viet Naam, the pronunciation varying according to which president of the United States you'd happen to be listening to. I listened to four of them. All four got paid pretty well. They gave more speeches than I do and they were all-stars; they're in the Hall of Fame.

My hero, the old man, wasn't an all-star. He was just a tiny shrunken, bald old man in brown pants and a flannel shirt. His name was Elroy Birdall. and old Elroy was smart. He was hard to fool. Like the famous all-star once said, "You can fool some of the people all of the time, and all the people some of the time, but you can't fool all the people all the time." There should have been an extra clause in that statement to include Elroy Birdall. He hardly ever got fooled. I did get fooled for a while. The Gulf of

Tonkin business fooled me; it fooled a lot of people, including many hundred members of Congress and forty-eight members of the U.S. Senate. They passed a resolution named after the Gulf of Tonkin. The resolution legitimized the war I didn't want to die in. Anyhow, twenty years ago, when old Elroy and I talked about the Gulf of Tonkin, he said a smart thing. The thing he said was this: he said "Crap." He said another smart thing: "There should be a law," he said "if you vote for a war," he said "you have to go fight in it in the front lines, or else you have to send your mother." "A law" he said.

Well, I'm sorry to be talking about these terrible things to you. America gave me Viet Nam. I spent twenty years giving it back. What happened was this: When I got drafted, I decided to run away. I lived in Minnesota, which is a state north of Mexico, adjacent to the Canadian border. Nobody in my generation had trouble pronouncing Canada. So I packed a bag and I drove north to a river called the Rainy River, which separates Minnesota from Canada. To think things over for a while, I stopped at a fishing resort called the Tip Top Lodge, which was just a bunch of old yellow cabins along the Rainy River. Elroy Birdall was the caretaker, and for six days in the summer of 1968 Elroy watched over me as I made my decision. He asked no questions, but he knew there was a war on. He knew that, he knew my age, he saw the terror in my eyes, he heard me squealing in my sleep, he knew Canada was just a boat ride away. Even so, he didn't press me. He offered no advice, he fed me and gave me a place to lie low. Elroy, in the summer of 1968, was simply there, like the Rainy River and the late summer sun. And yet by his presence, his mute watchfulness, he made it real. He was a witness, like God, or like the gods, who look on in absolute silence as we live our lives, as we make our choices, or fail to make them. He was a hero. I wasn't. I went to Viet Nam.

The Common Core Standards "Publisher's Criteria" document (2012) suggests that several times per year, students should move from reading excerpts, passages, and shorter texts to the study of a longer work, typically a novel or play. The very strong implication is that these readings are to be guided by the teacher, and focus students on a deep and close analysis of the text and its craft. In this chapter, we take three commonly taught novels and show how the lessons in this book can help you create a sequence of thinking and discussion opportunities of just this kind—and still help kids fall in love with books.

But first, let's remember that this particular type of methodical book study is only one part of a balanced diet of reading experiences. In fact, if deep analysis of long works is done poorly or excessively, it can alienate young people from books for good. If students feel peppered and punished by a relentless barrage of teacher questions, nobody wins.

Independent, recreational, or "pleasure" reading is the foundation of reading development. There's nothing more important than the experience of getting lost in a book and staying up all night to finish it. Or falling in love with an author, hunting down all of her books, and reading them one after another. Or becoming fascinated with a genre, and gobbling up fantasies, war stories, historical novels, mysteries, or sci-fi tales. These are the joyful experiences that can transform students into lifelong readers, year in and year out, and far beyond school.

As grown-up readers, the great majority of the fiction or poetry we read, we read once, savor it, and then move on. Maybe we'll tell a friend or spouse about the book, especially if we want to recommend it. And, if we happen to be in a book club at that time, we might engage in some analysis of the chosen book. But mostly, we just read for the pleasure of well-crafted language, the joy of an absorbing plot, the chance to meet fascinating characters, the delight of being transported to another place and time, and the opportunity to marinate in themes that move us—love, brotherhood, courage, family, faith, conflict, justice. No second readings, no close readings—just reading.

The sheer volume of this unmonitored reading practice matters too. We have plenty of research showing that at every age level, reading more pages in school and at home each day is associated with higher reading scores (Allington 2011).

All of this independent experience counts, big-time. Along the way, we acquire fluency, vocabulary (some that we never hear spoken aloud) stamina, sentence structures, knowledge of genre schemes, and so much more. We constantly build (mostly below the level of awareness) the knowledge we need to become better readers—and writers.

Studying a Novel

Now, assuming that those wide independent reading experiences are in place, there's room for kids to downshift and study a meritorious book in detail, in a community of fellow readers. If done well, slowing readers down to think deeply and discuss the text can actually add spice and fun to reading. But engagement and ownership must be established and maintained if kids are to benefit fully.

To show what we mean, we've assembled a sequence of our lessons for three oft-taught books:

The Giver, by Lois Lowry

To Kill a Mockingbird, by Harper Lee

The Great Gatsby, by F. Scott Fitzgerald

Here, just as with the text sets, we've drawn upon the lessons in Chapters 3–9 to create a series of teaching suggestions. The three novels we have picked are just examples; you can combine any of the book's thirty-seven strategy lessons to find a sequence that will work for any novel or play.

Unless otherwise indicated, the suggested activities take place after students have read the specific chapters listed. There are many other possible lessons and sequences; our point is not to single out any particular lessons, but to show a few possible paths through a book.

We suggest that you use the literature circle format for ongoing reading, note taking, and postreading small-group discussion. In other words, while you will orchestrate several focused whole-class lessons on the way through the book, kids' baseline setup will be ongoing groups of four or five. This allows for more active participation opportunities and ensures a high level of positive peer pressure, so kids keep up and join in. Students who read ahead (something we always encourage) must monitor themselves to not "talk ahead," giving away events from later in the book.

▶ *The Giver* by Lois Lowry

Getting the Novel Started

The Giver has been a favorite of teenagers (and adults, and plenty of younger kids) for twenty years now. While dystopian novels have been around forever, Lois Lowry's 1993 Newbery winner unquestionably paved the way for *The Hunger Games, Above, Feed, The Eleventh Plague,* and a dozen other scary-future yarns. *The Giver* is widely taught as a whole-class novel in middle schools, but it has also been the subject of frequent censorship attempts. The title has even appeared on the American Library Association's list of the Top Ten Challenged Books—quite an irony, considering that the book portrays a community where most books, knowledge, and history are banned.

TEACHER READ-ALOUD (Lesson 3.2) *The Giver* is a perfect choice for starting with a read aloud. The first four pages of the book (up to "*Apprehensive*, Jonas decided. That's what I am") introduce the protagonist, unveil a strange community, create an atmosphere of mystery, and evoke plenty of puzzling questions. Establish pairs and then have kids read along as you read aloud, with expression.

PAIR SHARE (Lesson 3.1) Now, have partners discuss their response to and questions about the story so far. Invite them back to a whole-class discussion centered around predicting what might happen in the pages to come. Be sure to have kids talk about what "released" might mean.

Working Through the Book

Text Annotation *(Lesson 4.1)*

CHAPTERS 2–9: One of the major themes of *The Giver* is *rules*—the need for rules, the nature of rules, following and breaking rules, and the potential tyranny of rules. As the book unfolds, dozens of rules are gradually mentioned, and in combination they define the nature of Jonas' community. Have students keep an ongoing list of the accumulating rules and define what they endorse or prohibit.

Text on Text *(Lesson 7.2)*

CHAPTER 9: In the middle of this chapter, Jonas receives his assignment as The Receiver, and it includes a quite dramatic list of eight instructions. Blow up this section and place this text on chart paper. Then have students do a three-person text-on-text (page 149) write-around in the margins. Have them focus on what these rules might tell us about the duties of The Receiver. Discuss the possibilities, and then have students recheck these thoughts as they read further.

One-Minute Write *(Lesson 3.3)*

CHAPTER 16: This is a pretty climactic chapter, with Jonas giving away memories without authorization, talking about the concept of love with his puzzled parents, and deciding to stop taking the pills prescribed to quell his "stirrings." Have students stop at the last page of this chapter and write for one minute about where they predict the story will go from here, and then share with a partner.

Take a Position *(Lesson 8.1)*

CHAPTER 23: The ending of the book is intentionally ambiguous. Either Jonas and Gabe have sledded into a warm and well-lit town in Elsewhere, where singing people are waiting to welcome them, or perhaps they have frozen to death as Jonas hallucinates the magical sled ride, so suspiciously reminiscent of the first memory The Giver offered him. Many other interpretations are also possible. Have students choose their own explanation of the book's ending and share with each other, using quotes from the book to support their position. This could be developed into a polished formal literary essay, if desired.

Don't tell the kids too early, but Lowry has spoken on this subject:

I will say that I find it an optimistic ending. How could it not be an optimistic ending, a happy ending, when that house is there with its lights on and music is playing? So I'm always kind of surprised and disappointed when some people tell me that they think that the boy and the baby just die. I don't think they die. What form their new life takes is something I like people to figure out for themselves. And each person will give it a different ending. (www.random-house.com/teachers/guides/give.html)

But who says the author is always right? Perhaps the ending with its powerful implications of doom and death and release came from her own unconscious—and now she is trying to reel it back in. Or satisfy the widest possible audience. Or placate the book banners? (Do we detect a whiff of the same kind of backsliding David Chase engaged in when viewers objected to Tony Soprano's possible demise?) Such impertinent questions, and great for kids to chew on.

Connecting the Novel with Nonfiction Resources

There are some great beyond-the-book nonfiction topics that arise from *The Giver*. Google or follow the provided links to find great materials.

Utopian Communities

For centuries, humans have tried to establish perfect—sometimes called "utopian"—communities. Many of these experiments were tried in America in the nineteenth and twentieth centuries. Often, these communities required their members to sacrifice or give up certain individual rights or pursuits or pleasures for the good of the group. Google "utopian communities" and you'll find information on scores of different ones.

Book Censorship

In *The Giver*, books are prohibited by The Rules. Ironically, *The Giver* itself has been a frequently banned or challenged book in U.S. schools. Objectors have pointed to the book's violence, "occult themes," and sexual explicitness as reasons to remove it from school shelves. (Whew, we totally missed the sex part.) Invite kids to discuss whether this book seems ban-worthy. What might be the damage to young readers? The American Library Association has many programs designed to protect citizens' access to books of their choice. Learn more at www.ala.org/advocacy/banned.

Surveillance and Privacy

In *The Giver*, citizens have relinquished almost all privacy, and live surrounded by speakers and screens that cannot be turned off. The *Washington Post* recently reported on a plan to attach electronic monitoring devices to American school students.

$1.1 million-plus Gates grant: "Galvanic" bracelets that measure student engagement

by Valerie Strauss

In the "you-can't-make-up-this-stuff" category, the Bill and Melinda Gates Foundation is spending about $1.1 million to develop a way to physiologically measure how engaged students are by their teachers' lessons. This involves "galvanic skin response" bracelets that kids would wear so their engagement levels could be measured. (6/11/12)

Have students discuss any connections between the book and this news item. What if some kind of "discipline wand" were linked to such a bracelet?

▶ *To Kill a Mockingbird* by Harper Lee

Getting the Novel Started

In the beginning, students have to worry most about characters and setting. The early 1930s time period and the rural setting of Maycomb, Alabama, puzzle many students, particularly kids with no direct connection to the southern United States. You can use either or both of the following prereading activities depending on the needs of your students. Tapping prior knowledge and applicable personal experience is the goal of Find an Expert. Starting to make character inferences and plot predictions is the goal of Literary Networking. And if you are confident that your kids can dive right in, then go straight to Reading with Questions in Mind.

Find an Expert *(Lesson 7.1)*

In the chart (page 286), key background items have been pulled from the story. If you have students mix and mingle five minutes at a time over several days, the completed chart will reveal who the classroom experts are on a variety of topics that emerge in the forthcoming chapters. Then, when collard greens come up in Chapter 1—and again in Chapter 6—call on your experts to share their knowledge. Also, be sure to take a glance at the finished charts to see if there are certain topics on which no one is an expert. For those items, *you* are going to have to be the expert, so get prepared!

Literary Networking *(Lesson 9.1)*

The first couple of *Mockingbird* chapters introduce a substantial number of characters, and students struggle at first to keep them all straight, particularly since half of the characters also have nicknames! Getting kids to share and speculate about the characters they will soon encounter greatly diminishes reading confusion. And when they run across the lines they saw on their cards (page 287), kids will tackle the text with greater confidence.

Reading with Questions in Mind *(Lesson 4.4)*

CHAPTER 1, FIRST PARAGRAPH: Ask students, "What is the question that the author wants us to raise at the very beginning of this story?" Once kids have brought up "How did Jem break his arm?" tell them we will keep this question in mind for the rest of the book.

TITLE: What does the title have to do with the story? Another question to keep in mind as students read.

Working Through the Book

Frozen Scenes *(Lesson 7.3)*

In creating dramatic "still-lifes," students enjoy a chance to collaborate as they review and conceptualize the text. Listed below are a few chapters that cry out for some succinct captions and dramatic statues. Plus, it's fun for a class to see how different each group's interpretation is when they've all read the exact same words.

CHAPTER 6: The Boo Radley obsession of Jem, Scout, and Dill surpasses common sense. Students love portraying their attempts to take that peek into the Radley window.

CHAPTER 10: Just when Jem and Scout conclude their father is old and useless, he turns out to be a crack shot when he takes down the rabid dog Tim Johnson.

CHAPTERS 28–31: Bob Ewell exacts his final revenge when he attacks Jem and Scout on Halloween. Thank goodness Boo Radley was paying attention!

Character Interview Cards *(Lesson 7.5)*

CHAPTER 8: When Miss Maudie's house burns down, students can review the chapter while playing a reporter and various characters. Possible interview characters:

Scout	Mr. Avery
Jem	Arther (Boo) Radley
Atticus	Fireman
Miss Maudie	

Character Text Messages *(Lesson 9.2)*

CHAPTER 10: What might Jem and Scout text each other as they watch Atticus reveal his marksmanship?

Two-Column Notes *(Lesson 6.3)*

CHAPTER 15: Set up two-column notes. Left-hand column: Reasons for Defending Tom Robinson. Right-hand column: Reasons for Not Defending Tom Robinson. Students work in pairs to brainstorm items for both columns. They may use text details from Chapters 1–15 as well as nonfiction text and background knowledge information.

Human Continuum *(Lesson 7.4)*

CHAPTER 15: After completing the two-column notes, have students line up in a human continuum in response to this question: Given the pros and cons of defending Tom Robinson, should Atticus continue to defend him?

Tweet the Text *(Lesson 4.6)*

CHAPTERS 17, 18, 19, AND 25: Students are independent reporters sending tweets to those following the trial; then later in Chapter 25 they are reporting on Tom Robinson's death.

Connecting the Novel with Nonfiction Resources

There are some plenty of historic and present-day topics that arise from *To Kill a Mockingbird*.

Understanding Jim Crow

When the jury convicts Tom Robinson of raping Mayella, students are absolutely astonished that Tom is convicted *without any evidence*. Plus, it is clearly apparent to everyone (readers and fictional characters) that Bob and Mayella Ewell are lying. How could this happen? This is a good time to introduce students to the history of Jim Crow justice. Though Lee was inspired by the Scottsboro trials, a better piece of history study for high school students is the murder and subsequent trial of Emmett Till. An excellent video for students to watch is the PBS *American Experience* documentary "The Murder of Emmett Till." An accompanying website is available that includes articles on segregation as well as the actual *Look* magazine post-trial interview of Emmett's murderers where they openly admit that they killed him. (See http://www.pbs.org/wgbh/amex/till/.)

Modern-Day Discrimination

After reading *To Kill a Mockingbird*, students often conclude, "Well, thank goodness the United States isn't like *that* anymore." After all, that novel took place in the early 1930s, and now it's over eighty years later. Yes, we did get some very important civil rights laws passed, but even with those laws, minorities and people of color still face discrimination. A great nonfiction read that opens students' eyes to this is *Zeitoun* by David Eggers. Abdulrahaman Zeitoun, a longtime New Orleans resident and local contractor, remained in his neighborhood after the levee flood following Hurricane Katrina. Solely because of his Syrian heritage, he was arrested as a terrorist and held unjustly, in brutal conditions, for over a month. This took place in 2005. After the literature circle training provided by *To Kill a Mockingbird*, *Zeitoun* is a great follow-up whole-class book. Eggers writes in a style that is simple yet deeply moving, and students have no problem leading their own discussions as they move back and forth between the injustice faced by Tom Robinson and that faced by Abdulrahaman Zeitoun.

Has eaten collard greens	Visited Alabama or Mississippi
Has an annoying cousin	Toured a Southern plantation
Has a favorite neighbor	Knows about head lice
Has gotten a pet vaccinated for rabies	Takes care of a younger sibling
Has eaten at the "kiddie" table	Collects coins
Visits relatives on major holidays	Has an older brother

When he was nearly thirteen, my brother Jem got his arm badly broken at the elbow.	Jem brightened. "Touch the house, that's all?"
It was then that Dill gave us the idea of making Boo Radley come out.	Dill nodded.
When enough years had gone by to enable us to look back on them, we sometimes discussed the events leading to his accident.	Jem was the product of their first year of marriage; four years later I was born, and two years later our mother died from a sudden heart attack.
Inside the house lived a malevolent phantom. People said he existed, but Jem and I had never seen him.	When we slowed to a walk at the edge of the schoolyard, Jem was careful to explain that during school hours I was not to bother him. I was to stick with the first grade and he would stick with the fifth.
My father, Atticus Finch, went to Montgomery to read law.	Our summertime boundaries were Mrs. Henry Dubose's house two doors to the north of us, and the Radley Place three doors to the south.
A baseball hit into the Radley yard was a lost ball and no questions asked.	Miss Caroline inspected her roll-book. "I have a Ewell here, but I don't have a first name . . . would you spell your first name for me?" "Don't know how. They call me Burris't home."
Atticus liked Maycomb, he was Maycomb County born and bred; he knew his people, they knew him.	Dill was from Meridian, Mississippi, was spending the summer with his aunt, Miss Rachel, and would be spending every summer in Maycomb from now on.
"I won't say you ran out on a dare . . . if you just go up and touch the house."	"He's one of the Ewells, ma'am. They come first day every year and then leave."

NOTE: You might be reluctant to use this book given the fact that Mr. Zeitoun has been repeatedly accused of domestic violence against his ex-wife. However, take a look at Kathy Zeitoun's statement:

> *Reached by telephone Friday, Kathy Zeitoun said her ex-husband more recently had become a much different person from the one described in the book with his behavior turning violent toward his family. "Over time, it just started getting aggressive, more and more way out of hand," she said. "He was a good man, he changed too much."*(Cain Burdeau, Associated Press, "Police: Katrina Hero Plotted Ex-wife's Murder," August 10, 2012)

What to make of this? How could a previously loving person become violent? Whether it is prison or war, the toll is tremendous. Untreated post-traumatic stress disorder sometimes manifests itself in dangerous behavior toward oneself and others. Though they were unacknowledged, Mr. Zeitoun describes experiencing PTSD symptoms. If students bring up this sad subsequent chapter in the lives of Abdulrahaman and Kathy Zeitoun, then it is absolutely appropriate to research the effects of PTSD (see www.helpguide.org/mental/post_traumatic_stress _disorder_symptoms_treatment.htm). We also have a text set about PTSD in our companion book, *Texts and Lessons for Content-Area Reading* (Heinemann, 2011).

▶ *The Great Gatsby* by F. Scott Fitzgerald

Getting the Novel Started

The Great Gatsby is not the kind of novel suitable to start reading cold. The first five pages can be very confusing for adolescent readers. There's a lot to establish: Nick's attitude toward others; his unreliable narration; his background as a Yale graduate, World War I veteran, and now bond salesman-in-training. Just as in *To Kill a Mockingbird*, there is a ton of background to absorb. Students need help to understand the geography of Manhattan, Long Island, and East Egg and West Egg, as well as cultural phenomena like Prohibition and everything else the Roaring Twenties conjures up.

Two-Column Notes *(Lesson 6.3)*

It is helpful for students to grasp the concept of "old school" wealth before they begin reading *Gatsby*. For this, show the video "America's Castles." All the kids need to watch are the segments on The Breakers and Marble House. As students watch, have them use two-column notes. On the left, they list mansion facts and details and on the right they jot down their corresponding reactions. Almost every student we've ever had has been amazed that something the Vanderbilts called a "summer cottage" had over a hundred rooms. However, this background knowledge helps students picture the grandeur of East Egg as well as the unlimited wealth Gatsby tossed around so casually at his parties.

Teacher Read-Aloud/Pair Share *(Lessons 3.2 and 3.1)*

CHAPTER 1: Start reading the novel aloud to the whole class in order to dodge some of the early comprehension potholes. Give your reading some drama, but stop frequently, sometimes pointing out what you are thinking, sometimes asking students to turn to a partner to discuss a specific line.

Visual Images

CHAPTER 1: Once you get to the paragraph that starts "I lived at West Egg . . . " (it's around the fifth page), it's time to stop and show kids some visuals depicting "the Eggs."

Luckily, these images are easily obtainable via Google Maps. Type in "Great Neck Long Island." Zoom in to point out East Egg and West Egg; zoom out to show the Eggs' location in relation to Manhattan.

As students continue reading, you can help with other visual references that students might not picture: Long Island and Manhattan, images of Central Park, the Upper West Side, the Plaza Hotel, the Valley of Ashes, Dr. Eckleburg's eyes. Fitzgerald's subtle descriptions seem to assume we all live in Manhattan, but if your kids are like ours, all they visualize about Manhattan is maybe the Statue of Liberty. Luckily all the NYC images you'll need are easily searchable.

Gatsby also offers the opportunity to examine art depicting this era. We've found the best phrase to Google is "Jazz age artwork."

Denotation/Connotation *(Lesson 6.1)*

CHAPTER 1: Ask students to jot down what comes to mind when they encounter these words: *arrogant, cruel, contempt, hulking.* Discuss mental pictures, whether the words are positive or negative. Tell students to watch for these words as they read and notice which character they are describing. After reading, talk about why Nick might have chosen those words since he is the narrator telling the story. How might different words have changed our first impressions of Tom Buchanan?

Reading with Questions in Mind *(Lesson 4.4)*

CHAPTERS 1–2: Once you have read aloud and discussed the first five or so pages, you might say: *Now that we've gotten past the beginning and have some understanding of the narrator, Nick, and the setting, I want you to start thinking about this question: Who's the biggest jerk? Which character is the most selfish? The most unreliable? The most dishonest? The one who most takes advantage of other people and situations? By the time you have finished Chapter 2, you will have met all the main characters. Some of them will seem like sure-fire winners for the "Biggest Jerk Award." However, keep observing all of them as you read on. You might be surprised.* As students continue to read, remind them to keep this question in mind—possibly even annotating accordingly—and bring the "jerk" factor up for regular discussion.

Working Through the Book

Discussion Questions/Follow-Up Questions *(Lesson 5.3)*

CHAPTER 2: Before moving students into larger discussion groups using the literature circle format, it's often helpful for students to first discuss a chapter with just one partner. This keeps engagement and skill practice at a high level. As students read individually, they should jot down discussion questions as well as page numbers (as indicated in the first two columns of the handout on page 293). When the kids meet with their partners, they take turns initiating a discussion based on their initial question and then following up with additional questions, which they jot down in the right-hand column.

Take a Position *(Lesson 8.1)*

CHAPTERS 1–9: Take your pick of the symbols: Daisy's green dock light, the Valley of Ashes, Dr. Eckleburg's eyes, East Egg versus West Egg. Have students pick a symbol and trace it through the novel, using text evidence to explain its meaning.

Arguing Both Sides *(Lesson 8.3)*

CHAPTERS 4–9: Students can argue these issues as they arise or even return to them as they learn more through further reading. And later, these oral arguments can turn into full-fledged argument papers.

- Should Nick have reintroduced Daisy to Gatsby when he knew it would likely lead to an affair?

- Should Gatsby have continued to pursue Daisy once she was married to Tom?

- Should Gatsby have tried to protect Daisy from consequences of the "hit and run"?

- Should Gatsby be admired or despised?

- If it's offered, should Nick take a job with Wolfsheim?

Film/Book Comparison

The CCSS explicitly ask students to compare the same work across different media. Most of the time we wait until the book is finished before showing the film, as if watching the movie is some kind of final reward for everyone: the kids get to zone out for a few days while we grade all those essay tests. However, it's often more interesting to compare media midreading. By that point students have a pretty clear internal picture of what each character looks like, sounds like, et cetera. Then, when you show the film, the kids are often shocked that the casting director pictured someone so completely different—or not. By the time you read this, there will be three full versions of *Gatsby* at your disposal:

> **1926—SILENT FILM TRAILER.** No copies of the original film remain, yet this trailer available on YouTube offers proof of its existence. Would be fun to compare this trailer with the 2013 one.

1974—ROBERT REDFORD AND MIA FARROW. Offers excellent tutelage in regard to setting and 1920s fashion and follows the book faithfully. However, the acting is so leaden and unconvincing that the kids never beg to finish the film after we've watched it for one period.

2000—PAUL RUDD AND MIRA SORVINO. Made for TV. The kids like the fact that they actually know who Paul Rudd is, and the acting is better. Downside: this one starts with Gatsby's murder—Really?! And the sets look low-rent compared to the 1974 version.

2013—LEONARDO DICAPRIO. It may be awhile before you can get your hands on this DVD. However, go to YouTube and watch the trailers for a taste of Baz Luhrmann's interpretation.

Point-of-View Correspondence

AFTER CHAPTER 9: This activity is actually a combination of the Point-of-View Note Taking (Lesson 6.4) and Written Conversation (Lesson 5.1). Once the book is completed, have students partner up. First, everyone writes a letter to Daisy from Nick: *At the end of the book, it's pretty clear that Nick is fed up with Tom and Daisy. They skipped town. They didn't go to Gatsby's funeral or even send some flowers. And then, when Nick runs into Tom in Manhattan, he finds out that their dealings with George Wilson resulted in Gatsby's murder. Write a letter explaining your feelings. Be sure to use text details additional to the ones we've just mentioned.*

Give students some time to write. Remind them to give their letters a closing that reflects Nick's state of mind.

When everyone is just about done, announce one more minute to wrap it up. Remind students again to include a closing and signature from Nick. Then have students trade papers. *Now you are all writing as Daisy. Read the letter from Nick and respond. Remember that Daisy has never taken responsibility for anything in her entire life. Like before, use text details to capture her character and defend herself as she tries to convince Nick that she is the real victim here.*

As before, give students time to read and then respond. As students finish up, call time, and have them trade back. The results are usually hilarious, but also reflect a keen understanding of character and plot. If time permits, have a few pairs confer and then pick one of their pieces to read to the class as Nick and Daisy. Encourage dramatic interpretation.

Connecting the Novel with Nonfiction Resources

There are some great nonfiction articles that connect with *The Great Gatsby*. Look them up; the Internet is your friend!

- "As for Empathy, the Haves Have Not," Pamela Paul, *New York Times*, December 30, 2010.

  Possible explanation for why it was so easy for Daisy and Tom to brush off the deaths of Myrtle and Gatsby.

- "The Chemist's War: The Little-Told Story of How the U.S. Government Poisoned Alcohol During Prohibition with Deadly Consequences," Deborah Blum, *Slate.com*, February 19, 2010.

  Surprising information about the U.S. government's attempts to enforce prohibition.

- "Love Notes Drenched in Moonlight; Hints of Future Novels in Letters to Fitzgerald," Dinitia Smith, *New York Times*, September 8, 2003.

  Reveals how real-life circumstances and people influenced Fitzgerald's fictional characters.

- "Coal Ash: 130 Million Tons of Waste," *60 Minutes*, August 15, 2010, www.cbsnews.com

  Who knew coal ash was so toxic? Lucky for Myrtle and George that they ended up dead by the end of the novel. Thanks to their daily ingestion and inhalation of coal ash, the Valley of Ashes sequel would have depicted them dying slow and painful deaths without health insurance. The *60 Minutes* site also offers the video version of the episode.

- http://learning.blogs.nytimes.com/2010/08/03/teaching-the-great-gatsby-with-the-new-york-times/

  This site has links to lots of resources and additional related nonfiction articles connected to *The Great Gatsby*.

DISCUSSION QUESTION/FOLLOW-UP QUESTION NOTES

Page #	Discussion Questions	Follow-Up Questions

EXTENDING THE TEXTS AND LESSONS

Need More Readings?

Not a problem. This chapter outlines several ways for you to grow your inventory of great short texts for lessons in literature—or in writing, language, speaking and listening.

We hope you have found that the common thread in most of our selections is that they are *great reads*. They're pieces that adults would *choose* to read, not just texts that have been certified "important" or that showcase a literary device that teachers think they have to cover.

Fellow English teachers! We all picked this job largely because we love books, reading, and authors. We have chosen and read tons of books over our lives. We are reading nerds—and we are *experts on literature*. We need to trust our own sense of what kids might love. No lexile score or Coh-Matrix Common Core leveling number can catch each fickle adolescent's attention. But on our good days, we can.

Short Fiction

More than half the readings in this book come from a single literary goldmine called "short-short stories." The two of us have been fans, collectors, geeks, and wonks of this genre for decades. We're telling you, for English teachers, this is the mother lode of brief, read-in-class-length selections we can use to teach every skill and strategy in the book. And, as you teach lessons with these jewels, you'll also be preparing your students to meet every state and national standard, as well as score big on the PARCC, Smarter Balanced, or whatever other high-stakes assessment your state has signed up for.

There are a number of recent collections of these "short-shorts," books filled with stories that range from a teeny fifty-five-word maximum (*World's Shortest Stories*), to one typed, double-spaced page (*Micro Fictions*), to pieces that soar up to three or four pages. And as a teacher, you can use them in your classroom without paying the permission fees we have rendered for publishing them in this book.

So here is our master bibliography of short-shorts: this may the most precious gift we have to offer. We've starred the ones that have the *really* short stories, and from which we've drawn the most. One suggestion: before you jump on Amazon and order every one of these, check them out from the local library for a preview perusal.

SHORT STORY BIBLIOGRAPHY

Biguenet, John. 2001. *The Torturer's Apprentice: Stories*. New York: Ecco.

Cheuse, Alan, and Caroline Marshall, eds. 1991. *The Sound of Writing*. New York: Anchor.

*Eggers, Dave. 2007. *One Hundred and Forty Five Stories in a Small Box*. San Francisco, CA: McSweeney's.

Fraustino, Lisa Rowe, ed. 1998. *Dirty Laundry: Stories about Family Secrets*. New York: Viking.

Frosch, Mary, ed. 1994. *Coming of Age in America: A Multicultural Anthology*. New York: New Press.

Gallo, Donald R., ed. 1988. *Visions: Nineteen Short Stories by Outstanding Writers for Young Adults*. New York: Dell.

Lobel, Arnold. *Fables*. 1980. New York: Harper & Row.

Krull, Kathleen. 2000. *Lives of Extraordinary Women: Rulers, Rebels (and What the Neighbors Thought)*. New York: Harcourt.

Manguso, Sarah. 2007. *Hard to Admit and Harder to Escape*. San Francisco: McSweeney's.

*Masih, Tara L. 2009. *Field Guide to Writing Flash Fiction: Tips from Editors, Teachers, and Writers in the Field*. Brookline, MA: Rose Metal.

Mazer, Harry. 1997. *Twelve Shots: Outstanding Short Stories about Guns*. New York: Delacorte.

*Moss, Steve, ed. 1998. *The World's Shortest Stories*. Philadelphia: Running.

*Moss, Steve, and John Daniel, eds. 1999. *The World's Shortest Stories of Love and Death*. Philadelphia: Running.

*PEN/Faulkner Foundation, comp. 2000. *Three Minutes or Less: Life Lessons from America's Greatest Writers*. New York: Bloomsbury.

*Phillips, Helen. 2011. *And Yet They Were Happy*. Teaticket, MA: Leapfrog LLC.

*Shapard, Robert, and James Thomas, eds. 2007. *New Sudden Fiction: Short-Short Stories from America and Beyond*. New York: W.W. Norton.

*Shapard, Robert, and James Thomas, eds. 1986. *Sudden Fiction: American Short-Short Stories*. Salt Lake City: G.M. Smith.

*Shapard, Robert, and James Thomas, eds. 1989. *Sudden Fiction International: 60 Short Stories*. New York: W.W. Norton.

Sieruta, Peter D. 1989. *Heartbeats and Other Stories*. New York: Harper & Row.

*Smith magazine, ed. 2009. *I Can't Keep My Own Secrets: Six-Word Memoirs by Teens Famous & Obscure*. New York: HarperTeen.

*Stern, Jerome, ed. 1996. *Micro Fiction: An Anthology of Really Short Stories*. New York: W.W. Norton.

*Thomas, James, and Robert Shapard, eds. 2006. *Flash Fiction Forward: 80 Very Short Stories*. New York: W.W. Norton.

*Thomas, James, Denise Thomas, and Tom Hazuka, eds. 1992. *Flash Fiction: Very Short Stories*. New York: W.W. Norton.

*Unferth, Deb Olin. 2007. *Minor Robberies*. San Francisco: McSweeney's.

Weiss, M. Jerry, and Helen S. Weiss, eds. 1997. *From One Experience to Another: Award-Winning Authors Share Real-Life Experiences Through Fiction*. New York: Tor.

---

*Short-short stories, mostly two pages or less.

Poetry

If you want to reignite your own engagement in poetry, just log onto YouTube and watch fifteen minutes of the slam poetry. Holy versification, Batman! And good luck stopping at fifteen minutes. This is red-blooded, full-bore poetry, featuring some of the coolest verse and most youth-friendly performances of any literary form today. While there are many slam events and poets around the country, the official governing body is Poetry Slam, Inc., at www.poetryslam.com.

Brave New Voices is the youth slam, with great examples at http://youth speaks.org/bravenewvoices/.

And for another video view of slam in action, you can view Young Chicago Authors' documentary "Louder than a Bomb" on YouTube.

Thus energized, you can grow your poetry repertoire further at your school or local library. Both probably have underutilized poetry sections that are just waiting for you to come and browse. You'd be surprised how easy it is to get lost in the poetry section of the library. Take a look at the spines, find a title that speaks to you, and just start flipping through and skimming. Not grabbing you? Reshelve it and try another. In no time, you will be sitting on the floor between the stacks of books, immersed in poetry, completely unaware that you've been hanging out in the library for a couple of hours.

Don't forget your textbook. A typical middle or high school English textbook has poems all over the place, sometimes in plain sight, sometimes tucked into an obscure corner of the page. See what's there that you can use. The kids already have copies (no photocopying necessary) and since poems are generally short, a few sticky notes will work for the note taking/annotation.

So where do our favorites come from? Here are some of the collections we have discovered over the years, and a couple of how-to-teach poetry books from our colleagues Holbrook and Salinger. As we said before, try to get your hands on a preview copy before you go nuts on Amazon!

POETRY BIBLIOGRAPHY

Alexie, Sherman. 2005. *Face*. New York: Hanging Loose Press.

Collins, Billy, comp. 2005. *180 More: Extraordinary Poems for Every Day*. New York: Random House Trade Paperbacks.

Collins, Billy, comp. 2003. *Poetry 180: A Turning Back to Poetry*. New York: Random House Trade Paperbacks.

Cormier, Robert. 1999. *Frenchtown Summer*. New York: Delacorte.

Gordon, Ruth, ed. 1993. *Peeling the Onion: An Anthology of Poems*. New York: HarperCollins.

Hempel, Amy, and Jim Shepard, eds. 1995. *Unleashed: Poems by Writers' Dogs*. New York: Crown.

Hesse, Karen. 1997. *Out of the Dust*. New York: Scholastic.

Holbrook, Sara, and Michael Salinger. 2010. *High Definition: Unforgettable Vocabulary-Building Strategies Across Genres and Subjects*. Portsmouth, NH: Heinemann.

Holbrook, Sara, and Michael Salinger. 2006. *Outspoken! How to Improve Writing and Speaking Skills Through Poetry Performance*. Portsmouth, NH: Heinemann.

Holbrook, Sara. 2003. *By Definition: Poems of Feelings*. Honesdale, PA: Wordsong/Boyds Mills.

Holbrook, Sara. 1996. *I Never Said I Wasn't Difficult: Poems*. Honesdale, PA: Boyds Mills.

Holbrook, Sara. 1998. *Walking on the Boundaries of Change: Poems of Transition*. Honesdale, PA: Boyds Mills.

Hyett, Barbara Helfgott. 1986. *In Evidence: Poems of the Liberation of Nazi Concentration Camps*. Pittsburgh, PA: University of Pittsburgh.

Knudson, R. R., and May Swenson, comps. 1988. *American Sports Poems*. New York: Orchard.

Neruda, Pablo. 1995. *Odes to Opposites*. Comp. Ferris Cook, Trans. Kenneth Krabbenhoft. New York: Bullfinch.

Nye, Naomi Shihab. 2005. *19 Varieties of Gazelle: Poems of the Middle East*. New York: HarperTempest.

Rubin, Robert Alden, ed. 1993. *Poetry Out Loud*. Chapel Hill, NC: Algonquin of Chapel Hill.

Salinger, Michael. 2009. *Well Defined: Vocabulary in Rhyme*. Honesdale, PA: Wordsong.

Sones, Sonya. 2001. *What My Mother Doesn't Know*. New York: Simon & Schuster for Young Readers.

Soto, Gary. 1994. *Neighborhood Odes*. New York: Scholastic.

Images: Comments and Suggestions

Looking for images? Here's a quick review.

- As you have seen in this book, for many literature lessons we search for and project images that help students understand the time, place, culture, and flavor of different literary works. Google Images usually gets the job done for these general historical and literary images.

- Don't forget to study whatever textbooks you have sitting around, old or new. Whoever made those books was trying to enrich them with relevant photos and artworks. All of the illustrations, pictures, and paintings will give the source information. Once you've got that, it's just a matter of visiting either the museum website or Google Images.

- Visit your local art museum and keep tabs on the pieces you might be able to use in the classroom. Once you get home, find the images online. Also, most art museums have substantial teacher resource centers. Need some help incorporating images into a unit? Give the resource center a call. They will be delighted to help you since that is their mission!

- Browse museum websites. The Smithsonian Museum of American Art (http://americanart.si.edu/collections/), the National Gallery of Art (http://www.nga.gov/collection/index.shtm), and the National Portrait

Gallery (http://www.npg.si.edu/collection/permanent.html) are all great places to begin. Then, if you're not totally art-overloaded, you can always visit this mega-virtual mother of all online museums: The Museum of Online Museums (http://www.coudal.com/moom/).

Home-Grown Texts

We wrote a couple of the readings in this book, using pseudonyms. No, we didn't sign them "Pat Conroy" or "Virginia Euwer Wolff." Sometimes, writing your own mentor text can be quicker and more fun than scouring the Internet for some rare genre. Yeah, it sounds like a chore, but sometimes, creating your own microfiction or twelve-line poem is the fastest solution. And when we do, we are sharing ourselves with kids as writers, a bit of much-neglected modeling.

Also, don't forget all those talented young writers right in your classroom. Remember Lorian Dahkai's "I Am From" poem (page 152)? That's a piece of student work that sets up a lesson as well as any professional author's piece might. When you use a student work as mentor texts, you kill several birds with one stone. You honor and encourage the author; it becomes a goal for everyone to be selected; readers can give useful feedback to the writer; and readers get to interview the author—in person.

Selections from Your Basal Textbook or Anthology

In the Shoptalk section of many lessons, we have offered suggestions about how you could teach the typical selections found in the major textbook series. Take a look back at those notes if you've missed them. Summing it up, we think that our lessons can help you:

- "Update" your textbook with fresher stories, poems, and images
- Teach the traditional literary elements (figurative language, dialogue, allegory, narrative structure, foreshadowing) with engaging, read-in-class text
- Develop text-dependent thinking with literature that matters
- Have alternative text choices for too-hard or too-easy textbook readings
- Help you build text sets of related readings within or across genres
- Discriminate among and avoid textbook exercises that don't build comprehension

Until Next Time

Thanks for listening, friends and colleagues. This is our fourth book written together, and we are unlikely to stop with this one. And thanks for sharing, too. Our best ideas have always come from the kids we meet in your classrooms, as we travel and work in schools. Please stay in touch through the website with your success stories, complaints, interesting student work, or professional musings. Vent if you need to; we're here.

This is a tough time to be a teacher, and you guys just keep pushing ahead. Thanks for the inspiration, and know that what you do makes a lifelong difference. Years from now, your ex-students will remember your passion for literature, not some standards they met or tests they endured. And a few of them will pay you the ultimate compliment, by becoming English teachers themselves.

Smokey Daniels
Santa Fe, New Mexico

Nancy Steineke
Brookfield, Illinois

APPENDIX

HOW THE LESSONS CORRELATE WITH THE COMMON CORE STANDARDS

		COMMON CORE COLLEGE AND CAREER READINESS ANCHOR STANDARDS FOR READING									
		1	2	3	4	5	6	7	8	9	10
Chapter 3	**Sharing Literature Aloud**										
3.1	Pair Share	x			x		x				Addressed in all lessons
3.2	Teacher Read-Aloud				x		x				
3.3	One-Minute Write		x		x	x					
3.4	Teacher Think-Aloud	x	x				x				
3.5	Partner Think-Aloud	x				x					
Chapter 4	**Smart-Reader Strategies**										
4.1	Text Annotation	x	x	x	x						Addressed in all lessons
4.2	Connections and Disconnections	x	x								
4.3	Drawing Text Details	x	x		x						
4.4	Reading with Questions in Mind	x		x	x						
4.5	Inferring Meaning	x			x						
4.6	Tweet the Text		x			x					
Chapter 5	**Lively Discussions**										
5.1	Written Conversation	x		x		x	x				Addressed in all lessons
5.2	Thirty-Second Look	x			x			x			
5.3	Follow-Up Questions		x	x			x			x	
5.4	Save the Last Word for Me	x	x	x	x						
5.5	Literature Circles	x	x	x	x		x				
Chapter 6	**Closer Readings**										
6.1	Denotation/Connotation	x			x						Addressed in all lessons
6.2	Setting the Scene	x						x			
6.3	Two-Column Notes	x	x	x							
6.4	Point-of-View Note Taking	x			x	x		x			
6.5	Seeing a Character	x			x			x			
6.6	Metaphorically Speaking	x	x	x	x						
6.7	Rereading Prose	x	x	x							
6.8	Rereading Poetry	x	x	x	x						

		COMMON CORE COLLEGE AND CAREER READINESS ANCHOR STANDARDS FOR READING									
		1	**2**	**3**	**4**	**5**	**6**	**7**	**8**	**9**	**10**
Chapter 7	**Up and Thinking**										
7.1	Find an Expert	X	X	X							
7.2	Text on Text	X			X	X	X				
7.3	Frozen Scenes	X		X		X	X				Addressed in all lessons
7.4	The Human Continuum	X	X	X			X				
7.5	Character Interview Cards	X	X		X		X				
Chapter 8	**Literary Arguments**										
8.1	Take a Position	X	X	X	X	X	X				
8.2	Finish the Story	X		X			X				Addressed in all lessons
8.3	Arguing Both Sides	X		X							
Chapter 9	**Coping with Complex and Classic Texts**										
9.1	Literary Networking	X	X	X	X						
9.2	Characters Texting	X	X	X							
9.3	Opening Up a Poem	X	X		X						Addressed in all lessons
9.4	Stop, Think, and React	X	X	X	X						
9.5	Reading with Expression	X			X						
10	**Text Sets**										
10.1	Memory	X	X	X	X		X	X		X	
10.2	Citizenship	X	X		X	X		X			
10.3	Life Stories	X	X		X	X	X	X	X	X	
10.4	Mothers and Daughters	X	X	X	X	X	X			X	Addressed in all lessons
10.5	Narcissism	X	X		X	X	X	X		X	
10.6	Labels	X	X	X	X	X	X	X		X	
10.7	Abuse	X	X	X	X	X				X	
10.8	Soldiers and Heroes	X	X	X	X	X	X	X	X	X	

WORKS CITED

Allington, Richard. 2011. *What Really Matters for Struggling Readers*, 3rd ed. New York: Allyn and Bacon.

Coleman, David, and Susan Pimentel. 2012. *Revised Publishers' Criteria for the Common Core State Standards in English Language Arts and Literacy, Grades 3–12*. Washington, DC: National Governors Association.

Common Core State Standards for English Language Arts & Literacy in History/Social Studies, Science, and Technical Subjects. 2010. National Governors Association Center for Best Practices and the Council of Chief State School Officers, www.corestandards.org/assets/CCSSI_ELA%20Standards.pdf.

Daniels, Harvey. 1994. *Literature Circles: Voice and Choice in the Student Centered Classroom*. Portland, ME: Stenhouse.

Daniels, Harvey, et al. 2011. *Comprehension Going Forward*. Portsmouth, NH: Heinemann.

Daniels, Harvey, and Nancy Steineke. 2011. *Texts and Lessons for Content-Area Reading*. Portsmouth, NH: Heinemann.

Daniels, Harvey, and Nancy Steineke. 2006. *Mini-lessons for Literature Circles*. Portsmouth, NH: Heinemann.

Daniels, Harvey, and Steven Zemelman. 2004. *Subjects Matter: Every Teacher's Guide to Content-Area Reading*. Portsmouth, NH: Heinemann.

Daniels, Harvey, Steven Zemelman, and Nancy Steineke. 2005. *Content-Area Writing: Every Teacher's Guide*. Portsmouth, NH: Heinemann.

Harvey, Stephanie, and Harvey Daniels. 2009. *Comprehension and Collaboration*. Portsmouth, NH: Heinemann.

James, Charity. 1972. *Young Lives at Stake: The Education of Adolescents*. New York: Agathon Press.

Pearson, P. David, and Meg Gallagher. 1983. "The Instruction of Reading Comprehension." *Contemporary Educational Psychology* 8, 317–344.